THE EXPLOSION OF POP, MINIMALISM, AND PERFORMANCE 1958–1964

THE EXPLOSION OF POP, MINIMALISM, AND PERFORMANCE 1958–1964

BARBARA HASKELL

with an essay on The American Independent Cinema
by JOHN G. HANHARDT

Whitney Museum of American Art, New York
in association with W. W. Norton & Company,
New York, London

Dates of the exhibition: September 20–December 2, 1984
Copyright © 1984
Whitney Museum of American Art
945 Madison Avenue
New York, New York 10021

LIBRARY OF CONGRESS CATALOGING IN PUBLICATION DATA

Haskell, Barbara.
    Blam! the explosion of pop, minimalism, and performance,
1958–1964.
    Published in connection with an exhibition held at the
Whitney Museum, Sept. 20–Dec. 2, 1984.
    Bibliography: p.
    1. Arts, American—Exhibitions.   2. Avant-garde (Aesthetics)
—United States—History—20th century—Exhibitions.
I. Hanhardt, John G.   II. Whitney Museum of American Art.
III. Title.
NX504.H36   1984   700'.973'07401471   84-7304
ISBN 0-87427-000-6 (Whitney Museum of American Art;
softcover edition)
ISBN 0-393-01935-7 (W. W. Norton & Company; hardcover
edition)

This publication was organized at the Whitney Museum of
American Art by Doris Palca, Head, Publications and Sales;
Sheila Schwartz, Editor; Elaine Koss, Associate Editor; and
Amy Curtis, Secretary/Assistant.
Designer: Bruce Campbell
Typesetter: Trufont Typographers, Inc.
Printer: Eastern Press, Inc.

PHOTOGRAPH CREDITS

The photographs reproduced have been supplied in the majority of
cases by the owners or custodians of the works of art or by the
photographers, as credited in the captions. The following list
applies to photographs for which an additional acknowledgment
is due. Numbers refer to figures.

Harry N. Abrams, Inc., New York: 2; Tom Arndt: 90; Bob Benson:
138; Ferdinand Boesch: 9; Scott Bowron: 95; Rudolph Burckhardt:
4, 5, 6, 21, 23, 103, 105, 112, 115, 117, 119, 126, 127, 129, 130, 135,
136, 147, 153, 154, 155; Francesco Cantarella: 43; Leo Castelli
Gallery, New York: 99, 141, 143; Catalogue 1962 Wiesbaden
Fluxus 1982: 52; Geoffrey Clements: 84, 104, 108, 125, 151; John
Cohen: 29, 31; Rainer Crone: 98; Bevan Davies: 96; Roy Elkind:
74; Flow Ace Gallery, Los Angeles: 146; Jack Gunter: 132; Mark
Heddon: 145, 148; George Franklin Hurych: 16; Scott Hyde: 14,
25; Kate Keller: 15; Robert Mates: 152; Robert R. McElroy: 54, 85;
Dennis McWaters: 22; Albert Mozell: 11; The Museum of
Contemporary Art, Chicago: 91; The National Gallery of Canada,
Ottawa: 132, 133, 134; Claes Oldenburg: 17, 18, 19, 81, 149; Eric
Pollitzer: 56, 92, 93, 94, 109, 113, 116, 122, 124, 152; Nathan Rabin:
10; Seymour Rosen: 107; Walter Russell: 110, 144; Tim Rautert:
140; Marc Schuman: 102; Duane Suter: 3; Frank J. Thomas:
156; Jerry L. Thompson: 106, 118, 128; Dan Walworth: 101;
Virginia Zabriskie Gallery, New York: 1; Dorothy Zeidman: 142

Frontispiece: Jim Dine in his Happening *The Smiling Workman*
at the Judson Gallery, Judson Memorial Church, New York, 1960.
Photograph by Martha Holmes, *Time* magazine.

CONTENTS

SPONSORS OF THE EXHIBITION

Asher B. Edelman

Henry and Elaine Kaufman Foundation

The Leonard and Evelyn Lauder Fund

Howard and Jean Lipman Foundation, Inc.

Robert and Meryl Meltzer

Robert and Jane Meyerhoff

National Endowment for the Arts

Dorothy and Lawson Reed, Jr.

The Billy Rose Foundation, Inc.

Charles Simon

Laura-Lee Woods

Anonymous Donor

Funds for this catalogue were provided, in part, by the
Edith C. Blum Foundation

FOREWORD

During the decade following the end of World War II, the achievements of the Abstract Expressionists brought American art to a position of international pre-eminence for the first time, and the aesthetics and ideology of Abstract Expressionism came to dominate the art of the 1950s. However, late in that decade, a number of artists who were to have a major influence in the 1960s and 1970s started to search for alternative forms of expression. We now realize that the period from 1958 to 1964 was a critical time of transition in American art, as the unquestioned hegemony of Abstract Expressionism began to falter and the new movements of Pop Art and Minimalism emerged. This was also the period when young American artists began to receive more recognition in Europe than in the United States, and European museums and private collectors began to assemble collections of contemporary art that far exceeded those of their American counterparts. The Whitney Museum of American Art is pleased to offer the public an opportunity to examine, through this exhibition and accompanying book, the issues explored by American artists during those turbulent and amazingly creative years.

On behalf of the Trustees and staff of the Whitney Museum, I extend our appreciation to the lenders of the exhibition for their generous cooperation throughout the organization and presentation of this endeavor. We are also grateful for the support of the National Endowment for the Arts, which continues its commitment to twentieth-century American art with a grant for this exhibition. Finally, we sincerely appreciate the assistance of the individuals and foundations listed in the front of this book who believed in the importance of this project and whose financial help has made the exhibition possible.

TOM ARMSTRONG
Director

ACKNOWLEDGMENTS

In seeking to review the period 1958 to 1964, I have been fortunate in receiving an exceptionally full measure of goodwill and support from many of the individuals who actively participated in the events of those years. In particular, I would like to thank Richard Bellamy, Walter De Maria, Martha Edelheit, Red Grooms, Dick Higgins, Sidney Janis, Ivan Karp, Alison Knowles, Roy Lichtenstein, Jackson Mac Low, Robert Morris, Claes Oldenburg, Yvonne Rainer, Lucas Samaras, George Segal, Anita Simons, and La Monte Young for their willingness to share with me their recollections of the period. I am indebted as well to Barbara Moore, who was more than generous in making available her research material on Fluxus and who offered important clarifications on the Fluxus section of the manuscript. My thanks also go to William Agee, Leon Botstein, and Robert Rosenblum for their insights and advice about the manuscript, and to Marcia Siegel for her suggestions about the section on dance.

I am immensely grateful to the individuals and institutions who consented to lend valuable and fragile works to the exhibition; without their generosity this presentation would have fallen far short of its goal of bringing together seminal works from the period. The same is true for those artists who agreed to re-create earlier Happenings sets and environments, thereby enabling the public to experience again these transient artworks.

Neither the exhibition nor the catalogue could have been successfully realized without the unflinching commitment shown by Tom Armstrong, Director of the Whitney Museum, and by members of the Board of Trustees, in particular, Flora Biddle, Victor Ganz, and Howard Lipman. Their support joined an extraordinary effort made by the entire staff of the Whitney Museum. In this regard, I would especially like to thank Jennifer Russell, Pat Brownstone, Linda Gordon, Dana Stein-Dince, and Sheila Schwartz.

I have been fortunate to have had an especially high level of assistance from the staff that worked with me. Susan Cooke, a superior research assistant, not only took responsibility for compiling the Chronology and Bibliography, but was also intimately involved in virtually every aspect of the organization of the exhibition and catalogue. Her work has been the mainstay of the project. I am equally grateful to Deborah Leveton for her fortitude throughout the project and for her efficient handling and careful attention to the multitude of details that inevitably arose. Others in the department who made a briefer, but nonetheless significant and highly appreciated, contribution were Vera Cvikevich, Suzanne Dickerson, Elizabeth Evans, Louis Grachos, George Greos, and Mary Jo Marks.

I owe a large measure of gratitude to Oliver Lundquist for his assistance with the difficult and complex job of designing the installation. Robert R. McElroy, John Cohen, Al Giese, and Peter Moore generously made their photographic archives available and patiently filled numerous requests for prints. My thanks go to them as well as to Arlene Carmine, Tibor de Nagy, David Farneth, Fred Hughes, Olivia Motch, and Virginia Zabriskie for their help in assembling catalogue material. In addition, the Leo Castelli, Sidney Janis, and David Anderson galleries were particularly generous in supplying photographs for the catalogue.

Most of all, I would like to thank the individuals and foundations whose belief in this project and support of its presentation were essential in guaranteeing its realization. It is, of course, customary to thank individuals whose contributions make exhibitions possible. In this case, the thanks are more than routine, for the present donors contributed far more than financial backing: they contributed moral and professional support at a critical time in the exhibition's development. My hope is that this exhibition and catalogue merit the faith they have displayed.   B.H.

In the preparation of "The American Independent Cinema 1958–1964," a number of research libraries and individuals provided valuable assistance. I am grateful to Anthology Film Archives, The Museum of Modern Art's Film Study Center, Jonas Mekas, P. Adams Sitney, Raymond Carney, Robert Breer, Amos Vogel, and Callie Angell.   J.G.H.

BLAM!

THE EXPLOSION OF POP, MINIMALISM, AND PERFORMANCE 1958–1964

BARBARA HASKELL

INTRODUCTION

Between 1958 and 1964, the arts in America underwent a dramatic upheaval. Within this seven-year period, a group of young artists re-evaluated and ultimately overturned the ideology and formal strategies associated with art of the past. These were transition years in which the individuals later identified with the art of the 1960s and 1970s forged a new aesthetic by adapting the premises of Abstract Expressionism to unprecedented kinds of subject matter. In the process, they established a radically different sensibility—one whose style and notoriety were to have a lasting impact on the philosophy of art-making and on the relationship between art and society.

The onset of this artistic era was publicly heralded in 1958 by two exhibitions in New York, in which Jasper Johns and Robert Rauschenberg presented works incorporating everyday objects and motifs hitherto considered inappropriate for art. In that same year, Allan Kaprow constructed his first environment out of found objects and taped electronic music, and enacted his first public Happening. These presentations reflected the influence of composer John Cage's theories about the interchangeability of art and life. Cage's twenty-five-year retrospective concert in New York in May 1958 and the class he taught that academic year on experimental music composition at the New School for Social Research encouraged a variety of artists from all disciplines to venture into non-narrative and non-traditional forms of performance. Out of these experiences artists evolved fresh paradigms for music, theater, dance, sculpture, and painting which found expression in Happenings, Fluxus, the Judson Dance Theater, and Pop Art. Other artists, meanwhile, responding in many cases to the same stimuli, were formulating a more abstract style which came to be known as Minimalism—seen, for example, in Frank Stella's first Black paintings of 1958. Examining the emergence of these various styles synchronistically reveals the uniquely close interaction that existed between artists in all media during this period, an interdisciplinary exchange that exerted a critical impact on the evolution of the new aesthetic.

The artists whose work stamped the aesthetic character of the sixties began their careers in the shadow of Abstract Expressionism. For the five years following 1958 their art retained much of the rawness, spontaneity, emotionalism, and surface gesture of their predecessors. It was not until the beginning of 1964 that the revisionism which had begun in 1958 took firm hold: in painting and sculpture, a hard-edged, seemingly depersonalized style superseded the rough, relatively handmade quality of the artists' formative work; in the performance arts, media attention and the shift to more blatantly dramatic styles caused artists to move in separate directions, severing the camaraderie and closely knit community that had prevailed since 1958. Looking back, Yvonne Rainer described the spirit of those earlier times as "a dare-devil willingness to 'try anything,' the arrogance of our certainty that we were breaking ground, the exhilaration produced by the response of the incredibly partisan audiences. . . ."[1] But at the end of 1963, a curtain descended and a new chapter began.

While the sixties as a decade has received extensive discussion, the years between 1958 and 1964 have never been examined as a self-contained, interdisciplinary period.[2] This is due, in part, to the widespread acclaim bestowed on the artists' post-1964 work and, in part, to the critical habit of discussing the decade of the sixties as if it were a homogeneous entity. The advantage of some twenty-five years' perspective confirms different chronological distinctions.

This essay is not intended to present a comprehensive history of American art during the years 1958 to 1964. It does not include, for example, the Color Field and figurative painters, but instead focuses on those artists whose shared origins and parallel ideologies formed an intellectually cohesive aesthetic.[3] In this way, the discussion isolates those concerns and visual modes that most profoundly served as the models for the art of the next generation. Even though the condition of art at any given moment is, as Donald Judd noted, "messy,"[4] and, like E. M. Forster's description of daily life, "full of false clues and sign-posts that lead nowhere,"[5] such an approach offers important insights into the motivations for aesthetic change and the degree to which the artists who came to maturity in the early sixties built upon and transformed past styles in the process of forging new aesthetic principles.

The Backdrop for Revolt

The aesthetic upheaval of the years 1958–64 was staged against the backdrop of Abstract Expressionism, a style which had been in ascendancy since World War II. Notwithstanding the existence of other modes of expression, this New York–based school of painting dominated the aesthetic signature of the 1950s. By the end of the decade, it had attained a level of international prestige and influence unparalleled in American art.

Abstract Expressionism or, more precisely, Action Painting, its gestural manifestation, was predicated on the communicability of subjective feeling and inner emotions by means of the pictorial "act." It posited an art "inseparable from the biography of the artist," wrote Harold Rosenberg, one of the decade's foremost critics.[6] Personal expression was the exalted virtue. Art was viewed as a vehicle of metaphor and symbol, transcribed onto canvas through a painterly vocabulary of loose, freely applied, thick paint.

As practiced by its progenitors—Willem de Kooning, Jackson Pollock, and Franz Kline, for example—Abstract Expressionism was a fiercely liberating, powerful style. But by the late 1950s, a crisis clearly had arisen. In the hands of second- and third-generation followers, Abstract Expressionism seemed to have lost its authenticity and conviction. To the younger generation of artists who began their careers in the late fifties, Abstract Expressionism's original practitioners were heroic, mythical figures. But it seemed easier for their followers—Milton Resnick, Joan Mitchell, and Alfred Leslie, among the best—to imitate the superficial aspect of Abstract Expressionism's thickly brushed, bravura painting style than to absorb its generative spirit. By 1958 these epigones numerically dominated the art scene to such an extent that the initial power of Abstract Expressionism had become diluted. For a younger generation, Abstract Expressionism seemed "like a fire that had burned itself into cold embers," as Walter De Maria later observed.[7] To the young artists arriving in New York at the end of the decade, expressive paint handling had degenerated into a decorative, academic mannerism. When *Art News* ran a two-part series of interviews in 1959 on the subject of whether or not a new academy existed, the answer was uniformly affirmative.[8] Friedel Dzubas summed up the sentiments of many: "Why is it that after an evening of openings on Tenth Street, I come away feeling exhausted from the spectacle of boredom and the seemingly endless repetition of safe sameness? I wonder why people—especially young people—continue to do something which in its results is as dreary and dim as a late Victorian front parlor, and as respectable."[9]

Paradoxically, at the very time that Abstract Expressionism was perceived as exhausted and bankrupt, it simultaneously exerted a hegemony so absolute that it offered young artists no room to maneuver. There seemed to be nothing more that could be done within its style: "De Kooning had already painted all my paintings," Tom Wesselmann declared.[10] When asked what had precipitated his break with the past, Roy Lichtenstein replied: "Desperation. There were no spaces left between Milton Resnick and Mike Goldberg."[11] At some point every generation feels the need to explore territory different from that occupied by its elders. "Must we remain the obedient children of our ancient fathers? Isn't it about time we went for a stroll on our own in 1959?" George Sugarman asked.[12] Clearly the moment was propitious for a change.

The Aesthetics of Junk

The first wave of the assault against Abstract Expressionism occurred within its very ranks as artists such as Al Held, Ray Parker, and Robert Goodnough reacted against the formlessness of Abstract Expressionism by organizing their brushed areas of paint into more discrete, legible shapes. Yet ultimately their efforts did not resolve the question that plagued the upcoming generation: whether in fact subjective states could be transmitted. To younger artists, the existential rhetoric surrounding Abstract Expressionism no longer seemed viable. In response, a number of them during the 1950s began to search for an art that would focus on the "real" world rather than on abstraction. Indeed, even stalwarts like de Kooning and Pollock had grown restless with abstraction by the mid-fifties and had begun to reinsert figurative references into their work. Both had even gone so far as to introduce bits of everyday reality—de Kooning with newspaper reproductions of Marilyn Monroe; Pollock with cigarette butts, glass, and other debris accumulated during the process of painting. Still, the predominant idiom within Abstract Expressionism, especially that practiced by the Tenth Street School (the name given to the younger generation of Abstract Expressionists), did not condescend to traffic in images of the concrete and material.

To the artists who arrived in New York in the late fifties, the spiritual and philosophical aspirations of the original Abstract Expressionists were awesome; yet these same aspirations generated resentment because they excluded references to the external world. Younger artists chafed at being allowed to deal with universals but not to paint what could be seen or touched. "We found it amazing," George Segal recalled later, "that so much avant-garde twentieth-century art was rooted in physical experiences of the real world and suddenly the Abstract Expressionists were legislating any reference to the physical world totally out of art. This was outrageous to us."[13]

An early model for inserting the real into art was assemblage, the three-dimensional equivalent of collage.[14] On the surface, assemblage was not a form threatening to Abstract Expressionism. Collage, after all, had been a viable aesthetic option since the early twentieth-century *papier collés* of Pablo Picasso and Georges Braque. The Dadaists, convinced that art could be created out of anything whatsoever and determined to undermine venerated cultural standards, extended the Cubist collage technique into sculpture. By the heyday of Surrealism in the 1920s, found objects had become an accepted part of the artist's vocabulary.

In the late fifties assemblage exploded onto center stage. Richard Stankiewicz and Jean Follett had been making junk sculpture since the early 1950s, but only began to achieve a modicum of success later in the decade (Figs. 1, 2). Louise Nevelson had her first show of found-object constructions in

Fig. 1. Richard Stankiewicz, *Chain People*, 1960. Iron and steel, 50 × 16 × 17" (127 × 40.6 × 43.2 cm). Collection of Hanford Yang.

Opposite: Allan Kaprow's environment *An Apple Shrine* (see Fig. 7).

15

Fig. 2. Jean Follett, *Untitled*, 1955. Mixed media construction, 60 × 84″ (152.4 × 213.4 cm). Present whereabouts unknown.

Fig. 3. Robert Rauschenberg, *Canyon*, 1959. Combine-painting: oil, pencil, paper, metal, photograph, fabric, wood, on canvas, plus buttons, mirror, stuffed eagle, cardboard box, pillow, and paint tube, 81¾ × 70 × 24″ (207.6 × 177.8 × 61 cm). Collection of Ileana and Michael Sonnabend, on indefinite loan to The Baltimore Museum of Art.

1959, followed by shows of the European assemblagists Eduardo Paolozzi and Jean Tinguely in 1960. And Leo Castelli (who would play a major role in the promotion of Pop Art) added the assemblagists Lee Bontecou and Edward Higgins to his gallery in 1959 and 1960, respectively. The critical respect accorded these sculptors in America made it increasingly legitimate to use refuse from the environment as raw material for art. But however radical this work was, it was not an overt challenge to artistic authorship because these purloined materials were transformed into abstract or anthropomorphic images. They had no specific content of their own, no explicit referential value external to the work of art. Stankiewicz and Paolozzi combined their junk materials into witty, human surrogates reminiscent of the Constructivist assemblages of Picasso, Julio Gonzalez, and David Smith; Nevelson and Follett integrated their found objects into unified pictorial designs by treating them as abstract compositional elements purged of all references to their previous lives. Nevertheless, inherent in assemblage from the start was an impatience with the distinction between art and life. To those dissatisfied with Abstract Expressionism's detachment from perceptible reality, the interjection of commonplace materials by means of assemblage was seen as a way of rescuing art from overly subjective and rarefied realms and bringing it back into contact with the ordinary and the "real."

The artist who extended the referential implications of found objects was Robert Rauschenberg.[15] Even in his first New York exhibition, in 1953, he had gone beyond the bounds of decorum with a series of black paintings that incorporated dirt, scrap metal, rocks, and pieces of lumber he had collected off the street. The next year Rauschenberg exhibited a group of all-red paintings, also thickly encrusted with urban debris. But now the separate elements were more distinguishable than they had been in the black series. Although the show astonished visitors, nothing in this or subsequent Rauschenberg exhibitions prepared the art community for the work in his 1958 Castelli show.

Fig. 5. Robert Rauschenberg, *Pilgrim*, 1960. Combine-painting: oil, pencil, paper, fabric, on canvas, plus wood chair, 79¼ × 53¼ × 18⅝" (201.3 × 135.3 × 4.3 cm). Museum Folkwang, Essen, West Germany.

These pieces went far beyond assemblage in the type and the scale of found objects employed—stuffed birds, doors, pillows, tires (Fig. 3). Rauschenberg's uncompromising acceptance of "inappropriate" materials unequivocally marked him as a renegade. He embraced the referential associations of his derelict and banal objects but, unlike the Surrealists, did not capitalize on the narrative overtones produced by their juxtapositions. His objects were simply themselves: blunt, undisguised things with paint on them. The results infuriated critics, who assumed his sole purpose was an insidious attack on art. The component materials of his "combines"—the word he used to describe works that were neither paintings (because they were freestanding) nor sculptures (because painting figured so prominently in them)—seemed utterly too ephemeral and pedestrian to qualify as high art (Figs. 4, 5). There were few sales; "no one wanted junk in their house," Ivan Karp later explained.[16]

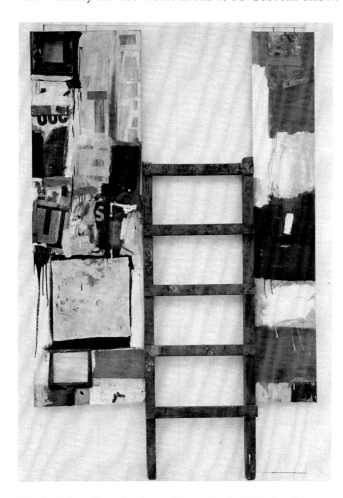

Fig. 4. Robert Rauschenberg, *Winter Pool*, 1959. Combine-painting: oil, paper, fabric, metal, transparent tape, wood, on canvas, plus wood ladder, handkerchief, and button, 89½ × 58½ × 4" (227.3 × 148.6 × 10.2 cm). Collection of Mr. and Mrs. Victor W. Ganz.

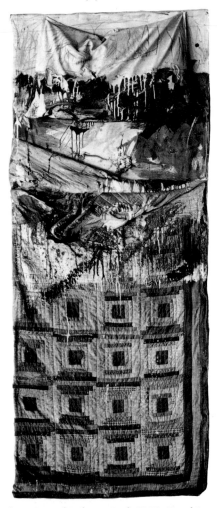

Fig. 6. Robert Rauschenberg, *Bed*, 1955. Combine-painting with bed: oil and pencil on pillow, quilt, sheet, on wood supports, 75¼ × 31½ × 6½" (191.1 × 80 × 16.5 cm). Collection of Mr. and Mrs. Leo Castelli.

The aesthetic lessons of Abstract Expressionism, however, were not entirely lost on Rauschenberg. Instead of rejecting its virtuoso brushwork, he simply applied it to mundane objects (Fig. 6)—a conjunction that marked the first break with the orthodoxy of Abstract Expressionism. Rauschenberg's innovative use of materials which evoked the grit of everyday street life, although distasteful to many, became a rallying point for younger artists.

It was Allan Kaprow who took the next step by uniting Rauschenberg's treatment of found objects and perishable urban refuse with what he felt were the spatial implications of Pollock's paintings.[17] For Kaprow, Pollock's large-scale, all-over canvases had become environments in their own right, extending psychologically beyond the rectangle into the room and enveloping the viewer. In Pollock's

hands, he argued, the "act of painting" had become a ritual in which painting was merely one of the materials. To go beyond Pollock meant going beyond painting.

Pollock, as I see him, left us at the point where we must become preoccupied with and even dazzled by the space and objects of our everyday life, either our bodies, clothes, rooms, or, if need be, the vastness of Forty-Second Street. Not satisfied with the *suggestion* through paint of our other senses, we shall utilize the specific substances of sight, sound, movements, people, odors, touch. Objects of every sort are materials for the new art: paint, chairs, food, electric and neon lights, smoke, water, old socks, a dog, movies, a thousand other things which will be discovered by the present generation of artists . . . . The young artist . . . will discover out of ordinary things the meaning of ordinariness. He will not try to make them extraordinary. Only their real meaning will be stated.[18]

Kaprow's assemblages began to extend further and further from the wall into the space of the room, making literal what had only been implied by Pollock's non-hierarchical canvases. In his exhibition at the Hansa Gallery in New York in the fall of 1958, Kaprow created an encompassing, maze-like environment. Viewers made their way through strips of slashed and painted colored fabric suspended from the ceiling in rows, interspersed with sheets of plastic, crumpled cellophane, tangles of Scotch tape, and Christmas lights. Once every hour five tape machines located around the gallery played electronic music.[19]

This environment, as well as Kaprow's subsequent ones, differed markedly from the European precedents established by Kurt Schwitters' *Merzbau*, the Surrealists' enveloping exhibition installations, and by Frederick Kiesler, the architect-designer whose installation design for the opening of Peggy Guggenheim's Art of This Century Gallery in 1944 called for pictures to be suspended in midair or obliquely projected on poles from the walls. While allied technically to these earlier forms, Kaprow's environments remained fundamentally indebted to and nourished by Abstract Expressionism: he translated its energy, improvisational technique, and textural attributes into actual materials (Fig. 7). His cluttered, seemingly disordered arrangement of street junk suggested flux and impermanence, an association with Abstract Expressionism furthered by his gestural handling of paint. Indeed, visually, Kaprow's environments seemed a natural extension of the Abstract Expressionist sensibility.

Kaprow's works were nevertheless quite different from their Abstract Expressionist antecedents: they mark a shift from a subjective abstraction toward a more objective, unmediated relationship with the environment. By interjecting soiled and untidy artifacts of the street, Kaprow, along with Rauschenberg, evolved a new vernacular realism. This attraction to concrete objects would shortly lead artists into Happenings and, from there, into Pop Art.

Kaprow's environments sufficiently shocked the public to warrant his (and Rauschenberg's) inclusion in a March 1958 *Newsweek* article entitled "Trend to the 'Anti-Art.' "[20] The article named Kaprow as one of the dangerous radicals on the art horizon whose work threatened to overthrow sacrosanct values. The art community's perception of the work was similar but its conclusion was different: a year after his appearance in *Newsweek*, Kaprow was selected as one of the up-and-coming artists in the prestigious *Art in America* New Talent Awards.[21]

There were several galleries in New York City that supported such alternative expressions. The prototype was the Hansa Gallery, later described by George Segal as "an embryo that hinted at most of the major directions in art in New York."[22] Founded as an artists' cooperative in 1952 by former students of Hans Hofmann, the gallery served as the epicenter for a group of artists who were seeking ways to modify what they viewed as the restrictive content of Abstract Expressionism, either with figurative images or with found objects. Its membership included the assemblagists Stankiewicz and Follett as well as Jan Müller and Lester Johnson, two figure painters working in a heroic, humanistic style. Kaprow, along with Robert Whitman and Segal, formed the gallery's younger contingent.[23]

The gallery supported itself on monthly dues.[24] Sales, despite low prices, were a rarity. Ivan Karp,

assistant gallery director under Richard Bellamy for two years, recalls that it was a sensation to sell a painting for $350.[25] Attendance was so meager that much of the time Bellamy sat on a battered rug in the center of the gallery and read poetry.[26]

There existed no common ground in these early days between uptown and downtown exhibition spaces in New York. The Hansa Gallery's location on Central Park South was a notable exception. For most younger artists the possibility of an uptown show was remote. Even Tenth Street in Greenwich Village, where the second-generation Abstract Expressionists showed, was beyond their reach. For them, activity took place in small, Lower Manhattan maverick establishments often run by artists. These galleries differed from the Hansa Gallery, being more like what are today called alternative spaces than commercial establishments.

The earliest was the City Gallery, run by artist

Fig. 7. Allan Kaprow's environment *An Apple Shrine* at the Judson Gallery, Judson Memorial Church, New York, 1960. Photograph by Robert R. McElroy.

Fig. 8. Documentation of Peter Schumann's *Totentanz* displayed in the Hall of Issues in the Judson Memorial Church, New York, 1962. Photograph by Peter Moore.

Red Grooms and his partner, Jay Milder. Grooms had come to New York from Nashville in 1956. In 1958, still feeling like an outsider, yet anxious to show his work, he decided to open a gallery in his studio. With the Hansa Gallery as his inspiration, Grooms showed deliberately crude, figurative work by artists such as Bob Thompson, Lester Johnson, and Mimi Gross. It was there that Claes Oldenburg and Jim (then Jimmy) Dine had their first public exposure in New York. Grooms moved the following year to the Lower East Side, where he opened the Delancey Street Museum. Here again he featured figurative art, environments, and what by then had become their temporal extension, Happenings. These successive galleries were models for other informal artist-run places, especially those emphasizing raunchy materials picked up off the street.

More public than Grooms' exhibition spaces were the Reuben Gallery and the Judson Gallery, both of which supported young, downtown artists whose work was impermanent, with strong expressionistic and figurative overtones. The Judson Gallery, which opened in late 1958, featured a lively assortment of experimental and then-unfashionable work from both visual and performing artists. Located in the basement of the Judson Memorial Church on Washington Square, the gallery was one aspect of a program initiated by Reverend Howard

Fig. 9. Lucas Samaras, *Untitled*, 1959. Cloth and plaster, 9¼ × 7½ × 7½" (23.5 × 19.1 × 19.1 cm). Collection of the artist.

Moody and his assistant minister, Bud (Bernard) Scott, to expand the church's social and political involvement with the neighborhood and draw upon the creative energies of the community. Not surprisingly, considering its location in the center of the country's most avant-garde art community, it soon became a locus of vital experimentation in dance, theater, poetry, and the visual arts.[27] It was here, for example, that the Judson Dance Theater developed its new language for dance; where many of the early Happenings were first staged; where the Judson Poet's Theater and Peter Schumann's Bread and Butter Theater performed; and where the Hall of Issues—a large room used for weekly community discussions about politics and aesthetics—was located. Functioning like a giant bulletin board, the hall was available on Sunday afternoons from two to five o'clock, or until the space was filled, to any artist who chose to pin, tack, or tape any manner of object around the room, be it a painting, poem, essay, newspaper clipping, or photograph (Fig. 8). The accumulated items remained on view until the following Wednesday, when the social, political, and aesthetic issues raised by them were discussed.

The second important nexus for the downtown community was the Reuben Gallery, opened by Anita Reuben in October 1959.[28] Initially located on Fourth Avenue, the gallery provided what at the time was a radical new kind of commercial exhibition space—bigger than uptown galleries yet more finished than the small storefronts along Tenth Street. More important, the gallery also advocated a new form of art. Anita Reuben opened her space with Kaprow's first public Happening and devoted her entire 1960–61 season to this transitory art form.

Perhaps because sales were marginal at best, there existed a free exchange of artists between the Judson and Reuben galleries, with many of those who showed regularly at the Reuben Gallery during its two years of existence—George Brecht, Kaprow, Robert Whitman, Jim Dine, Claes Oldenburg, Lucas Samaras, Red Grooms, Renee Miller (Anita Reuben's sister), and Martha Edelheit—exhibiting at the Judson Gallery as well. What united these artists was their desire to go beyond the rectangle, beyond painting as it had previously been practiced. As with other downtown artists, a kind of

vitality and frenzy infused their work. They explored new ideas with unremitting relish, combining figurative impulses with the physicality and textures of low city life. From this period (1959–60) came Samaras' plaster figures (Fig. 9); Oldenburg's figure paintings and *papier mâché* sculpture (Fig. 10); Dine's figurative and Rauschenberg-like assemblages (Fig. 11); Grooms' figurative paintings and collages (Figs. 12, 13); Miller's and Edelheit's painted, shaped constructions (Fig. 14); and Brecht's found-object boxes (Fig. 15). Using throwaway materials—cloth, plaster, cardboard, or paper—the artists appropriated the rubble of the city for both the subject and the materials of their work (Fig. 16).

To these artists, abstract art related only to art; they sought, instead, an art related to life. Being "real" meant imbuing their work with the grit and decay of the city. Oldenburg's sentiments about the need to present life rather than transmute it into

Fig. 10. Claes Oldenburg, *Woman's Leg*, 1959. Newspaper soaked in wheat paste over wire frame, painted with casein, 38½ × 16½ × 10″ (97.8 × 41.9 × 25.4 cm). Collection of Raymond Saroff.

Fig. 11. Jim Dine, *Greer Suit*, 1959. Oil and cloth (shown without frame), 62 × 24″ (157.5 × 61 cm). Collection of the artist.

abstraction could have stood as a general manifesto: "If you're a sensitive person," he wrote during this period, "and you live in the city, and you want to face the city and not escape from it you just have to come to grips . . . with the landscape of the city, with the dirt of the city, and the accidental possibilities of the city."[29]

This attitude was not unlike that held by Beat poets Jack Kerouac and Allen Ginsberg—both cultural heroes, comparable to movie stars, to this generation of artists.[30] In *Howl*, for example, Ginsberg had implicitly claimed that nothing was too pedestrian or commonplace for poetry; that the experience of the supermarket or superhighway was as appropriate a subject matter for poetry as the sublime. Moreover, the life-style of the Beat subculture, with its apparent absence of social pretensions, was regarded by young visual artists as the paradigm of what living the creative life meant.[31]

The downtown art scene in those days was remarkably intimate. Everyone knew everyone else—not through the bars that had functioned so effectively as the social meeting ground for the Abstract Expressionists, but through encounters at

Fig. 12. Red Grooms, *Portrait of Joan*, 1959. Oil on canvas, 58 × 59″ (147.3 × 149.9 cm). Collection of Louise and Virgil Le Quire.

Fig. 13. Red Grooms, *Policewoman*, 1959. Wood and metal, 45 × 29 × 10″ (114.3 × 73.7 × 25.4 cm). David K. Anderson Gallery, New York.

performance events and gallery openings attended by dancers, painters, sculptors, musicians, poets, and actors. Within this network of artists, aesthetic ideologies and loyalties were neither narrowly drawn nor mutually exclusive; visual artists mingled as freely with dancers and performing artists as with other painters and sculptors, with the result that aesthetic influences moved easily back and forth across disciplines. Still, the liveliness of the scene notwithstanding, audiences were small, collectors almost non-existent. To these artists, isolated from the commercial mainstream and living marginal, bohemian existences, the idea of making money seemed remote. Being outside the Establishment in a special cabal inspired a remarkable camaraderie, much like that which had developed among the Cubists and Dadaists. Alan Solomon's description of the Reuben Gallery as "almost a secret, a very 'in' thing, known only to a small group" applied to the entire range of downtown activities.[32] In retrospect it seems almost inevitable that members of such an exclusive yet alienated group would take it upon themselves to redefine the boundaries of art.

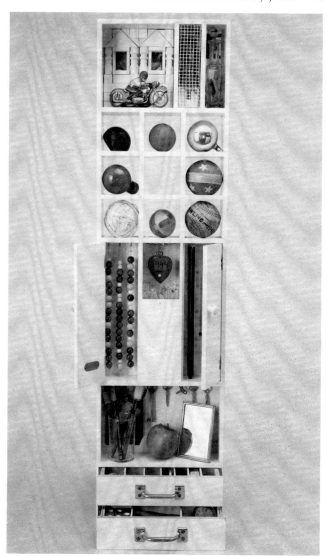

Fig. 15. George Brecht, *Repository*, 1961. Mixed media assemblage, 40⅜ × 10½ × 3⅛" (102.6 × 26.7 × 7.9 cm). The Museum of Modern Art, New York; Larry Aldrich Foundation Fund.

Fig. 14. Martha Edelheit, *Frabjous Day*, 1959. Canvas, sheet aluminum, oil, and collage, 58½ × 51½" (148.6 × 130.8 cm). Collection of the artist.

Working in this milieu, Oldenburg and Dine began to move beyond traditional forms of expression. Encouraged by Kaprow's environments, they too created totally encompassing found-object tableaux for their joint exhibition, "Ray-Gun," which opened at the Judson Gallery in January 1960.[33] Consisting of messy, cluttered arrangements of urban refuse, these "huge living constructions," as they were billed, exemplified the kind of break artists were making with Abstract Expressionism. Using techniques similar to Kaprow's, Oldenburg and Dine substituted found things for paint and canvas. And like Kaprow, they retained the "look"

Fig. 16. Jim Dine, *Bedspring*, 1960. Mixed media construction, 48 × 72 × 8″ (121.9 × 182.9 × 20.3 cm). Collection of Allan Kaprow and Vaughan Rachel.

Fig. 17. Jim Dine in his environment *The House* at the Judson Gallery, Judson Memorial Church, New York, 1960.

Fig. 18. Jim Dine with materials for his environment *The House* at the Judson Gallery, Judson Memorial Church, New York, 1960.

and spirit of their Abstract Expressionist predecessors, translating thickly impastoed bravura paint into three-dimensional material textures.

In Dine's environment *The House*, the gallery walls were completely obliterated with a dense accretion of paint-splattered rags, paper, found objects, scrawled words, and painted images (Figs. 17, 18).[34] As was true of all of Dine's work in this period, figurative references abounded: hidden within the accumulated debris were images of heads, eyes, and other body parts. Similarly, Oldenburg's tableau *The Street* was a jumble of two-dimensional, silhouetted figures and objects whose ragged, blackened contours and monochrome brown-black tones reeked of the decay and brutality of life in the Lower East Side slums (Fig. 19). Oldenburg invited the audience to add its own debris to the floor of *The Street* and encouraged other artists to pin up anything whatsoever on the "communication board" he had set up adjacent to the gallery.[35]

Anticipating the open attitude toward commercial imagery that would later find expression in Pop

Fig. 19. Claes Oldenburg's environment *The Street* at the Judson Gallery, Judson Memorial Church, New York, 1960.

Art, the text accompanying the two environments identified them as having "derived from American popular art, street art and other informal sources."[36] In a panel discussion the previous year, Oldenburg had already characterized this kind of art as a contemporary primitivism, achieved through the exploitation of popular culture.[37] This approach was again implied in the series of comic books Oldenburg, Dine, and various friends produced throughout the exhibition on the church's stencil machine.[38]

Oldenburg reinstalled *The Street* in May 1960 at the Reuben Gallery, where it underwent a slight transformation—the disheveled and debris-filled Judson Gallery version became substantially less dense and more ordered, almost antiseptic by comparison. Rather than tacking figures closely together against the wall and littering the floor with refuse, Oldenburg now isolated the fragmented silhouettes as discrete forms, suspending them from the ceiling or projecting them perpendicularly from the walls (Fig. 20). In this way the images began to assume an independent status—a step

that would lead Oldenburg into Pop Art sculpture.

This intense two-year period of what was known among its practitioners as "junk art" culminated in the exhibition "New Media—New Forms," presented in two stages at the Martha Jackson Gallery in June and September 1960 (Fig. 21). What made the show particularly noteworthy was its size—seventy-one artists participated—and its uptown location. The move uptown signaled a new status for this art form, from underground expression to mainstream phenomenon. The exhibition brought together for the first time a wide range of American artists with a predilection for found materials of street origin—Stankiewicz, Nevelson, Whitman, Kaprow, John Chamberlain, Follett, Oldenburg, Dine, Mark di Suvero, and Brecht—with European artists such as Schwitters and Jean Dubuffet. The predominant criterion for inclusion was the artists' use of junk or industrial debris.

The exhibition's broad scope resulted in the grouping of artists who in retrospect hardly seem to have been part of the same movement. John Chamberlain and Mark di Suvero, for example: al-

Fig. 20. Claes Oldenburg and Anita Reuben in Oldenburg's environment *The Street* at the Reuben Gallery, New York, 1960. Photograph by Charles Rappaport.

Fig. 21. "New Media—New Forms" at the Martha Jackson Gallery, New York, June 1960.

though both would later exhibit with Pop artists and former Hansa and Reuben Gallery artists at Bellamy's Green Gallery, their sculpture is more properly seen as a three-dimensional extension of the imagery and movement of Abstract Expressionism than as proto-Pop (Figs. 22, 23). While they never camouflaged the function or previous life of their component materials to the extent that Stankiewicz or Nevelson did, they nevertheless remained essentially indifferent to referential asso-

ciations. Thus, their inclusion in the exhibition was based primarily on the fact that their work was distinctly urban in character and constructed out of found, undisguised, chiefly industrial discards.

Much of the work by the younger assemblagists in Martha Jackson's exhibition aggressively highlighted a crudeness and ugliness in the city landscape. In this sense, the artists harked back to the Ashcan School, a group of American painters at the turn of the century who had likewise sought to depict urban life as it was, in all its common and seemingly ugly aspects.[39] Both groups incited critical wrath. Yet it was not the assemblagists' subject matter but their apparent presentation of untransformed materials that was taken by many as the greatest affront to good taste. Hilton Kramer, in an otherwise measured review, wrote:

> the bulk of the work in the "New Forms—New Media" exhibitions cannot be looked at twice . . . because the material itself has at no point been submitted to a conception that is sufficiently compelling to sustain itself as art. . . . Many of the assemblages of junk at the Jackson exhibition have no more connection with the *work* of art than those pieces of driftwood that people used to take home from their summer vacations.[40]

Even champions of the show were not certain how to view the lack of "transformation" in these new forms of junk art. Some perceived willful antagonistic protests; many, in an attempt to categorize this art, attached to it the then-ubiquitous label, Neo-Dada.[41] Indeed, in visually repudiating previously held conceptions of what art was supposed to look like and aspire to, the work did perpetuate Dada's anarchic spirit; nevertheless, the la-

Fig. 22. John Chamberlain, *Johnny Bird*, 1959. Welded and painted steel, 59 × 53 × 45½" (149.9 × 134.6 × 115.6 cm). Collection of Sydney and Frances Lewis.

bel clouded rather than illuminated the contemporary artists' intentions.

Ironically, it was precisely the lack of transformation in the works exhibited at the Jackson Gallery that proved to be a harbinger of the future. By tacitly asserting that the subject of the artwork could be identical with objects in the world, the assemblagists paved the way for the emergence of Pop Art, which simply replaced urban detritus with scavenged motifs from the mass media: "found objects" supplanted by "found images."

A year and a half after the "New Media—New Forms" exhibition, The Museum of Modern Art mounted "The Art of Assemblage." Despite the exhibition's timely scheduling, the emphasis on historical rather than contemporary manifestations of assemblage revealed the curator's apathy toward the more revolutionary aspects of the new work. The exclusion of Kaprow, Oldenburg, and Dine, for example, made for a pallid, timorous contemporary section, one which looked too reminiscent of earlier Dada and Surrealist experiments. The exhibition thus failed to galvanize much enthusiasm for or understanding of the innovative art forms.

It hardly mattered. By the time the show opened, many of the artists who might have been included had moved well beyond assemblage. Both Dine and Oldenburg had begun making the replications of common objects that became known as Pop Art. And Kaprow had abandoned the juxtaposition of found objects for a new art of juxtaposed events, launching, in the process, a new performance art movement which captured the attention of some of the most inventive artists of his generation.

Fig. 23. Mark di Suvero, *Ladder Piece*, 1961–62. Wood, steel, painted wood, 75″ high (190.5 cm). Collection of Philip Johnson; Promised Gift to The Museum of Modern Art, New York.

Happenings

Kaprow's mentor in venturing beyond the strictly visual arts was the composer John Cage.[42] In his class on experimental music composition at the New School for Social Research from 1958 to 1959, Cage expounded his theories about the viability of non-traditional sources of aesthetic material, and encouraged his students to experiment with theater events by assigning performance projects as part of the course. These weekly sessions were a seminal influence on Kaprow and others of his generation. At a time when acceptable aesthetic forms in the visual arts seemed limited to modes of Abstract Expressionism, Cage provided one of the few alternative models to which young artists could turn. Enthusiasm for his theories was not restricted to painters and sculptors. The small class also included filmmakers, musicians, and poets. Kaprow, Jackson Mac Low, George Brecht, Al Hansen, and Dick Higgins were among the regular students and often brought artist friends such as George Segal, Larry Poons, and Jim Dine. Kaprow later said of the course: "We all felt something terrifically exciting was going on in that class. I just couldn't wait to get back there every week."[43]

For Cage, the world itself was a work of art; he saw the aesthetic potential in the commonplace and accepted everyday noise as music. Making music was a means of revealing to people the beauty around them. The methods he chose were chance and indeterminacy. In Cage's 1952 composition *4'33"*, the pianist David Tudor had come out on stage, lifted the lid of the keyboard, and sat at the piano, without playing, for the duration of the piece. The random sounds and unexpected visual activities that happened within the time span constituted the work of art.

Cage's ambient sounds were like the found objects in assemblage. But his embrace of chance took "found art" one step further. By removing all traces of personal control in the making of sounds he radically redefined the function and meaning of art. To him, writing music was "an affirmation of life—not an attempt to bring order out of chaos nor to suggest improvements in creation, but simply a way of waking up to the very life we're living, which is so excellent once one gets one's mind and one's desires out of its way and lets it act of its own accord."[44] Only Marcel Duchamp with his ready-mades had come so close to obliterating the distinction between art and life. Yet Duchamp, in claiming the concept of the ready-made as his personal invention, had not relinquished his role as creator, nor had he fundamentally violated the uniqueness of the art object. Cage's work did both.

By the time Cage began teaching at the New School in 1958, he had been working as a composer for twenty-five years and was already considered a major force in the musical world. Pieces such as *4'33"* had played a key role in the musical community in legitimizing chance procedures (aleatory music) and ambient or "concrete" sound. The composers Earle Brown, Christian Wolff, Morton Feldman, and La Monte Young were particularly affected by Cage's theories.

Not satisfied with limiting himself to music, Cage had turned to theater early in his career, initially in "simultaneous" lectures—readings at which prerecorded tapes of his own voice played simultaneously with his live delivery. Shortly thereafter, Cage turned to a type of composition—exemplified by *Water Music* (1952)—in which the pianist pours water from pots, blows whistles under the water, uses a radio, and engages in various visual activities, such as playing with a pack of cards. Cage extended this interest in performance events while teaching during the summer of 1952 at Black Mountain College, an influential experimental school in North Carolina.[45] With several friends—Merce Cunningham, Rauschenberg, Tudor, and the poets M. C. Richards and Charles Olson—Cage organized an interdisciplinary performance consisting of music for piano and gramophone, poetry reading, dancing, lectures, films, and slides, all executed or exhibited by the performers independent of, but simultaneously with, one another.[46]

Although Cage himself did not continue these early forays into non-musical performance, he

Opposite: Claes Oldenburg in his Happening *Snapshots from the City*, 1960 (see Fig. 34).

taught its fundamental principles in his New School class. It was here that he described Surrealist and Dadaist soirées of the twenties and thirties. These theatrical events, with their capricious and dreamlike combinations of images and materials, obliterated conventional meanings in order to yield new ones. Robert Motherwell's 1951 anthology, *Dada Painters and Poets*, had already presented information about these soirées to an American audience. But it was not until Cage stimulated an interest in similar forms of theater that the book became a prized possession among artists. When isolated from their original political context, the Dadaist antics recorded in Motherwell's book lost their polemical edge and became additional models for an art of alogical juxtaposition.

Cage also advocated the theories of the French avant-garde playwright Antonin Artaud. Even before Artaud's book *The Theater and Its Double* appeared in English translation in 1958, it had already begun to exert a strong influence on American artists then beginning their own tentative performance activities. Artaud's radical prescriptions for theater—his pronouncements against narrative and his call for a primitive, ritualistic spectacle—provided a more emotional model than did Cage's. Artaud went further than most later Happening artists in proposing a "theater of cruelty," in which emotional involvement with the audience was achieved through an undercurrent of violence and suffering. But his admonition to circumvent traditional forms of theater found welcome listeners among younger American artists.

Kaprow, for one, was particularly affected by his experiences in Cage's class. His first experiment with an elaborate performance event occurred at a picnic for members of the Hansa Gallery at George Segal's farm in New Jersey several months before Kaprow showed his environmental piece at the Hansa Gallery in 1958 (p. 18). Structurally similar to Cage's 1952 Black Mountain performance, Kaprow's event called for members of the group to perform simultaneous but unrelated tasks: jumping through the props Kaprow and Segal had made from lumber and plastic sheeting; sitting in chicken coops rattling noisemakers; collectively painting a picture.[47]

This rather chaotic and unfocused event led to a more considered and public statement in *The An-*

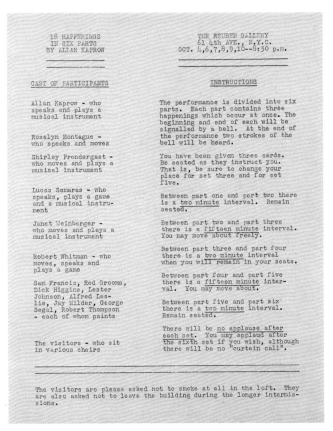

Fig. 24. Program notes for Allan Kaprow's *18 Happenings in Six Parts* at the Reuben Gallery, New York, 1959. Collection of Ellsworth Snyder.

thologist, a literary journal published at Rutgers University, where Kaprow taught art history. A 1959 issue of the journal included an article by Kaprow, "The Demiurge," calling for the creation of an entirely new art. At the end, Kaprow appended a section entitled "Something to Take Place: A Happening," in which he described a series of ordinary but disparate actions.[48] Although never realized as a performance, many of these elements found their way into Kaprow's *18 Happenings in Six Parts*, presented in the fall of 1959 for the opening of the Reuben Gallery (Fig. 24). For this ninety-minute piece, Kaprow divided the gallery into three sections with translucent sheets of plastic (Fig. 25). The performers, who included Kaprow, Whitman, Sam Francis, Alfred Leslie, and Segal, executed simple activities such as bending forward and extending their arms like wings, bouncing a ball, reading from placards, and playing records, as lights and slides went off and on in carefully programmed sequences.[49]

This piece was the first of what generically became known—to everyone save their creators—as

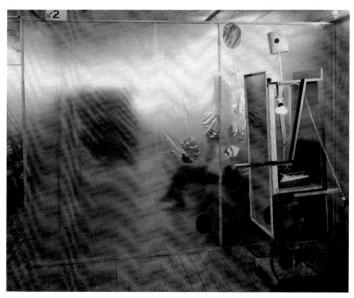

Fig. 25. Set for Allan Kaprow's *18 Happenings in Six Parts* at the Reuben Gallery, New York, 1959.

Happenings.[50] Extolling the concept of "total art," Happenings implicitly challenged the traditional separation between media. Why should artists limit themselves to painting or sculpture? Why musicians and composers only to sound? The idea of extending painting into actual space and time attracted a group of experimentally minded younger artists—among them, Whitman, Oldenburg, Hansen, Dine, and Grooms—all of whom knew Kaprow and, through interlocking friendships, one another.

What was especially critical to Kaprow was the Cagean notion of involving the audience, as in his instructions that viewers change rooms during the

Fig. 26. Allan Kaprow's environment *Words* at the Smolin Gallery, New York, 1962. Photographs by Robert R. McElroy.

Fig. 27. Allan Kaprow's environment *Yard* in the courtyard of the Martha Jackson Gallery during "Environments, Situations, Spaces," New York, 1961. Photograph by Robert R. McElroy.

Fig. 28. Allan Kaprow's Happening *The Courtyard* at the Mills Hotel, New York, 1962. Photograph by Lawrence Shustack.

performance of *18 Happenings in Six Parts*. This commitment to audience participation became of paramount importance in Kaprow's subsequent environments. In *Words* (1962), viewers were encouraged to write their own phrases on the constructed partitions; in *Yard* (1961), to walk on a pile of tires (Figs. 26, 27). As Kaprow's work developed, he came to view the involvement of the audience as an essential ingredient; eventually he would eliminate the separation between the viewer and the event altogether (p. 50).

Audience involvement was never as crucial to other Happening artists; their concern for viewer participation was manifested primarily by the forced proximity between audience and event. "Spectators" were crammed together in small spaces, often touching one another or brushing against the actors, who might be in front, above, or beneath them. This direct engagement of the viewer accounted for much of the impact of Happenings.[51]

Kaprow, under the influence of Cage, initially developed a detached and controlled approach to Happenings.[52] Less visually flamboyant than in the Happenings of other artists, his performers wore street clothes and executed deracinated commonplace tasks without emotional inflection. The relative spareness of Kaprow's sets and the absence of excessive physical displays can be attributed partially to the influence of Cage and partially to that of a dance performance given by Paul Taylor at Rutgers University in 1958. The performance consisted of Taylor, alone on the stage, executing single-gesture movements: at the sound of a woman's voice announcing the time, Taylor made movements such as turning his head, raising his arm, crouching, or twisting. After each "action" he returned to a neutral position and waited for the next time signal, which occurred at ten-second intervals.[53] A similar focus on carefully orchestrated, single gestures found its way into *18 Happenings in Six Parts*. In later works Kaprow became more absorbed in mythic and literary references. In *Tree* (1963), for example, a group of performers brandishing twigs advanced on a row of cars covered with hay—a reference to Birnam Wood in *Macbeth*; in *The Courtyard* (1962), a female figure suggested both Mother Nature and Aphrodite (Fig. 28).[54]

Red Grooms' Happenings, in contrast to Kaprow's, represented the physically flamboyant and improvisational side of Happenings.[55] Even before meeting Kaprow, Grooms had independently ventured into the performance arena with an event entitled *Play Called Fire*, staged at the Sun Gallery in Provincetown, Massachusetts, during the summer of 1958. He had earlier seen photographs in *Life* magazine of the French Action Painter Mathieu theatrically executing a painting in front of television cameras.[56] Inspired by these reports, Grooms had gone into the Provincetown gallery with various cans of paint and painted a canvas for twenty-five minutes before an incredulous public.

This notion of extending the "action" aspect of Abstract Expressionism into performance had been attempted earlier by the Gutai group of avant-garde artists from Osaka, Japan, whose work had been reported in *The New York Times* in 1957. The Gutai group, like Grooms, followed Mathieu's example in taking as their starting point the Abstract Expressionist focus on the act of creation. They turned the activity of painting into a performance by executing, before a live audience, such acts as throwing balls of colored pigment against blank canvases, modeling mud by rolling in it, and stamping footprints on large sheets of unrolled white vinyl.[57] The Gutai group's widely heralded

exhibition of paintings and documentary photographs at the Martha Jackson Gallery in September 1959 vindicated Grooms' earlier extension of Action Painting into theater.

But prior to the Gutai show, Grooms had heard about Kaprow's picnic Happening at Segal's, an event he described as "having opened things up for me by giving me license to do dumb things."[58] In the summer of 1959, he had also met Kaprow in Provincetown. Encouraged by Kaprow to pursue his theatrical interests, Grooms created his first non-narrative "play," *The Walking Man* (Fig. 29), that September. The set for this Happening, which retained the figurative and gestural character of his paintings, was assembled out of objects from the Provincetown dump—bedsprings, doors, tin cans, and other pieces of refuse. Grooms likened the result to an acrobat's apparatus in the circus, with the performers improvising their actions according to the dictates and logic of the materials rather than the logic of a narrative.[59]

Grooms' next Happenings, *The Burning Building* (December 1959) and *The Magic Train Ride* (January 1960), presented at the Delancey Street Museum and Reuben Gallery, respectively, captured even more the atmosphere of the circus and amusement park (Figs. 30–32). Spoken references to Dick Tracy, Orphan Annie, Tootsie, and the Statue of Liberty reinforced the connection with popular culture. Lasting just over ten minutes, these Happenings resembled fast-action Surrealist plays, in which non-actors engaged in a series of collage-like vignettes. Working at a frantic pace, Grooms had conceived and performed his three major Happenings in less than five months. But he soon began to

Fig. 29. Poster for Red Grooms' Happening *The Walking Man* at the Sun Gallery, Provincetown, Massachusetts, 1959.

30a.

30b.

30c.

30d.

30e.

Figs. 30a-e. Scenes from Red Grooms' Happening *The Burning Building* at the Delancey Street Museum, New York, 1959. The Firemen, Terry Barrell (left) and Jay Milder (right), do a clumsy dance (30a); the Pasty Man, Red Grooms, discovers the girl, Joan Herbst, in the Firemen's den, while the Soundman, Sylvia Small, reads a love poem (30b and 30c); the Firemen then gorge themselves on turkey, while the Pasty Man hides (30d); the Pasty Man escapes by somersaulting through the windows of The Burning Building (30e). Photographs by John Cohen (30a, 30d) and Max Baker (30b, 30c, 30e).

feel self-conscious about their lack of narrative continuity and his original fearlessness in assaulting more established forms of theater faltered.[60] In late 1960 Grooms went to Europe. The two years he spent there effectively removed him from active participation in Happenings and their aesthetic consequences. But the primitive energy and animalistic intensity of his events exerted an enormous impact on other early theater experiments, particularly those of Claes Oldenburg and Jim Dine.

Dine and Oldenburg first ventured into Happenings during the showing of their environments *The House* and *The Street* at the Judson Gallery in February–March 1960 (Figs. 17–19). Stimulated by the theatrical events being staged by Kaprow and Grooms, Oldenburg organized a series of performances under the aegis of his invented doppelgänger, Ray Gun. Called "Ray Gun Spex," the series presented Happenings by Oldenburg, Dine,

Fig. 31. Backdrop for Red Grooms' Happening *The Magic Train Ride* at the Reuben Gallery, New York, 1960.

Hansen, Kaprow, Whitman, and Dick Higgins.[61] Happenings themselves had been known only a few months, and only Kaprow and Whitman had previously created any work within this new art form.[62] As part of the series, Oldenburg and Dine printed money on the church stencil machine and—as if forecasting their later parodies on merchandising and commerce—distributed one million dollars to everyone buying a ticket to the performances. At intermission the audience could use this money to purchase the junk objects and debris which had been picked up off the street and were on display in the gallery lobby.

Of the six participants in "Ray Gun Spex," Oldenburg and Dine came the closest to fulfilling the prophetic implications of the word "spex"—an abbreviation for spectacle which meant burlesque in Oldenburg's native Swedish.[63] Oldenburg's Happening used *The Street* as its set: *Snapshots from the City* consisted of thirty-two posed tableaux which were briefly illuminated by periodic flashes

of light (Fig. 33). Straining to see the piece under these conditions was a way of involving and, to some later critics, brutalizing the audience.[64] Only by peering through an open door could viewers catch sight of the characters amid the tumble and debris of *The Street*. Conceived as a "painting in the shape of theater," as the Judson Gallery press release termed it, *Snapshots from the City* dealt with many of the themes implied in Oldenburg's environment—the danger, misery, and deprivation that prevails on the fringes of society. Performers wore elaborate costumes and executed loosely scripted actions based on character stereotypes, which would emerge in Oldenburg's subsequent Happenings (Figs. 34–36).[65]

Oldenburg's next Happening, *Blackouts* (December 1960), combined dream images with pieces of daily life—a baby's rattle, a cart, roller skates. This growing reliance on concrete things to convey meaning would eventually lead Oldenburg to abandon human figures in his sculpture and instead to

Fig. 32. Red Grooms as the Pasty Man and Terry Barrell as the Conductor in Grooms' *The Magic Train Ride* at the Reuben Gallery, New York, 1960. Photograph by John Cohen.

Opposite: Fig. 33. Pat Oldenburg (on ladder) and Tom Wesselmann (crouching below) in Claes Oldenburg's Happening *Fotodeath* at the Reuben Gallery, New York, 1961.

Fig. 34. Claes Oldenburg in his Happening *Snapshots from the City* at the Judson Gallery, Judson Memorial Church, New York, 1960. Photograph by Martha Holmes, *Time* magazine.

create objects which served as their surrogates. By 1962, when Oldenburg presented his ten-part cycle of Happenings in the context of his environment *The Store* (p. 70), he could write: "Nothing is communicated or represented except through its attachment to an object."[66] As his Happenings evolved, the psychological torment conveyed by scenes such as those in *Injun, I* (Fig. 37)—where bodies lay in the midst of charred rubbish—was eventually replaced with images of greater sensuality, optimism, and humor (Figs. 38, 39).

Dine's Happening *The Smiling Workman* revealed the almost demonic obsession he brought to all his work during this period. Lasting slightly more than thirty seconds, it consisted of Dine, dressed in a paint-splattered smock, with his face painted red, his mouth black, rapidly scribbling "I love what I'm doing" in orange and blue paint on an empty canvas; he then drank from the jars of paint, drenched himself with what remained, and fin-

Fig. 35. Claes Oldenburg as the Prop Man wrapped in newspaper in a rehearsal of his Happening *Store Days, II* at the Ray Gun Mfg. Co., New York, 1962. Photograph by Robert R. McElroy.

Fig. 36. Claes Oldenburg as the Prop Man and Pat Oldenburg as the Performer in Claes Oldenburg's Happening *Store Days, II* at the Ray Gun Mfg. Co., New York, 1962. Photograph by Robert R. McElroy.

ished by diving through the canvas (Fig. 40). As in his three other Happenings—*The Vaudeville Show*, *Car Crash*, and *A Shining Bed*, all performed at the Reuben Gallery in 1960 (Figs. 41, 42)—there was no elaborate script and Dine was the central performer. With the exception of the lighthearted *The Vaudeville Show*, these works were like nightmares in which fear of an unknown, yet ever-present, danger took hold.

Dine later repudiated his Happenings as immature and too much like the acting out of his obsessive daily life.[67] He felt the permanence of his paintings gave viewers time to absorb different levels of meaning; Happenings were too fleeting for this kind of reflective perception. Moreover, he resented the absence of critical standards. "Anyone could do anything and be liked," he later remarked. "The audiences were laughing at everything."[68]

Of the original Happening makers, Robert Whitman was the artist most involved in creating a the-

ater of abstract images. A student of Kaprow at Rutgers University, he had been the youngest member of the Hansa Gallery. The junk culture assemblages he showed there and later, at the Reuben Gallery (Figs. 43, 44), displayed a gentleness and quietude which would find expression in his Happenings, as would his essentially abstract approach. Whitman rejected character and narrative, preferring instead sequences and overlays of abstract pictorial images. In order to differentiate his intent from that of his colleagues, he disavowed the word "Happening," calling his works "theater pieces." Whitman's first such efforts, among them *E.G.* and *Duet for a Small Smell*, his contribution to "Ray Gun Spex," were visually informed by a found-object aesthetic (Figs. 45, 46). In later pieces—*The American Moon*, *Mouth*, and *Flower*— he turned to delicate materials like fabric and paper to orchestrate poetic, dreamlike sequences of nonnarrative imagery (Figs. 47–50). In contrast to the

Fig. 37. Lucas Samaras (left) and Claes Oldenburg in Oldenburg's Happening *Injun, I* at the Ray Gun Mfg. Co., New York, 1962. Photographs by Robert R. McElroy.

Fig. 38. Öyvind Fahlström (left), Milet Andrejevic (center), and Mariela Maza (right) in Claes Oldenburg's Happening *Nekropolis, I* at the Ray Gun Mfg. Co., New York, 1962. Photograph by Robert R. McElroy.

Fig. 39. Lucas Samaras (left), Pat Oldenburg (center), and Claes Oldenburg (right) in Claes Oldenburg's Happening *Sports* at the Green Gallery, New York, 1962. Photograph by Judy B. Ross.

meticulous precision of Kaprow's early pieces and the raw physicality of the other Happening artists, these later events were sparse, exuding an ethereal quality—"real matter being insubstantial," as Segal later described them.[69]

During the years 1958–64, performance events were as vital to the downtown art community as painting and sculpture. Although they absorbed the attention of a relatively small number of artists, they produced an atmosphere of frenetic energy and adventure. Yet the inherent transience of Happenings has made them seem, in retrospect, less significant than more permanent art forms. Since our understanding of them is based solely on documentation, it is difficult to envision the intensely charged climate in which they took place.[70] At the time, however, Happenings were perceived as a dramatic redefinition of the possibilities of art, as an overlapping and interpenetration of art forms resulting in a strikingly innovative form of expression.

However varied the approaches of individual Happening makers, their performances had a common denominator: they amalgamated the junk materials of assemblage, the gestural vocabulary of Abstract Expressionism, and Cage's theories of non-narrative performance. Since Kaprow, Oldenburg, and Dine had already merged Abstract Expressionism with found objects in their junk environments, the visual connection between Happenings and these environments was obviously

Fig. 40. Jim Dine in his Happening *The Smiling Workman* at the Judson Gallery, Judson Memorial Church, New York, 1960. Photograph by Martha Holmes, *Time* magazine.

Fig. 41. Jim Dine and Judy Tersch in Dine's Happening *Car Crash* at the Reuben Gallery, New York, 1960. Photograph by Robert R. McElroy.

close. Happenings displayed a similar crudeness, disorder, and textural richness. The costumes and sets in Happenings were constructed out of the same kind of urban, cast-off materials as those employed in environments—newspapers, junk, string, rags, cardboard, wood crates, and the like. Indeed, Oldenburg and Dine had used their environments *The Street* and *The House* as the sets for their first Happenings; and Grooms had exhibited the set from his Happening *The Magic Train Ride* at his 1960 Reuben Gallery show (Fig. 31). What Happenings added to the messy, object-oriented tableaux were actions, sounds, light, and movement. Happenings were like junk assemblages come to life— "the passive and active sides of a single coin," as Kaprow once described them.[71] Their impetus was the same: Oldenburg remarked that Happenings were intended (as were junk assemblages) to counter "the notion of a work of art as something outside of experience, something that is terribly precious."[72]

Just as the contiguous elements in assemblage were juxtaposed without narrative logic, the sequential actions in Happenings conveyed no sense of cause and effect. Happenings dispensed with a linear story line; like a series of anecdotes, they presented compartmentalized events in which each action was self-contained—no plots or stories, no character portrayals, no sense of time and

Fig. 42. Jim Dine in his Happening *The Vaudeville Show* at the Reuben Gallery, New York, 1960. Photograph by Robert R. McElroy.

Fig. 43. Robert Whitman, *Untitled*, 1958. Mixed media construction, 72 × 72 × 72" (182.9 × 182.9 × 182.9 cm). Installed at the Hansa Gallery, New York, 1959.

Fig. 44. Installation views of Robert Whitman's one-artist exhibition at the Reuben Gallery, New York, 1959.

Less obvious than the connection between Happenings and junk environments was that between Happenings and Action Painting. Yet Kaprow stressed repeatedly that Happenings had grown out of the demands for flux and process in advanced American art; that essentially they were Action Paintings with objects.[74] He was not alone in acknowledging this inheritance. "Sometimes," Oldenburg said, "I feel that what I'm doing with living material, with people and objects and situations is something like what they (de K[ooning] and P[ollock]) did with paint. I just have substituted material."[75]

In retrospect, the action component of Happenings was indeed a logical outcome of the "event" orientation of Abstract Expressionism. Grooms, for example, later credited the impetus for his Happenings to the atmosphere created by the words "Action Painting."[76] In the hands of artists like Pollock and de Kooning, the gestural tactics of Abstract Expressionism had been transformed into something resembling actual performance. Pollock could almost be described as "dancing" on top of his canvas in the act of painting; the painting itself, as Harold Rosenberg argued, was merely the record of this movement.[77] Happening artists took the next step by opening the curtain on the event, moving it from behind the scenes to center stage. This shift from private to public art-making affected the art-spectator relationship by making the spectator, at the very least, a tacit participant in the creative act. Moreover, by presenting actual gestures and movements, Happening artists "literalized" the action in de Kooning's and Pollock's paintings. This drive toward literalism ran through the period. It motivated the assemblagists' use of tangible objects as it later would the Pop artists' and Minimalists' use of concrete images and unambiguous forms.

The absence of plot and climax in Happenings provided a further analogue to Abstract Expressionist painting, in this case to its non-hierarchical character. The consequent difficulty of determining when a Happening was over recalls Rosenberg's maxim that an Action Painting was never fully complete but was forever in a state of becoming. Similarly analogous was the quality of spontaneity in both art forms. Because of financial restrictions and the legacy of Cage's attitude toward chance and

place.[73] Performers simply enacted dreamlike vignettes whose content and sequence eluded logical comprehension. Instead of the character-context matrices of traditional theater, the focus in Happenings was on the props, costumes, and sets. Where words were used they functioned as sounds, independent of meaning. The primary concern was the creation of vivid and arresting "pictures" whose potential for superimposed and constantly changing imagery offered a degree of invention far greater than that in more static art forms.

Fig. 45. Jim Dine dressed as the Ball Man in a rehearsal of Robert Whitman's theater piece *E.G.* at the Reuben Gallery, New York, 1960. Photograph by Robert R. McElroy.

Fig. 46. Final scene of Robert Whitman's theater piece *E.G.* at the Reuben Gallery, New York, 1960. Photograph by Robert R. McElroy.

Fig. 47. Robert Whitman, standing next to the set of his theater piece *The American Moon* (under construction) at the Reuben Gallery, New York, 1960. Photograph by Robert R. McElroy.

indeterminacy, most Happenings were presented with only sketchy instructions and few rehearsals.[78] (Kaprow's early, more orchestrated ones were exceptional.)

However, unlike Abstract Expressionist paintings, Happenings—impermanent and not replicable—were inherently uncommercial. They could be commissioned but not bought or sold; and they could not be collected. For Kaprow, this result was deliberate, an anti-capitalist effort to prevent the stockpiling of art by the rich.[79] Circumventing the marketplace was also a means of avoiding the pitfalls of success—a trap into which the first-generation Abstract Expressionists appeared to have fallen. According to Kaprow, the creative energy of vanguard artists in the 1950s had been dissipated by public acclaim and financial windfalls.[80] Even in his capacity as unofficial director of the Judson Gallery in 1960–61, he had cautioned against media attention and publicity seeking.[81] Only those on the fringes of society, he implied, could legitimately be creative. This view of the artist as an outcast, unappreciated in his own time, was commonly held by members of the Abstract Expressionist generation. For Kaprow, however, these very Abstract Expressionists had become insiders through their success.[82]

But even Kaprow sensed the public's inevitable cooption of this challenging art form. Operating

Fig. 48. Lucas Samaras in Robert Whitman's theater piece *The American Moon* at the Reuben Gallery, New York, 1960. Photograph by Robert R. McElroy.

outside the marketplace did not, in the end, guarantee artists their role as outsiders; the absence of a tradable commodity was no defense against public popularity and approval. Happenings rapidly acquired the veneer of chic. By 1964 there were signs that the seemingly unassimilable was becoming welcome. Museums had begun to commission performances in 1962—Kaprow at the Walker Art Center, Minneapolis, Oldenburg at the Dallas Museum for Contemporary Art. By that time, Oldenburg lamented, "the whole thing had become totally commercial."[83]

Perhaps because of this, the era of Happenings was relatively short-lived. Of the original Happening artists, only Whitman remained committed to large-scale theatrical productions. Kaprow continued producing Happenings but their form shifted in the middle sixties from the elaborate sets and carefully rehearsed scripts of his earlier works to a sparser kind of event enacted without an audience (p. 50). By 1960 Grooms had left for Europe and had ceased making Happenings; Dine virtually stopped then as well. Oldenburg remained with the genre only until 1966. Yet however brief their prime, Happenings had brought a sense of vitality to the art community that it was not quick to forget. In the process they had precipitated new attitudes about the possibilities of art-making which would radically redefine the direction of art.

Fig. 49. Chippie McClellan in a rehearsal of Robert Whitman's theater piece *Mouth* at the Reuben Gallery, New York, 1961. Photograph by Robert R. McElroy.

Fig. 50. Chippie McClellan and Judy Tersch in a rehearsal of Robert Whitman's theater piece *Mouth* at the Reuben Gallery, New York, 1961. Photograph by Robert R. McElroy.

Fluxus

During the period Happenings were being formulated in New York, a parallel mode of performance art, later identified with the Fluxus group, was emerging from Cage's class at the New School. These works differed from Happenings in their rejection of the physicality and gestural vocabulary of Abstract Expressionism, favoring instead a conceptual rigor and attentiveness to "insignificant" phenomena. In place of visually engaging costumes and sets, these Events (so-called to distinguish them from Happenings) were enacted in unadorned settings by performers wearing ordinary street clothes. They usually consisted of a unitary gesture, such as a light going on and off, or a line of performers shuffling across the floor. Typically, a deadpan wit pervaded the disciplined enactment of these isolated, quotidian actions. In Alison Knowles' *Proposition* (1962), performers came out to the performance area, made a salad, and exited; Emmett Williams' *Voice Piece for La Monte Young* (1963) instructed the performer to ask whether La Monte Young was in the audience and then leave.

Certain members of Cage's class created slightly more complex performance scripts based on the principle of chance advocated by Cage. The component words of Jackson Mac Low's poem *Peaks and Lamas* (1959) were determined by chance operations. For its performance, first enacted in Cage's class, Mac Low employed other chance procedures to determine when performers were to utter their lines and at what pitch and volume level. Since the spoken entrances of each performer varied, the effect resembled an atonal musical composition with words. Similarly, in George Brecht's *Motor Vehicle Sundown* (1960), each performer was given a set of differently shuffled instruction cards. At dusk, they were to go to their cars and execute such directions as turning headlights or radios on and off, honking horns, rolling windows up or down, operating windshield wipers, and switching on the glove compartment light. The time allotted for each activity having been determined by chance, the performance was over when all the participants

had finished their assignments and turned off the car motors. While somewhat reminiscent of *18 Happenings in Six Parts*, such scrupulously annotated performances differed markedly from the improvisatory permissiveness of most Happenings.

Out of Cage's class had also come overt challenges to the definition of what constituted artistic authorship. In *4'33"*, Cage had subverted his own subjective expression by forcing the audience to take an active role (p. 31). He had provided the composition's structure, but it was the audience, not he, who provided the sounds. Brecht, who believed that music was not merely what one heard or listened to, but was everything that happened, extended Cage's expansive attitude toward musical material to include visual phenomena.[84] In *Time-Table* (1961), Brecht instructed the performers to go to a train station and choose a number from the timetable. This number determined the duration of the piece—3:25, for example, translated into three minutes and twenty-five seconds. He considered everything that occurred in the train station within this designated time period to be part of the composition.

Cage's insistence that the audience provide the "music" in *4'33"* had conflated the role of the audience and performer. It had not, however, entirely obliterated the distinction between those who generated sounds and those who listened to them. The final break was only achieved by certain members of Cage's class, who simply eliminated the concept of "audience." Audience and performers became synonymous. In Dick Higgins' *Winter Carol* (1959), the performers were instructed to determine the composition's duration, then go outdoors for the specified amount of time and listen to the falling

```
              A Winter Carol
             (Contribution No. 6)

Any number of people may perform this composition.
They do so by agreeing in advance on a duration
for the composition, then by going out to listen in
the falling snow.

                                       New York
```

Opposite: George Brecht performing his *Three Aqueous Events* (see Fig. 59).

Fig. 51. Dick Higgins, 1959.

Fig. 52. Nam June Paik performing his *Zen for Head* in Wiesbaden, West Germany, 1962.

tinction between art and life beyond recognizability.

The often numerous components of Kaprow's later Happenings differed from the single-action character of Fluxus Events. In Robert Watts' *Casual Event* (1962), for example, one performer drove his car to a filling station, inflated the right front tire until it blew out, then changed the tire and drove home.

The mischievous subversion of conventional aesthetics undertaken by these Cage-inspired artists was reminiscent of Dadaist antics, as in the performances of the Rumanian Dadaist, Tristan Tzara. In one, the word "roar" was repeated 147 times followed by the non sequitur "Who still considers himself very charming."[85] Self-consciously radical, the latter-day heirs of Dada sought to provoke and outrage in order to jolt viewers out of self-satisfied assumptions about art. Their subversive attack on normative aesthetic taste carried an almost moralistic sense of mission: "The purpose of this series is not entertainment" read the program notes for a series of concerts given in 1960–61.[86]

Fig. 53. George Brecht, *Suitcase*, 1959. Mixed media assemblage, 7⅞ × 16⅛ × 11¹³⁄₁₆" (20 × 41 × 30 cm). Collection of Reinhard Onnasch.

snow (Fig. 51). No one was invited to "watch," a format drastically different from that of most Happenings, in which audiences were participatory if only by virtue of their cramped proximity to the performers.

The only Happening artist to dispense with the audience was Kaprow, whose later performance works consisted of a number of tasks executed at different times and in different parts of a given city. As a result, Kaprow could allow his performers control over the location, time, and manner of execution of these assigned tasks. In *Fluids* (1967), twenty hollow, rectangular ice blocks were built by an unspecified number of participants around the city during a three-day period. Once built, the blocks were left, unattended, to melt. Unlike Kaprow's earlier events, the only "audience" to observe these enactments was that which serendipitously took notice of the activity, unaware that they were viewing an art performance. That such events took place in the midst of ordinary life, rather than in a designated performance area, confounded the dis-

Fig. 54. George Brecht, *Iced Dice*, a realization of his word event "chair," in "Environments, Situations, Spaces" at the Martha Jackson Gallery, New York, 1961.

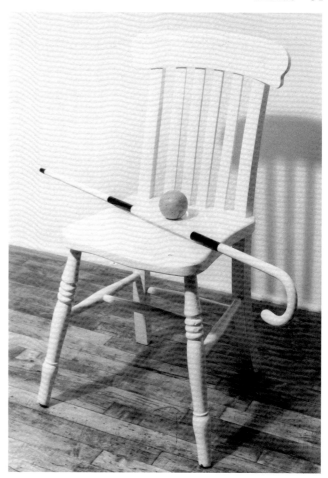

Fig. 55. George Brecht, *Chair Event*, c. 1960; reconstructed 1969. Painted wood chair, painted cane, and an orange, 35⅛ × 19 × 38″ (89.2 × 48.3 × 96.5 cm). Collection of Reinhard Onnasch.

Some of the discomfort caused by these events derived from their intimations of violence. When Yoko Ono sat passively onstage while members of the audience came forward and cut off pieces of her clothing until she was nearly naked, the effect was unnerving. Or when Nam June Paik came up to John Cage in a performance and proceeded to slash Cage's shirt, chop off his necktie, and pour a bottle of shampoo over his head before running from the room, the resultant laughter was of the nervous kind elicited by fear. This same commingling of humor and implicit violence can be seen in Paik's *Zen for Head* (Fig. 52), where the horror of "blood" dripping from his necktie plays against the pun of the title.

Despite the differences between these more conceptually based artists and those involved with Happenings and junk assemblages, the art world vanguard was sufficiently small in the years 1958–64 that initially the distinction between them was not rigidly drawn. Brecht, in particular, floated easily between these two worlds. A member of Cage's class, he was also a regular exhibitor at the Reuben Gallery. His 1959 show there featured a group of found-object sculptures which viewers could manipulate or change; *Suitcase* (Fig. 53), filled with discrete objects that could be taken out and rearranged at will, was typical. It was, in other words, an object on its way to becoming an Event, a characteristic underscored by the exhibition's title, "Towards Events."[87]

Brecht's union of sculpture and Event received a more radical articulation in Martha Jackson's 1961 exhibition "Environments, Situations, Spaces," in which Dine, Whitman, Kaprow, Oldenburg, and Walter Gaudnek participated. Kaprow created his environment *Yard* (Fig. 27) for the show, Dine a found-object environment of fabric, filled with hanging pots (Fig. 86), and Oldenburg his plaster reliefs of everyday commodities (Fig. 81). Brecht

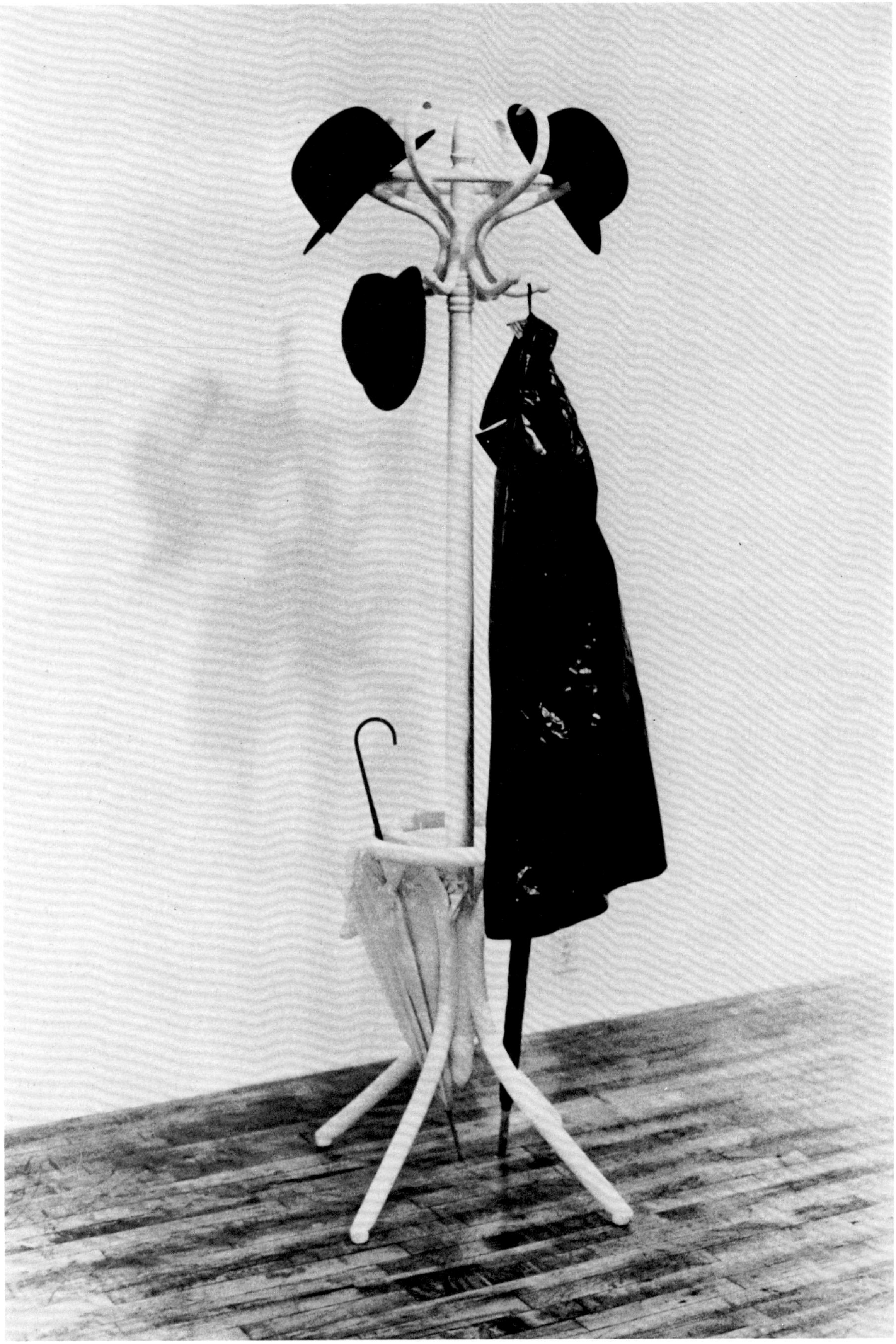

Fig. 56. George Brecht, *Clothes Tree*, c. 1963; originally installed in Brecht's New York loft; reconstructed 1969. Painted clothes tree with three hats, one coat, and two umbrellas, 72 × 27 × 29½" (182.9 × 68.6 × 74.9 cm). Collection of Reinhard Onnasch.

submitted two performance scores, one of which consisted simply of the word "chair." The "realization" of this score was a white wicker rocking chair which sat on the floor of the gallery for the duration of the exhibition (Fig. 54). It differed from the found objects in other artists' work in that it was functional; it could be sat upon and moved around. By occupying the border between art and utility, it confounded aesthetic categories. Hereafter most of Brecht's sculptures were realizations of performance scores (Figs. 55, 56). Because their implementation depended on available materials and individual interpretation, the same piece could potentially look quite different each time it was installed.

In addition to utility, the absence of painterly gesture on Brecht's objects contrasted markedly with the found objects and figurative work of his colleagues at the Reuben Gallery. *Sink* (1963), for example, was just an ordinary white porcelain sink, on which rested toothbrushes, soap, and a glass. Because of its seemingly dispassionate presentation of mundane, commercial objects, such work would initially be categorized as Pop Art. Yet the classification was inadequate. Brecht's reluctance to tamper with his component materials and his willingness to subvert his own control made his work more analogous to the ambient sound compositions of John Cage.

The activities of Brecht and other members of Cage's class were given added momentum by the arrival from San Francisco of La Monte Young in the fall of 1960. Young had been introduced to Cage's ideas while still a graduate student at the University of California, Berkeley, through Cage's published lectures and a summer workshop Young had attended in Darmstadt, West Germany, in 1959.[88] During the summer of 1960, Young had created a series of "musical compositions" which displayed his debt to Cage's theories regarding chance and audience involvement. *Composition 1960 #3* was typical:

Announce to the audience when the piece will begin and end if there is a limit or duration. It may be of any duration.

Then announce that everyone may do whatever he wishes for the duration of the composition.

Like Brecht, Young extended Cage's definition of music to include that which is only seen. *Composition 1960 #5* involved releasing a handful of butterflies into the air; *Composition 1960 #10* directs the performer to draw a straight line and follow it. Like Cage's emulation of the anecdotal style of Zen stories, these compositions were short and often paradoxical (Fig. 57).

Upon Young's arrival in New York in September 1960, his apartment became a meeting place for musicians, visual artists, dancers, and poets. Young's commitment to what he later called "the theater of the single event"[89] spurred other artists to contribute to this new genre. James Waring, the dancer with whom many of those later connected with the Judson Dance Theater worked, addressed the poem *Haircut* (1960) to Young: "Use a stop watch. Watch and time three minutes. During that time say 'haircut' as [sic] least, or as many times as you like."[90]

During this period, Brecht, quite independent of Young, had likewise shifted from complex orchestrations involving multiple performers to single-gesture actions. Typically restricted to short phrases or single words, Brecht's Events were more like Zen Buddhist *koans* than precise performance instructions (Fig. 58). *String Quartet* consists of the words "shaking hands"; *Three Aqueous Events* reads "ice/water/steam"; *Piano Piece* (1962) reads "vase of flowers on[to] a piano." Since Brecht believed that the task of the artist was simply to stimulate the viewer's imagination or perception, these cryptic phrases were to him equally valid as performance directives, physical entities, or states of mind; although they could be enacted, simply reading and thinking about them was sufficient to constitute realization (Fig. 59). Following Brecht, a number of other artists were encouraged to create similarly aphoristic Event-poems: Robert Watts' *Bean on a plate* (1962) and *I opened a book and the page was not there* (1962) (Fig. 60); or Yoko Ono's *Tape Piece I* (1963)—"take the sound of the stone aging"—and her *Sun Piece* (1962)—"watch the sun until it becomes square."

In the fall of 1960 Young became involved in several activities that led to what was later described as Fluxus. One was a series of concerts that he organized at Yoko Ono's loft at 112 Chambers

Composition 1960 #2

Build a fire in front of the audience. Preferably, use wood although other combustibles may be used as necessary for starting the fire or controlling the kind of smoke. The fire may be of any size, but it should not be the kind which is associated with another object, such as a candle or a cigarette lighter. The lights may be turned out.

After the fire is burning, the builder(s) may sit by and watch it for the duration of the composition; however, he (they) should not sit between the fire and the audience in order that its members will be able to see and enjoy the fire.

The composition may be of any duration.

In the event that the performance is broadcast, the microphone may be brought up close to the fire.   5·5·60

Composition 1960 #3

Announce to the audience when the piece will begin and end if there is a limit on duration. It may be of any duration.

Then announce that everyone may do whatever he wishes for the duration of the composition.   5·14·60

Composition 1960 #4

Announce to the audience that the lights will be turned off for the duration of the composition (it may be any length) and tell them when the composition will begin and end.

Turn off all the lights for the announced duration.

When the lights are turned back on, the announcer may tell the audience that their activities have been the composition, although this is not at all necessary.   6·3·60

Composition 1960 #5

Turn a butterfly (or any number of butterflies) loose in the performance area.

When the composition is over, be sure to allow the butterfly to fly away outside.

The composition may be any length but if an unlimited amount of time is available, the doors and windows may be opened before the butterfly is turned loose and the composition may be considered finished when the butterfly flies away.

           6·8·60

Piano Piece for Terry Riley #1

Push the piano up to a wall and put the flat side flush against it. Then continue pushing into the wall. Push as hard as you can. If the piano goes through the wall, keep pushing in the same direction regardless of new obstacles and continue to push as hard as you can whether the piano is stopped against an obstacle or moving. The piece is over when you are too exhausted to push any longer.

           2:10 A.M.
           November 8, 1960

Composition 1960 #6

The performers (any number) sit on the stage watching and listening to the audience in the same way the audience usually looks at and listens to performers. If in an auditorium, the performers should be seated in rows on chairs or benches; but if in a bar, for instance, the performers might have tables on stage and be drinking as is the audience.

Optional: A poster in the vicinity of the stage reading: COMPOSITION 1960 #6
by
La Monte Young
admission

(price)

and tickets, sold at stairways leading to stage from audience, admitting members of the audience who wish to join the performers on stage and watch the remainder of the audience.

A performance may be of any duration.

           July 2, 1960

Piano Piece for David Tudor #1

Bring a bale of hay and a bucket of water onto the stage for the piano to eat and drink. The performer may then feed the piano or leave it to eat by itself. If the the former, the piece is over after the piano has been fed. If the latter, it is over after the piano eats or decides not to.

           October 1960

Piano Piece for David Tudor #2

Open the keyboard cover without making, from the operation, any sound that is audible to you. Try as many times as you like. The piece is over either when you succeed or when you decide to stop trying. It is not necessary to explain to the audience. Simply do what you do and, when the piece is over, indicate it in a customary way.

           October 1960

Piano Piece for David Tudor #3

most of them
were very old grasshoppers

           November 14, 1960

Composition 1960 #7

to be held for a long time

La Monte Young
July 1960

Composition 1960 #10
to Bob Morris

Draw a straight line
and follow it.

           October 1960

Composition 1960 #13
to Richard Huelsenbeck

The performer should
prepare any composition
and then perform it as
well as he can.

           November 9, 1960

Composition 1960 #15
to Richard Huelsenbeck

This piece is little whirlpools
out in the middle of the ocean.

           9:05 A.M.
           December 25, 1960

Fig. 57. La Monte Young, compositions, originally printed in *An Anthology*, 1962.

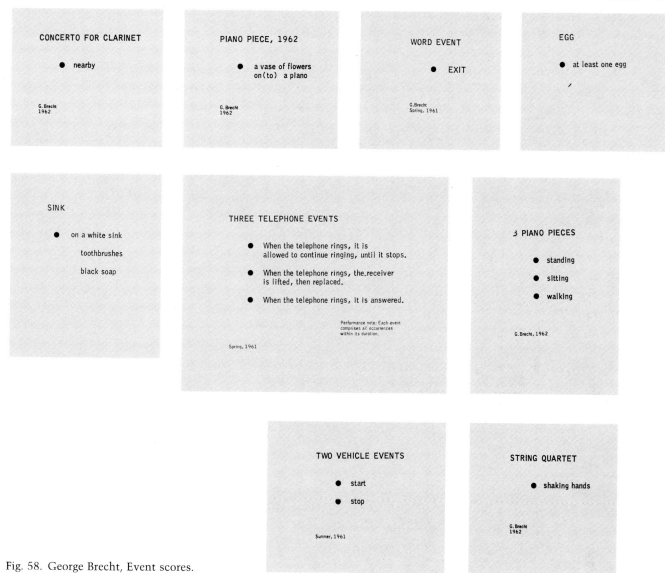

Fig. 58. George Brecht, Event scores.

Street. Included in the series were a group of Young's colleagues, also recently arrived from San Francisco—sculptors Walter De Maria and Robert Morris, dancer Simone Forti[91]—as well as artists Young had met in New York—musicians Joseph Byrd and Richard Maxfield, dancer Robert Dunn, poet Jackson Mac Low. Held from January to June 1961, the Chambers Street series, as it was informally dubbed, offered the first collective forum for the vanguard sensibilities that emerged as Fluxus.

Several months after the initial Chambers Street concert, George Maciunas, a Lithuanian émigré who had opened the AG Gallery on Madison Avenue, began to sponsor a series of similar events.[92] Earlier that fall (1960), Maciunas had enrolled in the continuation of Cage's class at the New School,

taught by Richard Maxfield, the composer of electronic music. Maciunas' introduction to Young, also enrolled, and to the kind of work produced in the class encouraged him to radicalize the presentations at his gallery. It was here, for example, that De Maria first exhibited his Minimalist plywood sculpture (p. 99) and where Mac Low's *Nuclei for Simone Forti* (1961) was first performed, a sequence of chance-derived nouns and verbs to be improvised upon by the performer.

In late 1960, Young had been asked to compile for the poetry magazine *Beatitude East* a special issue devoted to contemporary performance and literary work. When the magazine's regular editor abandoned the project and moved to California, leaving Young without any means of financing the publication, Maciunas offered to design and print the collection of material in the back room of his gallery. Owing to financial complications, the publication, ultimately called *An Anthology*, was not bound and distributed until 1963 (Fig. 62). However, even its compilation proved seminal to the development of Fluxus by bringing together artists who would form the core of American Fluxus and by introducing Maciunas to the idea of publishing artists' work.[93]

By the time *An Anthology* was released, Maciunas had been in Europe more than a year and had initiated a flurry of concerts under the general title of "Fluxus," the first of which took place in September 1962 in Wiesbaden, West Germany.[94] This concert marked the tenuous cohesion of a group of artists who would join together in publishing and performance ventures under the name of Fluxus. With Japanese and European artists prominent among them, the organization had a decidedly international tenor.

It was not until the spring of 1964, following Maciunas' return from Europe, that the first American Fluxus concert took place in New York. While Maciunas was abroad, Brecht and Watts had organized a series of events in May 1963 known as the Yam Festival; though it involved many of the Fluxus participants, it was not an official Fluxus Event.[95] The same was true of Charlotte Moorman's Festival of the Avant Garde. Presented annually beginning in 1963, the festival provided an important opportunity for vanguard composer-artists—Joseph Byrd, Philip Corner, Richard Maxfield, and La Monte Young—to be included in programs with such musical luminaries as Earle Brown, John Herbert McDowell, and Morton Feldman. Moorman's criteria for what qualified as music were broad. She was, after all, part of an art community that had considered the sound of vegetables being chopped (in Knowles' *Proposition*) or the *a cappella* recitation of a concrete poem by Emmett Williams to be valid musical expressions. It was in this all-inclusive spirit of music-making that Yoko Ono had premiered her composition *A Piece for Strawberries and Violin* at the Carnegie Recital Hall in 1961 (Fig. 61), and the New York Audio-Visual group (founded by Higgins and Al Hansen) met every Sunday morning to perform experimentally

Fig. 59. George Brecht performing his *Three Aqueous Events* included in "Happenings, Events, and Advanced Musics," organized by Al Hansen at Douglass College, Rutgers University, New Brunswick, New Jersey, 1963. Photograph by Peter Moore.

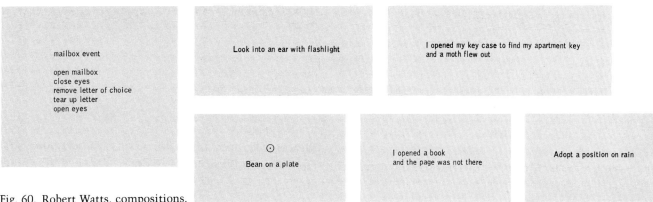

mailbox event

open mailbox
close eyes
remove letter of choice
tear up letter
open eyes

Look into an ear with flashlight

I opened my key case to find my apartment key
and a moth flew out

⊙

Bean on a plate

I opened a book
and the page was not there

Adopt a position on rain

Fig. 60. Robert Watts, compositions.

Fig. 61. Yoko Ono with the poster for her concert *A Grapefruit in the World of Park* at the Carnegie Recital Hall, New York, 1961. Photograph by George Maciunas.

an an an
OLOGY OF OLOGY OF OLOGY OF OLOGY OF OLOGY OF OLOGY OF

chance operations concept art anti-art indeterminacy improvisation meaningless work natural disasters

stories poetry essays plans of action diagrams music mathematics dance constructions compositions

BY GEORGE BRECHT, CLAUS BREMER, EARLE BROWN, JOSEPH BYRD, JOHN CAGE, DAVID DEGENER, WALTER DE MARIA, HENRY FLYNT, YOKO ONO, DICK HIGGINS, TOSHI ICHIYANAGI, TERRY JENNINGS DENNIS, DING DONG, RAY JOHNSON, JACKSON MAC LOW, RICHARD MAXFIELD, ROBERT MORRIS, SIMONE MORRIS, NAM JUNE PAIK, TERRY RILEY, DITER ROT, JAMES WARING, EMMETT WILLIAMS, CHRISTIAN WOLFF, LA MONTE YOUNG, LA MONTE YOUNG - EDITOR, GEORGE MACIUNAS-DESIGNER

notated music on everyday objects such as motor-cycles or bouncing balls.[96]

Paradoxically, it was Maciunas' return to the United States and his promotion of concert programs and published editions of artists' work that established Fluxus as an organization and simultaneously precipitated the departure of certain artists who previously had been colleagues. Most of those who left did so out of a distaste for Maciunas' aesthetic orientation. Of the San Francisco artists who had participated in Young's Chambers Street series and *An Anthology*, none were associated with Fluxus as an organization; Morris, who had removed his contribution to *An Anthology* prior to its binding (p. 100), wrote to Maciunas in 1964 that he wanted nothing more to do with Fluxus.[97] Kaprow, for his part, became angered by what he felt was the Fluxus artists' aesthetic irresponsibility and their condescending attitude.[98]

Splits began to occur even among those artists who had participated in the original Fluxus concerts in America—AY-O, Brecht, Anthony Cox, Higgins, Knowles, Ono, Hansen, Joe Jones, Ben Patterson, Watts. Many resented Maciunas' stridently pro-Soviet politics and his dictatorial attempts to impose his aesthetic ideas. At Karlheinz Stockhausen's *Originale* concert, presented at the Carnegie Recital Hall in September 1964 under the auspices of Charlotte Moorman's 2nd Annual New York Avant Garde Festival, Maciunas and Henry Flynt, another Fluxus member, picketed the performance and distributed vitriolic manifestos outside the theater. They were upset by the stranglehold they felt Stockhausen exercised over modern music and by what they took to be his patronizing attitude toward ethnic music.[99] Since the production included many Fluxus artists in its cast, the protest underscored the rift that had already developed within the group.

Still, the Fluxus spirit continued to flourish after 1964, in performance events and in the graphics and Fluxus objects produced under Maciunas' guidance. Using a typographical style similar to that in Dada publications, Maciunas tirelessly printed announcements, labels, and artists' broadsides.[100] He also encouraged a number of artists' newspapers, the prototype of which was Brecht's *V TRE*, a pas-

Fig. 63. *V TRE*, edited by George Brecht, including work by George Brecht, Diter Rot, Robert Morris, Claes Oldenburg, Ruth Krauss, Heinz Gappmayer, Angus MacLise, Jackson Mac Low, 1963.

tiche of found newspaper clippings, Brecht's own compositions, and contributions by other artists (Fig. 63).

Maciunas, in part because of his energy and organizational abilities, was unquestionably the primary force behind the ventures that occurred under the Fluxus imprimatur.[101] Yet Fluxus remained elusive; what it was or who was included within its orbit was always a source of debate.[102] The formative years of Fluxus nevertheless proved seminal to the development of a reductivist art which was to find expression in Minimalist sculpture and the Judson Dance Theater.

Opposite: Fig. 62. Title pages of *An Anthology*, 1963. Typography by George Maciunas.

The New American Dance

The conditions in dance in the late fifties were similar to those in the other arts. Stifled by the hold exerted over modern dance by its innovators, aspiring choreographers found themselves in an aesthetic cul-de-sac; only by changing the presumptive definition of dance did they feel they could break new ground. The emergence of the Paul Taylor, Erick Hawkins, and Alwin Nikolais dance companies during this period can be seen as part of the general challenge to modern dance as it then prevailed—to what was perceived as the gradual depletion and mannered stylization of modern dance's first revolutionary impulses.

Among those who actively participated in forging a new dance vocabulary were the group of dancers who formed the Judson Dance Theater: Steve Paxton, Deborah Hay, Fred Herko, Elaine Summers, Trisha Brown, Ruth Emerson, Yvonne Rainer, and Simone Forti.[103] The last four dancers had worked with Ann Halprin in her dance workshop near San Francisco. It was there that they formed friendships with the artists La Monte Young, Walter De Maria, and Robert Morris—friendships that were strengthened in 1960 when, during the course of the year, all arrived in New York.

Halprin championed a dance style unfettered by drama or psychological portrayal. Eager to liberate dance from the self-conscious, emotional introversion associated with Martha Graham, she encouraged natural movements, forcibly expanding the vocabulary of dance by assigning task-oriented activities such as sweeping the floor or pouring water from one can to another. To further insure against the artfulness of "dancing," she used everyday objects as props.

Working simultaneously on the East Coast was Merce Cunningham, who had participated in John Cage's Black Mountain "event" in the summer of 1952 (p. 31).[104] Like Halprin, Cunningham wanted to wrench dance away from narrative associations and symbolic conceits.[105] Under Cage's influence, Cunningham began introducing into his work natural, commonplace gestures: washing hands,

Fig. 64. Simone Forti, Steven Paxton, and Alex Hay (hidden) performing Forti's *Slant Board*, first presented at Yoko Ono's loft, New York, 1961; shown here in a later presentation at the School of Visual Arts, New York, 1967. Photograph by Peter Moore.

combing hair, filing nails, skipping, walking, and standing on one's hands. His union of ordinary "found movement" and invented dance movements was the dance equivalent of assemblage.

The Halprin-trained dancers arrived in New York in time for the inauguration of a dance class given in late 1960 at the Cunningham studio by the composer Robert Dunn and his wife, Judith, a member of Cunningham's company. Consciously using his experience as a student in Cage's New School class as a prototype, Dunn promoted an interdisciplinary mingling of dancers and non-dancers. As a composer, he had little interest in teaching choreographic method, and sought instead to stimulate his students by applying Cage's theories about chance and everyday life to dance. He encouraged his students to arrange their compositions through random procedures and to experiment with the incorporation of written texts and game assignments.

Simone Forti, a former Halprin protégé, was among those taking Dunn's class. Forti's dances, the first to rely exclusively on tasks and objects to structure movement, were performed at the Reuben Gallery in 1960 and in La Monte Young's Chambers Street series. *Slant Board* (1961) was typical of her work: for the dance, the performers were instructed to climb up an 8-foot-square inclined board by means of ropes (Fig. 64). They were al-

Opposite: Carolee Schneemann's *Newspaper Event*, 1963 (see Fig. 72).

Fig. 65. Trisha Brown and Steve Paxton in Brown's *Lightfall*, with music by Simone Forti; included in *Concert of Dance 4*, Judson Dance Theater, at the Judson Memorial Church, New York, 1963. Photograph by Al Giese.

Fig. 66. Yvonne Rainer and William Davis in "Love," a subsection of "Play" from her *Terrain*, Judson Dance Theater, at the Judson Memorial Church, New York, 1963. Photograph by Al Giese.

lowed to rest, but not to get off the ramp for the ten-minute duration of the piece. Forti's focus on a single action rather than on a sequence of actions connected her work conceptually to the Events of pre-Fluxus artists such as Young (p. 53). In her strategy, movement derived from the neutral execution of the task rather than from the dancers' display of personal expression. This "Minimalist" concept of dance also characterized the work of Steve Paxton, another Dunn class member, whose dances typically consisted of single activities—Paxton sitting on a bench eating a sandwich, or running in and out of a school office, removing furniture one piece at a time. Such dances had a profound impact on other artists, particularly Robert Morris, who were also moving toward a reductivist vocabulary in their art.

Dunn disbanded his choreography class in the fall of 1962, after a successful group performance that summer at the Judson Memorial Church.[106] Many of his students continued meeting together, first in Yvonne Rainer's studio and later in the basement of the Judson Church, which served as their official performance space. By this time, Happenings were on the wane and the artists who had initially participated in the Judson Gallery were exhibiting elsewhere. Thus, this dance collective, known as the Judson Dance Theater, assumed the gallery's earlier role of providing the venue for the informal gatherings of the downtown art community.

While the Judson group was never a homogeneous entity, certain commonly held attitudes did prevail, the most important of which was the no-

Fig. 67. Lucinda Childs rehearsing her *Carnation*, included in *Concert of Dance 16*, Judson Dance Theater, at the Judson Memorial Church, New York, 1964. Photograph by Peter Moore.

Fig. 68. Judith Dunn and Steve Paxton performing Dunn's *Index*, with music by Robert Dunn, included in *Concert of Dance 4*, Judson Dance Theater, at the Judson Memorial Church, New York, 1963. Photograph by Al Giese.

Fig. 69. Philip Corner's *Certain Distilling Processes*, included in *Concert of Dance 4*, Judson Dance Theater, at the Judson Memorial Church, New York, 1963. Photograph by Al Giese.

Fig. 70. Steve Paxton's *English*, included in *Concert of Dance 4*, Judson Dance Theater, at the Judson Memorial Church, New York, 1963. Photograph by Al Giese.

Fig. 71. Lucinda Childs performing her *Pastime*, included in *Concert of Dance 4*, Judson Dance Theater, at the Judson Memorial Church, New York, 1963. Photograph by Al Giese.

Fig. 72. Carolee Schneemann's *Newspaper Event,* included in *Concert of Dance 3,* Judson Dance Theater, at the Judson Memorial Church, New York, 1963. Photograph by Al Giese.

Fig. 73. Carolee Schneemann's *Meat Joy* at the Judson Memorial Church, New York, 1964. Photograph by Peter Moore.

tion that anything could be looked upon as dance. Since neither technical virtuosity (the dance equivalent of painterliness) nor choreographic skill was a pivotal issue, dancers felt free—as did Happening and Fluxus artists—to choose performers from other disciplines, with no previous "dance" training.

What held favor with the Judson dancers was the matter-of-fact deployment of "found" movements —walking, running, falling, rolling, and so on (Figs. 65–71). In Judith Dunn's *Acapulco* (1963), one dancer simply walked slowly toward center stage and brushed the hair of a dancer seated on a chair; in Alex Hay's *Colorado Plateau* (1964), Hay dragged and carried dancers from one position to another in accordance with the taped instructions of his voice.

The appropriation of pedestrian subject matter

was analogous to that in the other arts. So too was dance's denial of mythic revelation and the expression of personal emotions. Dance objectified movement, as had Fluxus Events, by replacing illusionistic time with real time, allotting, for example, the amount of time it takes to tie a shoe to the performance of that activity. Any reference to things or emotions beyond the literal or concrete was shunned.

This deliberately neutral presentation of material even included emotions: in one section of Yvonne Rainer's "love duet" *Terrain,* she delivered hackneyed expressions ("I love you," "I don't love you," "I've never loved you") in a flat monotone which one critic likened to the recitation of a grocery order.[107] This coupling of emotional "content" with impersonal execution paralleled the emotionally charged subject matter and depersonalized presentation audiences were finding in Pop Art, especially as practiced by Roy Lichtenstein and Andy Warhol.

The deracinated gestures in these dances, isolated from their quotidian contexts, became visible as abstract movement, as pleasing to watch as classic dance steps. For example, when Rainer emerged from a somersault to walk across the stage, the effect was riveting. In performing such stripped-down actions, the new dancers cleansed dance of artifice and ornamentation, asserting in the process the power and beauty of movement as movement.

Although most of the new dances shared the reductivist spirit of Fluxus, a few bordered on the baroque theatricality of Happenings—in particular, Fred Herko's costumed ballets, and Carolee Schneemann's orgiastic rituals in which the human body was used as another material placed within found-object "painting-constructions" (Figs. 72, 73). The caricatured violence in *War* (1963), a collaboration between Robert Huot and Robert Morris, opened with La Monte Young playing *Gong Music (for Henry Flynt)* for five minutes while the audience sat in darkness. When the lights went on, Morris and Huot, dressed in shaggy armor of collaged found objects, released two doves into the auditorium and then ran toward each other and began fighting with handmade stick weapons (Fig. 74). This dance, like subsequent Morris performances, was based on the strategy of allowing the performers' actions to emerge from the assigned task.

Fig. 74. Robert Rauschenberg's set for Paul Taylor's *The Tower* at the 92nd Street YMCA, New York, 1957. Mixed media construction, 119¼ × 16 × 48″ (302.9 × 40.6 × 121.9 cm). Collection of Mr. and Mrs. Victor W. Ganz.

Fig. 75. Robert Morris in his costume for *War*, a collaboration with Robert Huot, included in *Concert of Dance 4*, Judson Dance Theater, at the Judson Memorial Church, New York, 1963. Photograph by Mark Heddon.

The connection between Happenings and dance in the early 1960s was part of a larger interdisciplinary relationship. As dance critic Jill Johnston noted, "the Judson choreographers, the Pop artists, the Cage/Cunningham axis, the Lower East Side society, the Happenings creators and the Neo-Dada or Fluxus performers mixed incestuously in a broad network of social/personal/professional interests."[108] La Monte Young, Richard Maxfield, and David Tudor created music for a number of contemporary dances; visual artists such as Morris and Rauschenberg participated in performances as dancers; Cunningham, who earlier had been encouraged by Cage to structure his dance with chance techniques, frequently used Cage's music as an independent entity in his performances. Moreover, Cunningham obtained the services of Rauschenberg, Jasper Johns, Frank Stella, and Andy Warhol, among others, to design costumes and stage sets. Oldenburg created costumes for the dancer Aileen Passloff; Rauschenberg and Johns had designed sets and lighting for Paul Taylor as early as 1954 and 1957, respectively (Fig. 75). And James Waring, an important part of the downtown dance community though not a member of the Judson Dance Theater, commissioned music and solicited the assistance of visual artists—Rauschenberg, Brecht, Grooms, Whitman, Larry Poons, and Robert Indiana—to design decorations and costumes for his pieces (Fig. 76).

Fig. 76. Yvonne Rainer (left) and Valda Setterfield in James Waring's *At the Hallelujah Gardens*, James Waring and Dance Company, Hunter Playhouse, New York, 1963. Photograph by Peter Moore.

Fig. 77. Robert Rauschenberg in his dance *Pelican*, included in the Pop Art Festival at the America on Wheels skating rink, Washington, D.C., 1963; shown here in a later presentation at the First New York Theater Rally, 1965. Photograph by Peter Moore.

Fig. 78. Robert Morris performing his *Arizona*, included in *Concert of Dance 6*, Judson Dance Theater, at the Judson Memorial Church, New York, 1963. Photographs by Al Giese.

Fig. 79. Robert Morris and Carolee Schneemann performing Morris' *Site*, at the Sur + Dance Theater, Stage 73, New York, 1964. Photograph by Peter Moore.

In addition to participating as costume and set designers, several of those who turned to choreography were painters and sculptors—Schneemann, Alex Hay, Rauschenberg (Fig. 77), and Robert Morris. Typically, Morris' dance pieces were sequences of uninflected and non-referential movement. His first such dance, *Arizona* (1963), a concatenation of discrete, episodic activities, resembled in some ways the Paul Taylor dance which earlier had inspired Kaprow (p. 34): in the first five-minute section of *Arizona*, a tape-recorded voice minutely described the process of sorting cows, while Morris twisted his torso from side to side so slowly that the movement was barely perceptible (Fig. 78); in the second and third parts, again accompanied by an unrelated text, he threw a javelin into a target and unwound and then swung two blue lights on a string over the heads of the audience, who sat in darkness; in the final section he manipulated a T-square. *21.3* (1964) again offered an exaggerated economy of movement. Standing at a lectern, Morris mouthed the words of a tape-recorded passage from Erwin Panofsky's *Studies in Iconology* while executing gestures—pouring water into a cup—

which corresponded to extraneous sounds on the tape. However, as with *Arizona*, the gestures were separated from their language equivalent, in this case because Morris' mimed re-enactment of the text was intentionally out of sync with the recorded version by several seconds. By 1964, in *Site* (Fig. 79), Morris was unequivocally exploring in dance the same sort of concerns that were finding expression in his Minimalist sculpture (p. 99).

Parallels between the new dance and sculpture were not limited to Morris' work. Yvonne Rainer analyzed the reductivist tendencies in both media, observing that the elimination of technical virtuosity in dance corresponded to Minimalist sculpture's elimination of the artist's autobiographical markings.[109] The stress in dance and sculpture was on unselfconscious formal devices, devoid of all symbolic and psychological allusion. Rainer further suggested that Minimalist sculpture had replaced metaphorical content and autobiography with factory fabrication, unitary shapes, non-referential forms, and literalism, while the new dance had done so with found movement, equality of parts, neutral performance, and task-like activity.

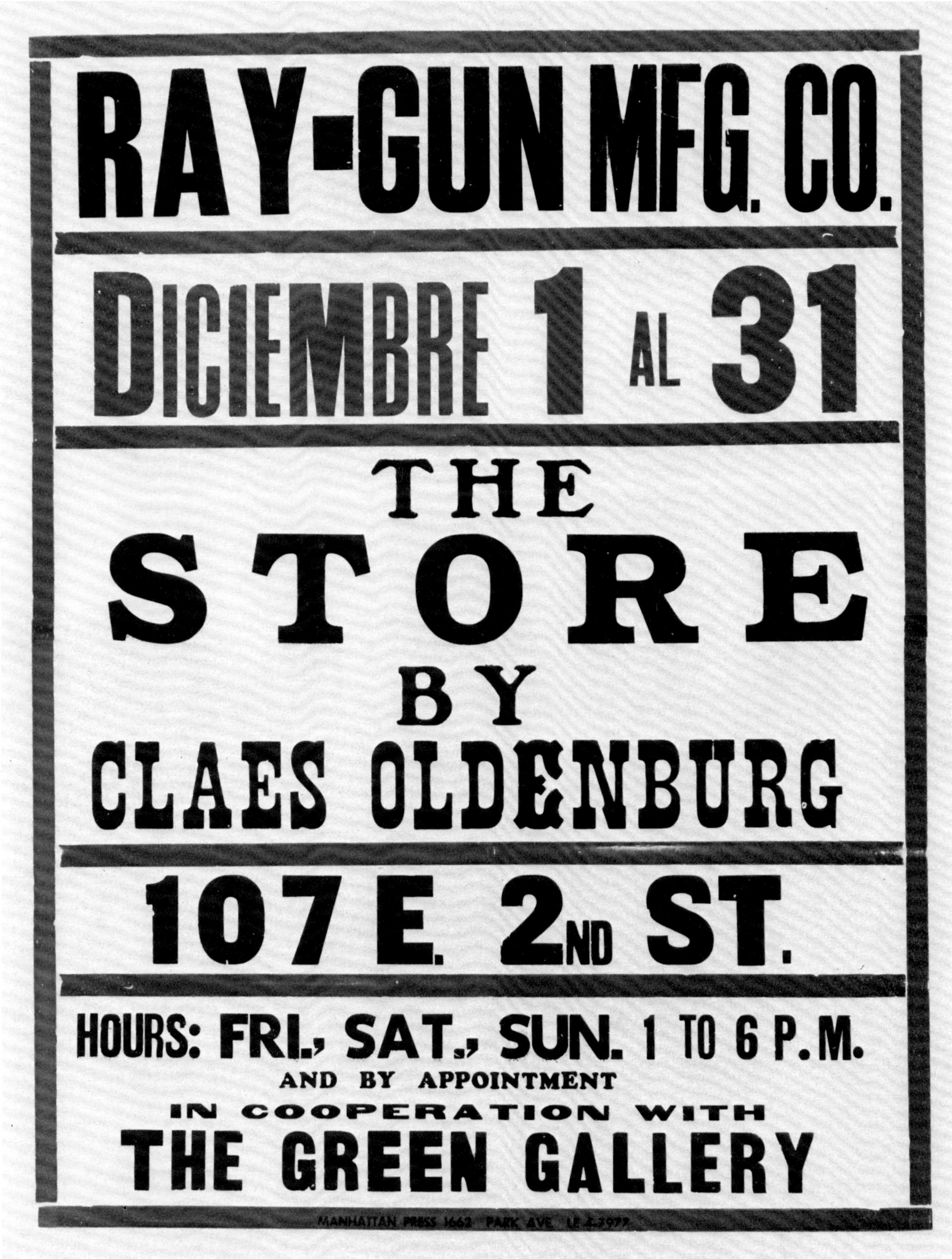

Fig. 80. Claes Oldenburg's poster for *The Store*, at the Ray Gun Mfg. Co., New York, 1961–62.

Pop Art

The impulse in the performing arts toward the tangible and the quotidian was transformed into more permanent works by the Pop artists. Just as their colleagues in other fields had shunned the symbolic and metaphoric conceits of predecessors, so too did Pop painters and sculptors strive to bring art back into contact with the concrete and the everyday.

For painting and sculpture, Martha Jackson's 1961 show "Environments, Situations, Spaces" provided the first look at this new development. This exhibition, in which Brecht had presented his word event (Fig. 54) and Kaprow his environment *Yard* (Fig. 27), had also included Oldenburg's new cycle of work, *The Store* (Fig. 81). *The Store* took the form of brightly painted plaster reliefs of everyday com-

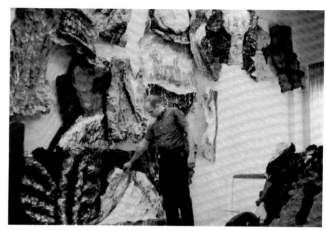

Fig. 81. Claes Oldenburg with his plaster reliefs for *The Store*, in "Environments, Situations, Spaces" at the Martha Jackson Gallery, New York, 1961. Photograph by Robert R. McElroy.

Fig. 82. Claes Oldenburg in his *Store*, at the Ray Gun Mfg. Co., New York, 1961–62.

Fig. 83. Claes Oldenburg, *Four Pies in a Glass Case*, 1961. Enamel on plaster in painted metal and glass case, 5¼ × 30 × 9" (13.3 × 76.2 × 22.9 cm). Collection of Robert K. Hoffman.

Fig. 84. Claes Oldenburg, *The White Slip*, 1961. Painted plaster, 41¾ × 29¼ × 3½" (106 × 74.3 × 8.9 cm). Whitney Museum of American Art, New York; Promised gift of Howard and Jean Lipman P. 55.80.

Fig. 85. Claes Oldenburg, *The Store*, at the Green Gallery, New York, 1962.

modities—shoes, foodstuffs, fragments of advertising signs. Suspended in the stairwell and front window of the gallery like a random display in a messy shop window, *The Store* manifested Oldenburg's increased involvement with commercial and manufactured objects. In contrast to the charred and torn relics of his *Street* (pp. 26, 27), these plaster reliefs were blatantly commercial in subject. *The Store* continued to evoke the culture of the Lower East Side, but it no longer commented on the bleak and despairing consequences of poverty and crime. Instead, the spirit of the installation was ebullient and sensual; it was about buying and selling.

Oldenburg's next version of *The Store* posed even more penetrating questions about the relationship between art and commerce. For two months beginning in December 1961, he ran a "business" in an actual storefront on East Second Street under the aegis of the Ray Gun Mfg. Co. (Figs. 80, 82). Using the typical small business as his model, he sold

plaster re-creations of foodstuffs and merchandise in the front half of the shop, while replenishing the inventory in his studio in the rear (Figs. 83, 84). In this way, Oldenburg conflated art and commerce. Yet, despite the verisimilitude of his storefront shop, it was not Oldenburg's intention to eradicate the distinction between art and life. For him the division between an art based on everyday objects and the objects themselves remained critical. Thus his motivation differed markedly from that of Cage and the Fluxus artists, whose advocacy of an art-life merger he disparaged: "The danger is to forget art and merely construct parables, to become a wise man rather than an artist. . . . No one can say that Cage with his mushroom picking . . . is not a super-wise man, but there is some argument about his being an artist."[110]

Oldenburg's switch in subject matter from human figures to objects was motivated by formal interests. He distrusted the merchandising of

American life as much as he had its poverty, but he saw in its products the potential for a more subtle manipulation of formal properties than that allowed with figuration. With *The Store*, Oldenburg transferred his figurative impulses from people to objects; from a representation of man to a symbol of man. Just as in his Happening *World's Fair, II* (1962) he implied that one of his characters could be judged by what the character had in his pockets,[111] so now he treated his wrinkled, bumptious objects as surrogates for the human body. Not only did he succeed in "mak[ing] hostile objects human,"[112] but he developed an iconography in which objects were identified with specific body parts: hamburgers were breasts, two adjacent disks were ears.

When Oldenburg opened the next incarnation of *The Store* at Richard Bellamy's Green Gallery in September 1962, he further equated objects and human anatomy. His sculptures were now on a human scale and soft—sewn out of canvas and stuffed with kapok in a manner reminiscent of the props in his Happenings (Fig. 85). Sagging and rearrangeable, they were, like the human body, prey to gravity. With the Green Gallery exhibition, Oldenburg brought *The Store* to Fifty-Seventh Street; the change of location from downtown to uptown represented, as Sidney Tillim noted at the time, Oldenburg's change of fortune as he progressed from blue collar to white.[113]

Jim Dine, meanwhile, had made a similar move toward the replication of commercial objects. Although the environment he created for the 1961 Jackson show (Fig. 86) harked back to his earlier found-object work, his concurrent paintings depicted commonplace objects isolated on the canvas against monochromatic fields, often of sensuous paint (Figs. 87, 88). Below these painted forms, Dine often inscribed their names—"shoe," "animal," or "tie." The effect of such word-image analogues was a sort of deadpan wit—far more playful than the demonic humor some critics had perceived in his Happenings.[114]

In 1962, the year Oldenburg began making his soft sculpture, Dine gave up painting replicas of objects and began affixing the real things to his canvases (Fig. 89). And the household paraphernalia he used was new—not worn or abandoned like the debris in his assemblages. The pristine, glistening pieces thus came to stand for the products of an industrialized society. And their very newness gave them anonymity, an impersonal detachment impossible to achieve with used objects.

Fig. 86. Jim Dine in his *Spring Cabinet*, in "Environments, Situations, Spaces" at the Martha Jackson Gallery, New York, 1961. Photograph by Robert R. McElroy.

Fig. 87. Jim Dine, *Black Zipper*, 1962. Oil and mixed media on canvas, 96 × 72" (243.8 × 182.9 cm). Collection of Ileana and Michael Sonnabend; on indefinite loan to The Baltimore Museum of Art.

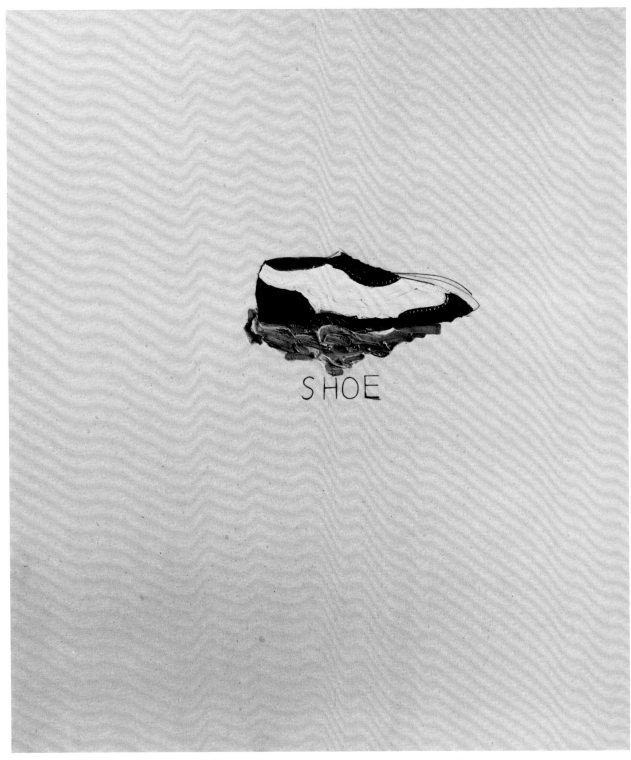

Fig. 88. Jim Dine, *Shoe*, 1961. Oil on canvas, 64 × 51½″ (162.6 × 130.8 cm). Private collection.

Fig. 89. Jim Dine, *Black Bathroom #2*, 1962. Oil drawing and china washbasin on canvas, 72 × 72″ (182.9 × 182.9 cm). Art Gallery of Ontario, Toronto; Gift of Mr. and Mrs. M. H. Rapp.

Fig. 90. George Segal, *The Dinner Table*, 1962. Plaster, wood, and metal, 72 × 120 × 120″ (182.9 × 304.8 × 304.8 cm). Private collection.

Yet Dine's work remained far more subjective than, say, Brecht's, whose similar repertory of objects was never treated to expressive paint handling. Nor did Dine entirely forfeit his figurative intentions; like Oldenburg, he simply transferred them to objects which became surrogate performers, acting out the mini-dramas of his unconscious, as he himself had done in his Happenings (p. 40).

Because Oldenburg and Dine retained the gestural style of their painterly forebears, they forged a link between Abstract Expressionism and what became known as Pop Art. Far from breaking irreverently with the past, they carried its style across new frontiers. "Lately I have begun to understand action painting," Oldenburg wrote. "By parodying its corn I have (miracle) come back to its authen-

ticity! I feel as if Pollock is sitting on my shoulder, or rather crouching in my pants!"[115] And Dine: "I tie myself to Abstract-Expressionism like fathers and sons."[116]

The third artist whose work bridged Abstract Expressionist style and Pop subject matter was George Segal. Segal matured aesthetically, as had Oldenburg and Dine, within an ambience of figuration and assemblage. A member of the Hansa Gallery, he had rebelled early on against what he felt to be Abstract Expressionism's proscription against incorporating everyday reality into art. Through his close friendship with Kaprow and the atmosphere generated by Kaprow's Happenings (p. 32), Segal was encouraged to transform the figurative images in his paintings into realistic, life-size plaster figures placed within environmental contexts (Fig. 90).[117] While adamantly rejecting the ephemerality of Happenings, Segal nonetheless embraced their banal subject matter. His plaster figures, their quotidian settings and actions, and the spectator involvement demanded by the tableau form of presentation constituted Segal's version of his friends' theatrical events. His works resembled frozen Happenings in which performers engaged in isolated and often private, self-involved actions—combing hair, bathing, eating (Fig. 91).

Segal's technique of molding the plaster directly on his models allowed for a remarkably literal transcription of idiosyncratic gestures and poses. With his figures placed in relatively sparse found-object sets, the result was a new, austere realism, not unlike that in later Pop images. Yet Segal's textural manipulation of the plaster surfaces, and his more blatantly figurative aspirations—to reveal how people relate to one another and to their surroundings—classed his work with that of Oldenburg and Dine.

Fig. 91. George Segal, *Woman Shaving Her Leg*, 1963. Plaster, metal, porcelain, and masonite, 63 × 65 × 30" (160 × 165.1 × 76.2 cm). Collection of Mrs. Robert B. Mayer; on long-term loan to the Museum of Contemporary Art, Chicago.

While Oldenburg, Dine, and Segal were wedding expressive handling with commercial subject matter, a second group of Pop artists—Andy Warhol, Roy Lichtenstein, Tom Wesselmann, and James Rosenquist—took the issue of merchandising and focused it on advertising images. Rather than replicating or using three-dimensional objects, these artists annexed the two-dimensional versions that appeared in advertisements, newspapers, and comics. Here finally was an art which irrefutably captured the modern media world.

The license to turn to this world had, to some extent, emerged from the atmosphere surrounding Happenings and junk environments. Although the second group of Pop artists had not directly participated in these events and installations, they were not immune to its appropriation of American popular culture. The allusion in Grooms' Happenings to Dick Tracy and Orphan Annie, Oldenburg's graffiti-like style and his silhouetted figures with word balloons coming out of their mouths in *The Street*, the creation of Ray Gun comics—all contributed to the artists' acceptance of popular imagery as viable sources for art. For Wesselmann, the contact with these art forms—and the impetus to pursue them—came through the Judson Gallery, where he was an early exhibitor, along with Dine, Oldenburg, and Marcus Ratliff. By 1962 the small-scale, figurative collages of his earlier years (Fig. 92) had become collages of advertising images and actual objects (Fig. 93). By 1963 these works were often situated on the floor, demanding a level of viewer involvement analogous to that in Happenings—the space of the artwork and that of the viewer being implicitly the same (Fig. 94). Experiencing them was like being jammed against the performers in a Happening. He reinforced the intrusion into the spectator's space by including television sets with ever-changing images or telephones that rang at periodic intervals.

In Lichtenstein's case, Happenings and junk environments vindicated the appreciation for the power of clichéd and parodied images expressed in his earlier work: semi-abstract Cubist renditions of Frederic Remington's cowboys and Indians from the mid-fifties and his loosely painted images of comic-strip characters from 1957–58 (Fig. 95).[118] But these predilections were not fully expressed until the summer of 1961, when he enlarged one of

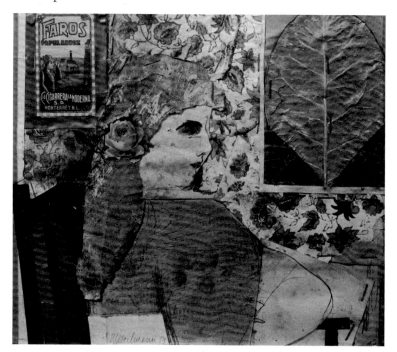

Fig. 92. Tom Wesselmann, *Portrait Collage #1*, 1959. Mixed media and collage on board, 9½ × 11″ (24.1 × 27.9 cm). Collection of Claire Wesselmann.

Fig. 93. Tom Wesselmann, *Still Life #17*, 1962. Mixed media and collage on board, 48 × 36″ (121.9 × 91.4 cm). The Morton G. Neumann Family Collection.

Fig. 94. Tom Wesselmann, *Bathtub Collage #2*, 1963. Mixed media, collage, and assemblage on board, 48 × 72 × 6½″ (121.9 × 182.9 × 16.5 cm). Private collection.

the cartoon images he had drawn for his children into a painting (Fig. 96). Radical though it was, Lichtenstein's move was in step with the times. He acknowledged that Oldenburg's blatantly trashy subjects and open confrontation with the issue of merchandising had affected him more than the work of Johns or Rauschenberg: "An Oldenburg 'Fried Egg' is much more glamorized merchandise and relates to my ideas more than Johns' beer cans."[119] He later credited Happenings with being "the greatest influence on my work."[120]

Lichtenstein had been brought into contact with Happenings and junk environments while teaching at Rutgers University with Kaprow and Robert Watts.[121] Warhol and Rosenquist, on the other hand, were relatively uninformed about the activities of the downtown art community. Both had been connected with commercial art—Warhol as an advertising illustrator, Rosenquist as a window designer at Bonwit Teller and as a billboard painter (Figs. 97, 98). Although Rosenquist's involvement with large-scale media images emerged primarily from this latter experience, he too was affected by what Lichtenstein described as the "kind of thing [that] was in the air."[122] Particularly in Rosenquist's sculptures and combination paintings (Figs. 99, 100), one can see his debt to the found-object tradition promoted at the Judson and Reuben galleries.

Warhol's annexation of media images apparently occurred almost as abruptly as had Rosenquist's. One day in 1960 he simply decided to paint replicas of what he most liked—the advertisements and cartoon images in cheap magazines (Figs. 101, 102). Given what at the time seemed Warhol's almost indiscriminate delight in everything around him, his apparent ignorance of Cage is ironic; more than any other contemporary painter, Warhol embodied Cage's affirmation that life needs no aesthetic mediation, that it is rewarding simply as it is. Cage found this principle particularly operative in Warhol's serial images: "Andy has fought by repetition to show us that there is no repetition really, that everything we look at is worthy of our attention. That's been a major direction for the twentieth century art, it seems to me."[123]

The model for replicating inherently two-dimensional images had been provided by Jasper Johns. Included in Johns' 1958 exhibition at the Leo Castelli Gallery were paintings from 1955 to 1958

Fig. 95. Roy Lichtenstein, *Mickey Mouse*, 1958. India ink and pastel on paper, 19 × 25" (48.2 × 63.5 cm). Collection of the artist.

Fig. 96. Roy Lichtenstein, *Look Mickey*, 1961. Oil on canvas, 48 × 69" (121.9 × 175.3 cm). Collection of the artist.

depicting flags, targets, and maps. But instead of transforming these motifs by setting them within an illusionistic painting space, Johns presented them verbatim, as two-dimensional objects (Figs. 103, 104). Moreover, since the shapes and internal details of his images pre-existed, Johns' strategy implied a forfeiture of artistic decision making.[124] And because his subjects were inherently two-dimensional, they were more like signs than palpable objects; they threw into question the relationship between the painted image and the "real" image. The query about whether his painting was a flag or a painting of a flag anticipated that asked about the commercial images in Pop Art; were they paintings of a soup can or paintings of an advertisement for a soup can?

Fig. 97. James Rosenquist, window display, Bonwit Teller, New York, 1959.

Fig. 98. Andy Warhol, window display, Bonwit Teller, New York, 1961.

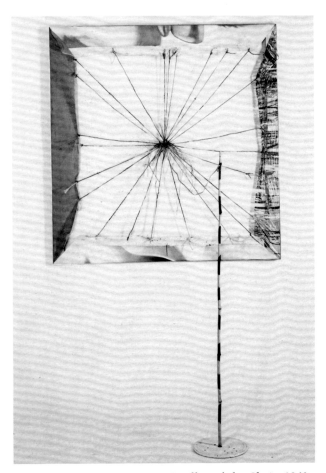

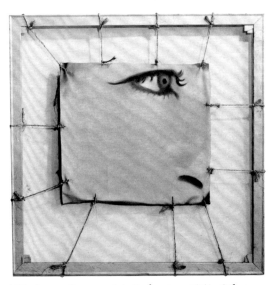

Fig. 100. James Rosenquist, *Bedspring*, 1962. Oil on canvas with twine, 36 × 36" (91.4 × 91.4 cm). Collection of the artist.

Fig. 99. James Rosenquist, *He Swallowed the Chain*, 1963. Paint, plastic, string, plus bamboo pole with canvas and wood base, 48 × 48 × 43" (121.9 × 121.9 × 109.2 cm). Collection of Richard Brown Baker; on loan to the Yale University Art Gallery, New Haven.

Johns himself did not pursue the implications of two-dimensional subject matter in his work. Instead, after 1960 he began to place actual found objects against his canvas fields, now rendered with a broader and more fluid painting style than he had used in his earlier work (Fig. 105). This union of found objects with an expressive paint surface clearly related these paintings more to Dine's and Oldenburg's work than to that of the media-oriented Pop artists. Yet it was undoubtedly Johns' earlier appropriation of two-dimensional subjects that paved the way for the Pop artists' subsequent appropriation of another kind of flat imagery—taken from the media.

In its developmental stage, the work of the media-based Pop artists was far looser and more painterly than the more hard-edged style with which they are generally associated. In Warhol's first advertising and cartoon paintings, for example, the imagery referred to the original advertisements, but the paint was loosely applied and contained remnants of Abstract Expressionist "drips" (Figs. 106, 102). Even his thirty-two-part series of Campbell's Soup Cans (Fig. 107) and his newspaper headlines, advertisements, and dance-step diagrams of 1961 and 1962 were still painted by hand (Fig. 108). It was not until late 1962 that he adopted the impersonal, mass-produced technique of the silkscreen. Ironically, even after this, his images retained a handmade look, owing to irregular inkings of the screen and uneven pressure in the printing (Fig. 109).

The paint handling in Rosenquist's works of 1961 and 1962 was likewise labored and heavy, and his palette dark (Figs. 110–12) in comparison with subsequent works. The steely edges and graduated tones that later became his trademark did not emerge until 1962, when he adopted the techniques of billboard paintings (Fig. 113). And Lichtenstein's first paintings based on advertisements or comic-strip images (Fig. 116) do not include the background of Ben-Day dots which he later used to simulate the mechanical and depersonalized look of industrial printing. Moreover, even after he added this technique, his paintings prior to 1964 appear stiff when measured against later works.

Still, in the context of Abstract Expressionism, Pop Art, even in its early stages, seemed defiantly

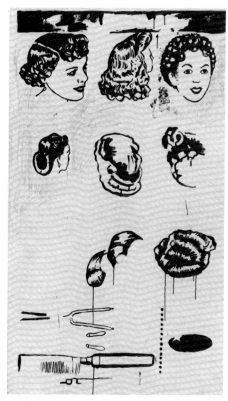

Fig. 101. Andy Warhol, *Wigs*, 1960. Oil and wax crayon on canvas, 70⅛ × 40″ (178.1 × 101.6 cm). Dia Art Foundation, New York.

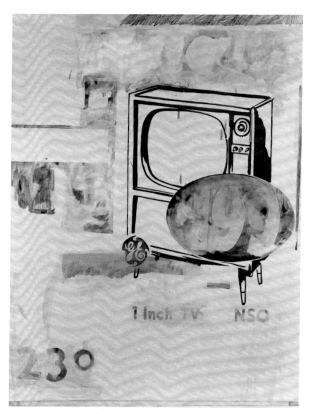

Fig. 102. Andy Warhol, *$199 Television*, 1960. Oil on canvas, 62¼ × 49½″ (158.1 × 125.7 cm). Collection of Kimiko and John Powers.

Fig. 103. Jasper Johns, *Target with Plaster Casts,* 1955. Encaustic and collage on canvas with objects, 51 × 44 × 3½″ (129.5 × 111.8 × 8.9 cm). Collection of Mr. and Mrs. Leo Castelli.

Fig. 104. Jasper Johns, *Three Flags*, 1958. Encaustic on canvas, 30⅞ × 45½ × 5″ (78.4 × 115.6 × 12.7 cm). Whitney Museum of American Art, New York; 50th Anniversary gift of the Gilman Foundation, Inc., the Lauder Foundation, A. Alfred Taubman, an anonymous donor (and purchase). 80.32.

Right: Fig. 105. Jasper Johns, *Fool's House*, 1962. Oil on canvas with objects, 72 × 36″ (182.9 × 91.4 cm). Collection of Jean Christophe Castelli.

impersonal. The use of pre-existing images and the near elimination of visible paint handling militated against the expression of emotions. "I want my painting to look as if it had been programmed. I want to hide the record of my hand," Lichtenstein said.[125] And Warhol went so far as to announce that "somebody should be able to do all my paintings for me. . . . The reason I'm painting this way is that I want to be a machine."[126] For artists in this period, the desire to reduce overt subjectivity was compelling: it was the predominant bond between works of apparent stylistic diversity.[127] Implied by the assemblagists' interpolation of found objects, the diminution of unbridled subjectivity had been taken even further in "concrete" music and in the straightforward enactment of "concrete" movement in Fluxus and dance. It had been the inspiration behind Cage's and others' promotion of chance techniques. (That Cage's advocacy of chance emerged out of Zen Buddhist precepts against individual ego did not lessen its impact on the arts.)

In literature, the subversion of subjectivity characterized Alain Robbe-Grillet's "objective novels," in which things and events were substituted for the psychology of human motivation.[128] Susan Sontag applauded the lack of interpretive analysis and metaphor in contemporary art as a means to put viewers back in touch with their intuitions.[129] Other writers deplored it. Irving Howe later described the literary sensibility of the age as shallow, escapist, and nihilistic. He lambasted the "relaxed pleasures and surface hedonism" of the period and asked whether such indifference to morality and ideas was "compatible with a high order of culture or a complex civilization."[130]

Yet even for those distrustful of excessive displays of subjectivity, the Pop painters' adoption of cool, detached techniques that mimicked commercial art posed a severe challenge to the notion of artistic originality and authorship. Lichtenstein and Warhol came in for particular abuse over this issue. Their paintings were denounced as mere enlargements of other images, so close to their sources that their art was pointless. In fact, these artists brought to their work a sophisticated level of formalist invention and decision making which

Fig. 106. Andy Warhol, *Dick Tracy*, 1960.
Oil on canvas, 70½ × 52⅝"
(179.1 × 133.7 cm). Private collection.

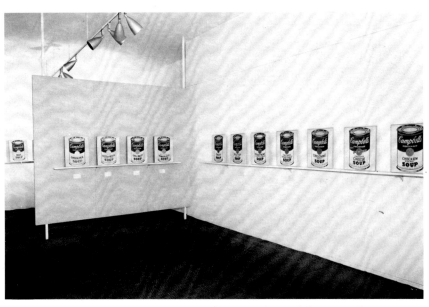

Fig. 107. Installation view of Andy Warhol's one-artist exhibition at the Ferus
Gallery, Los Angeles, 1962.

Fig. 108. Andy Warhol, *Before and After, 3*,
1962. Synthetic polymer on canvas, 74 × 100"
(188 × 254 cm). Whitney Museum of American
Art, New York; Gift of Charles Simon (and
purchase). 71.226.

Fig. 109. Andy Warhol, *Elvis*, 1964. Silkscreen
on canvas, 82 × 60" (208.3 × 152.4 cm). Collection of Peppino Agrati.

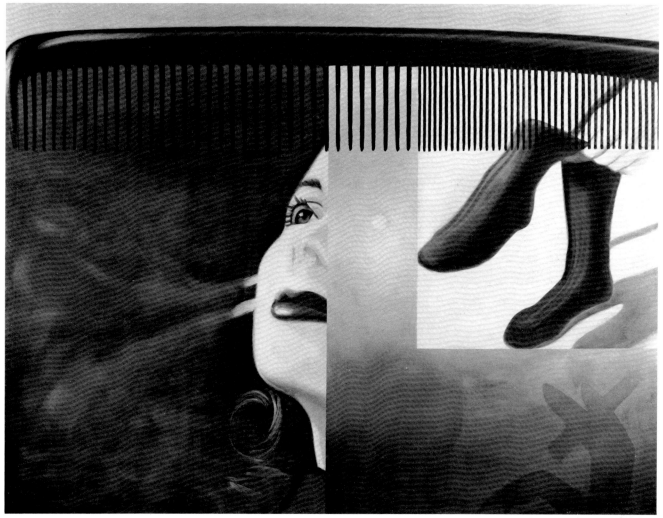

Fig. 110. James Rosenquist, *The Light That Won't Fail, I*, 1961. Oil on canvas, 72 × 96″ (182.9 × 243.8 cm). Hirshhorn Museum and Sculpture Garden, Smithsonian Institution, Washington, D.C.

even a cursory comparison with the original models reveals (Figs. 114, 115). More important, detractors failed to comprehend that Pop artists, through their choice and manipulation of images, were proposing a new kind of subjectivity—one that did not rest on the artist's expressive gesture.

From our present-day perspective, it is clear that Pop artists chose mass-produced images as vehicles through which to explore contemporary culture. As Oldenburg wrote in 1963: "It is the false and cynical treatment of real emotion, as in today's publications, that fascinates me and yields more truth."[131] By the 1950s, modern media—television, advertising, comic books—had become key transmitters of values in American life.[132] Information came to people primarily secondhand, through media sources. The messages and imagery from these

sources had assumed a normative validity, representing universal fantasies, determining assumptions about love, death, and propriety. They were the nearest thing to models for personal and public modes of thought and behavior. Behind the clichés and simpleminded appeals lay some measure of truth to which the culture subscribed.

Yet the judgments Pop artists made about the culture represented by these images remained ambiguous. Their art was neither exclusively celebratory nor satirical. Though Lichtenstein conceded that he drew his imagery from the most despicable and abhorrent aspects of American life, his treatment of these images was far from disparaging.[133] The fantasies of heroism and romance portrayed in his comic-book stereotypes could be viewed either as profound or as mocking (Figs. 117–119). Again, though Oldenburg announced

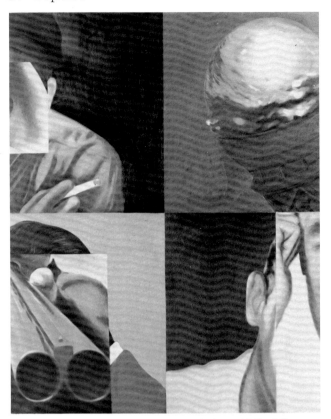

Fig. 111. James Rosenquist, *Four 1949 Guys*, 1962. Oil on canvas, 60 × 48″ (152.4 × 121.9 cm). Hara Museum of Contemporary Art, Tokyo.

that he detested American culture, he nonetheless assembled a "museum" of kitsch items, many of which he used as models.[134] One must remember too that these were the peak years of camp—the celebration of the outrageous, the exaggerated, the artificial.[135] In this spirit, Warhol's portraits of public personalities could simultaneously exalt and denigrate the celebrity's status as cultural icon. His serial images of Marilyn Monroe—the face repeated but never altered, save by color—reveal how superficial is the knowledge of a person with whom the culture assumes such familiarity (Fig. 120). The disquieting suggestion of death which pervades many of these early portraits is made more explicit in Warhol's serial depictions of disasters (Fig. 121).[136] The very repetition of the images reflects the way the horror of such events becomes neutralized by constant exposure in newspapers and on television.

In a subtle but definitive way, Warhol's images—and those of other media Pop artists—transferred subjectivity to the viewer. Warhol's pictorial treatment of the subject was the same, whether it was a car crash or soup can. Thus it offered no ready commentary on the depicted scene. In contrast to the celebratory art practiced by American Regionalists like Thomas Hart Benton or the satirical work of left-wing social commentators like George Grosz and Ben Shahn, Pop Art forced viewers into a more

Fig. 112. James Rosenquist, *The Lines Were Deeply Etched on the Map of Her Face*, 1961–62. Oil on canvas, 66 × 78″ (167.6 × 198.1 cm). Collection of Mr. and Mrs. Robert Meltzer.

Fig. 113. James Rosenquist, *Two 1959 People*, 1963. Oil and assemblage on canvas, 72 × 93⅛″ (182.9 × 236.5 cm). Rose Art Museum, Brandeis University, Waltham, Massachusetts; Gevirtz-Mnuchin Purchase Fund.

Fig. 114. Package design. Source of Roy Lichtenstein's *The Refrigerator*, 1962.

Fig. 115. Roy Lichtenstein, *The Refrigerator*, 1962. Oil on canvas, 68 × 58" (172.7 × 147.3 cm). Collection of Mr. and Mrs. Peter M. Brant.

Fig. 116. Roy Lichtenstein, *Kitchen Range*, 1961. Oil on canvas, 68½ × 68½" (174 × 174 cm). Australian National Gallery, Canberra.

decisive role in determining the image's meaning.

Viewer participation in Pop Art was further encouraged by the public and standardized nature of the imagery. Everybody could talk about a painting of Marilyn Monroe in a way not possible with Abstract Expressionist canvases since Pop Art's images reflected not individual experiences but general ones. By invoking cultural rather than personal symbols, they empowered an otherwise diverse audience to make judgments and form opinions, thus shifting the responsibility for interpretation to each individual. The most public images thereby came to have the deepest connection to the viewer's private experience.

Because of the accessibility of its imagery, Pop Art was thrust almost instantly into the forefront of the art world. Unlike Happenings and junk environments, which remained essentially downtown phenomena, Pop Art was acclaimed by established uptown galleries and widely discussed in the press. Most astonishing was that this notoriety came almost overnight. Before 1962, Pop artists were known, if at all, to only a handful of people. By February 1962, Dine, Rosenquist, and Lichtenstein had opened financially successful one-man exhibitions uptown; by September, Oldenburg had a similar triumph. In March 1962, the first article dealing with this new art as a cohesive movement appeared.[137] That the critic's assessment of "Neo-

Dada" (its initial designation) was unfavorable did not matter. For by September it had attracted enough attention for Sidney Tillim to write that it was the "most talked-about art movement of the moment."[138]

The coalescence of this art into a definable movement was ensured by "The New Realists" exhibition, mounted by the Sidney Janis Gallery in the fall of 1962.[139] Janis' stature in the art world was sufficiently unassailable that his prescient as-

Fig. 117. Roy Lichtenstein, *Blam*, 1962. Oil on canvas, 68 × 80" (172.7 × 203.2 cm). Collection of Richard Brown Baker, on loan to the Yale University Art Gallery, New Haven.

Fig. 118. Roy Lichtenstein, *Emeralds*, 1961. Oil on canvas, 67⅝ × 67⅜″ (171.8 × 171.1 cm). Private collection.

Fig. 119. Roy Lichtenstein, *Masterpiece*, 1962. Oil on canvas, 54 × 54″ (137.2 × 137.2 cm). Collection of Agnes Gund.

sertion—these artists "may already have proved to be the pacemaker[s] of the 60s"—was not easily dismissed.[140] Janis' gallery was too small to accommodate the show, and he was forced to open a secondary space in a ground-floor storefront on Fifty-Seventh Street (Fig. 122). Thus by coincidence but most fittingly, Pop Art from the beginning managed to bypass the exclusivity of the gallery circuit and reach out to a mass audience.

The exhibition, wrote Harold Rosenberg, "hit the New York art world with the force of an earthquake. Within a week tremors had spread to art centers throughout the country. . . . There [was] no greater aesthetic virtue in copying a de Kooning than in copying the design on a beer can."[141] "The point of the Janis show," Thomas Hess explained, "was an implicit proclamation that the New had arrived and it was time for all the old fogies to pack."[142] Pop Art did indeed appear to throw everything into shadow. Even Abstract Expressionism seemed "wiped out" by Pop Art, as Red Grooms later remarked.[143] One unidentified leading modernist was quoted at the time as saying, "I feel a bit like a follower of Ingres looking at the first Monets."[144]

Understandably, such instant notoriety spawned detractors among critics and fellow artists. For the Abstract Expressionists, Pop artists seemed like charlatans, their specious achievement an insult to genuine aesthetic values. In response to the installation of "The New Realists," all the Abstract Expressionists in Janis' gallery except de Kooning resigned. They especially resented the alacrity with which Pop Art captured the attention of the art world. Having struggled for years before attaining success, they viewed the Pop artists as Johnny-come-latelies.[145] For those who subscribed to the myth of the artist as impoverished outsider, Pop artists seemed to have capitulated to mainstream money. Dine's and Oldenburg's meteoric rise from downtown to uptown galleries was regarded, even by certain of their peers in the downtown community, as traitorous, a symbol of having "sold out."[146]

Art critics comprised an even more vociferous phalanx of opposition against Pop Art. With the exception of a few—such as Gene Swenson and Lawrence Alloway—the major critics attacked it.[147] They especially railed against Pop for its exorcism of metaphor and symbol and its un-

Fig. 120. Andy Warhol, *Twenty-Five Colored Marilyns*, 1962. Acrylic on canvas, 89 × 69″ (226.1 × 175.3 cm). Fort Worth Art Museum; The Benjamin J. Tillar Memorial Trust, acquired from the collection of Vernon Nikkel, Clovis, New Mexico.

who [are] insensible to the values of genuine culture. . . ."[150] Pop Art's refusal to pass judgment on its ostensibly debased subject matter only fueled critics' consternation. Max Kozloff's reaction was typical: "There is a moral dilemma implicit in these latest vulgarities. . . . Are we supposed to regard our popular signboard culture with greater fondness or insight now that we have Rosenquist? Or is he exhorting us to revile it. . . . If the first, the intent is pathological, and if the second, dull."[151]

The hostility these critics felt toward Pop Art must be seen against the background of the political climate of the 1930s and 1940s. Many of the leading proponents of Abstract Expressionism had been partisans of left-wing politics in the thirties. Following the disenchantment with Communism occasioned by the Moscow trials of 1936–38 and the Russo-German non-aggression pact of 1939, the art community entered an era of anti-Stalinism and de-politicalization. In this context, representational art, particularly that with a nationalist

transformed presentation of subject matter. According to Peter Selz, curator at The Museum of Modern Art, "The interpretation or transformation of reality achieved by the Pop Artist, insofar as it exists at all, is limp and unconvincing. It is this want of imagination, this passive acceptance of things as they are that make these pictures so unsatisfactory at second or third look. They are hardly worth the kind of contemplation a real work of art demands."[148]

Equally rich as a source of critical abuse was Pop Art's vernacular subject matter. Lichtenstein's statement that "the one thing everyone hated was commercial art" was all too true.[149] The intellectual snobbery which prevailed in Abstract Expressionist circles could not abide such overt trafficking in philistine culture. Already in 1936 Clement Greenberg, one of Abstract Expressionism's best-known defenders, had denounced kitsch, which he likened to "ersatz culture . . . destined for those

Fig. 121. Andy Warhol, *White Burning Car II*, 1963. Silkscreen on canvas, 106 × 82″ (269.2 × 208.3 cm). Hessisches Landesmuseum, Darmstadt; Karl Ströher Collection.

Fig. 122. Installation views of "The New Realists" exhibition at the Sidney Janis Gallery, New York, 1962.

character, was viewed as a propaganda tool of totalitarianism. Abstract art, on the other hand— specifically Abstract Expressionism—was welcomed as politically neutral and associated with freedom and internationalism.[152] To the advocates of Abstract Expressionism, Pop Art's representational style and its blatant American subject matter seemed to hark back to the socialist art of the thirties which they had so fiercely repudiated.

The banality of Pop Art's imagery violated as well the mythic and heroic dimension which had come to be associated with art in the 1950s. The notion of art as a lofty, moral enterprise, identified with abstract levels of truth, had been implicit among the Abstract Expressionists, who had prided themselves on their psychic distance from the vagaries of vernacular life. Mark Rothko and Adolph Gottlieb had avowed that "only that subject-matter is valid which is tragic and timeless."[153] For them, art was serious, remote, and "aristocratic"; that it remained ineffable and beyond the understanding of all but a small coterie of initiates only confirmed its specialness. Appropriating the mundane without apparent transformation undermined the mystery of art; it seemed to demythologize art and desanctify the artist. Artists and their supporters became ordinary citizens, no longer members of a select intelligentsia. In retrospect, this "democratizing" may have been one of Pop Art's most problematic aspects for the general public, which viewed fine art as embodying some mysterious and secret knowledge; many were suspicious of an art whose imagery mirrored their daily lives.

The vehement rejection of Pop by the critics created a radical reversal of roles, for it was left to the public, the galleries, and the popular press to take the lead in promoting Pop Art. Major articles on Pop appeared in periodicals such as *Life* and *Time* as soon as they did in art journals. A new type of collector emerged, as eager in some cases to embrace the artists' life-style as their art. Given the critical community's loss of credibility, these collectors turned to gallery dealers for aesthetic validation. Sidney Janis, Leo Castelli, and Richard Bellamy, among others, replaced critics as aesthetic arbiters. By the time critics caught up with the public's enthusiasm, the promotion of Pop was no longer an issue.

The mass popularity of the new art precipitated a subtle shift in the role and expectations of artists: works of art were heralded almost as soon as they were produced; artists achieved renown and financial success at remarkably young ages. Johns had set the example, being only twenty-eight when his first one-man exhibition sold out; his achievement was duplicated by this new generation of artists. Culturally, as Kaprow had feared for the Happening makers (p. 46), artists moved from being outsiders to insiders, from proverbially impoverished creators working on the fringes of society to newfound darlings of the jet set and high society. This altered relationship between art and society was to be one of the lasting legacies of this period.

Minimalism

The same dissatisfaction with unbridled subjectivity and emotionalism that inspired Pop Art, Fluxus, and the new dance prevailed among the group of artists who worked within the tradition of geometric abstraction. This tradition had been sustained throughout the heyday of Abstract Expressionism by a small, less visible group of artists, including Ad Reinhardt, Joseph Albers, Ellsworth Kelly, Ralston Crawford, and George Ortman. It had found additional expression during the 1950s in the work of the Chromatic Abstractionists—Barnett Newman and Mark Rothko, among others—whose spare forms and broad color areas exerted a profound influence on younger artists.[154] Still, the essentially mystical tone of the Chromatic Abstractionists and their commitment to art as a form of moral statement separated them from their emulators, who adapted their geometric style for less metaphysical ends.

The first artist to accept geometric abstraction but abrogate its subjectivity and metaphorical aspirations was Frank Stella. In 1958, directly after graduating from Princeton University, Stella began a series of paintings in which he replaced the loose forms and gestural brushstrokes of his earlier Action Painting with an increasingly anonymous, geometric structure and impersonal facture (Figs. 123, 124). A year later, when his Black paintings were included in The Museum of Modern Art's "Sixteen Americans" exhibition, their seemingly mindless configurations and detached execution stunned and baffled most viewers (Fig. 125). The charges flung against them—that they were boring and monotonous; that anyone could do them—were the same as those that greeted Pop Art.[155]

Yet, as with the earliest manifestations of Pop, what looked impersonal and emotionless in the context of the late 1950s now seems rich and almost loosely painted, with manifold variations in surface handling and edge. In retrospect, the dark palette and iconic presence of these paintings radiate an almost religious aura, which William Rubin

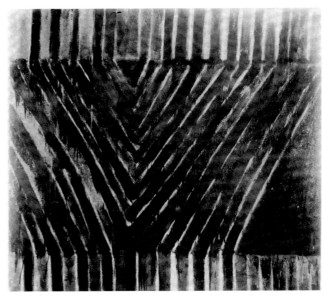

Fig. 124. Frank Stella, *Delta*, 1958. Enamel on canvas, 85⅜ × 97" (216.8 × 246.4 cm). Collection of the artist.

hinted at in 1960 when he wrote of being "mesmerized by their eerie, magical presence."[156] Even the titles Stella ascribed—alluding to death, fascism, and the urban underworld—belie the strictly formal explanations of the paintings that he initially offered.[157]

As Stella's work evolved, the edges of his color bands became more regular and his surfaces "harder." But never did the physical act of painting cease being important to him. "When I'm painting the picture," he explained, "I'm really painting a picture. . . . The thrill, or the meat of the thing, is the actual painting. I don't get any thrill out of laying it out. . . . I like the painting part, even when it's difficult. It's *that* which seems most worthwhile to address myself to."[158]

But the absence of painterly gesture and the commonplace geometric patterns of Stella's work defied any imputation of subjectivity and private symbolic meaning, much as did Pop Art's quasi-mechanical replication of found public images. Warhol said he wanted to be a machine; Stella, apparently contradicting himself, said it was enough for him to have a good idea; he would be just as happy if someone else, or a machine, made his pictures according to his specifications.[159] He denied that his paintings carried references to anything

Fig. 125. Frank Stella, *Die Fahne Hoch*, 1959. Black enamel on canvas, 121½ × 73" (308.6 × 185.4 cm). Whitney Museum of American Art, New York; Gift of Mr. and Mrs. Eugene M. Schwartz and purchase through the generosity of the John I. H. Baur Purchase Fund, Charles and Anita Blatt Fund, Peter M. Brant, B. H. Friedman, Gilman Foundation, Inc., Susan Morse Hilles, The Lauder Foundation, Frances and Sydney Lewis, Albert A. List Fund, National Endowment for the Arts, Sandra Payson, Philip Morris Incorporated, Mr. and Mrs. Albrecht Saalfield, Mrs. Percy Uris and Warner Communications Inc.   75.22.

beyond their own palpable physical reality. There "aren't any particularly poetic or mysterious qualities [in the Stripe paintings]," he asserted.[160] "My painting is based on the fact that only what can be seen there *is* there. . . . What you see is what you see."[161] Since Stella's paintings were not records of inner psychological states, no special knowledge was required to decipher them; because their meaning lay in the material surface of the painting, it was theoretically available to everyone.

As with the Pop painters, it was Johns who provided the structural model for Stella's radical critique of Abstract Expressionism. By painting a flat subject and making that painting identical with its format, Johns had eliminated the sense of a shape on a background and thus any reference to three-dimensional spatiality (Fig. 104). Whereas the Pop artists found in Johns the license to commandeer two-dimensional imagery, Stella was inspired by his abstract formal strategies. He covered the entire canvas with a single motif, thereby eliminating all sense of foreground and background. He thus duplicated Johns' flat surface, but removed all associative meaning by abandoning recognizable imagery. Adopting the structure of Johns' flags—their repetitive stripes and bands parallel to the framing edge—Stella conflated the external shape of the painting with its internal motif or surface pattern. The result was so totally divested of extrapictorial significance that it seemed to be more an object in itself than a painting, an effect enhanced by Stella's

Fig. 126. Installation view of Frank Stella's one-artist exhibition at the Leo Castelli Gallery, New York, 1964.

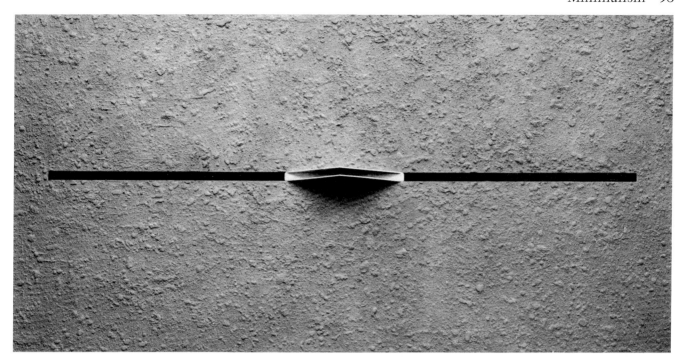

Fig. 127. Donald Judd, *Untitled*, 1962. Light cadmium red oil and wax on liquitex and sand on masonite and wood, with aluminum and black oil on wood, 48 × 96 × 7½" (122 × 243.8 × 19 cm). Private collection.

three-inch-wide stretcher bars. This painting-object was as palpably present as anything else in the viewer's space. The object-like quality became even more pronounced in Stella's work after 1961, especially in his Copper and Purple series, where traditional rectangles gave way to polygons or radically shaped perimeters (Fig. 126).

It was the bold, immediate impact of Stella's paintings that attracted Donald Judd and Carl Andre, who were fascinated by the "objectness" of his work and its implications for sculpture.[162] Stella's influence on Andre, who was a close personal friend, was more visual than theoretical. For a time in the early 1960s, Andre worked in Stella's studio, turning the notched corners and zigzag patterns of Stella's paintings into sculptural equivalents. The original versions of most of these sculptures were later burned as firewood when Andre left them behind after one of his frequent moves. Not until 1964, when he was asked to participate in a show at The Hudson River Museum, did Andre rebuild any of them. Other of Andre's Minimalist works from this period existed only as drawings or as small models until the early seventies; at this time he began executing earlier designs, probably on larger scales than had originally been envisaged.

Judd's relationship to Stella's work was based on the adamant objection both artists had to the European compositional formula of balancing one part of the painting or sculpture against another.[163] While still a painter, Judd had begun embedding found objects into his encrusted paint surfaces (Figs. 127, 128). These interpolated objects were abstract, but they functioned like the found objects in assemblage, eliminating painted illusionism by providing an image that was actual rather than depicted. In 1962, after having spent eight years as a painter, Judd turned to sculpture because of the inherent limitations he perceived in painting (Figs. 129, 130).[164] Painting seemed incapable of satisfying his desire for more rigorous, non-illusionistic concreteness. With real space, he was able to rid his art of the illusionistic deceit he saw as endemic to painting, while simultaneously achieving a physical presence not possible in painting. "Actual space," he explained, "is intrinsically more powerful and specific than paint on a flat surface."[165] Because Judd placed a high premium on the impact of indivisible images, he turned, as had Stella, to symmetry and modular repetition. This allowed him to circumvent the balancing of separate compositional elements. Like others of his generation, Judd denied the existence of symbolic meaning or of a higher reality in his sculpture. He repudiated any

Fig. 128. Donald Judd, *Untitled*, 1962. Light cadmium red oil on liquitex and sand on masonite with yellow Plexiglas, 48 × 96 × 2½" (121.9 × 243.8 × 6.4 cm). Private collection.

Fig. 129. Installation view of Donald Judd's one-artist exhibition at the Green Gallery, New York, 1963–64.

significance save the sculpture's own obdurate "thereness." Asked once what he considered art to be about, Judd answered, "about what I know."[166]

Such insistence on the tangible and concrete was one of the major themes of the avant-garde of the 1960s.[167] In contrast to Abstract Expressionists, these artists put greater faith in the truth of con-

crete facts than in the abstract theories which gave these facts cohesion and supposed clarity. The Pop artists, Fluxus, and dance practitioners had injected into their work the palpable artifacts and gestures of the outside world. As Rauschenberg said when he attached real objects to canvases, "I don't want a picture to look like something it isn't.

I want it to look like something it is."[168] So too with the Pop Art media painters whose work was synonymous with what it represented: "It doesn't look like a painting *of* something," Lichtenstein remarked, "it looks like the thing itself."[169] Minimalists such as Judd and Stella attained a similar objectivity by eschewing all aesthetic deception and illusionism, and insisting on the obdurate physical presence of their objects. No discrepancy existed in their work between what the eye registered and what was actually there. If an image suggested three dimensions, it was created in three dimensions; shapes were not depicted, they were real; for Judd, even color was intrinsic to the material, rather than something applied to the surface.

Judd's predominantly plywood works from 1961 and 1962 were executed according to pragmatic construction considerations. Not being a skilled carpenter, he often kept his materials raw and unsanded. The result was a "soft" surface and a more handmade look than he later obtained when he became more rigorous about mechanical exactness and refinement. In late 1963, improved finances allowed him to turn to metal and to employ outside fabricators. He also began to organize his pieces into units of equal size separated by either equidistant or mathematically based intervals (Fig. 131). (The connection between music and Minimalist sculpture, already noted in the works of La Monte Young and Fluxus artists [p. 67], existed for Judd as well; for his attraction to pre-existing mathematical systems as the structural bases for his compositions had its analogue in the work of musicians like Milton Babbitt.)

The artist closest in spirit to Judd was Dan Flavin. Flavin's early Cubist-derived collages made from crushed tin cans were exhibited at the Judson Gallery in 1961 (Fig. 132). These were followed by works such as *Gus Schultze's screwdriver (to Dick Bellamy)* and *Barbara Roses*, whose single-image format recalled the pre-Pop assemblages of Oldenburg and Dine (Figs. 133, 134). Even after he began to structure light bulbs and fluorescent tubes into severe compositional arrangements (Fig. 135), Flavin's motivations remained consistent with found-object art. What differentiated these later works was his rejection of the gestural conceits of Abstract Expressionism. The banality and un-

Fig. 130. Donald Judd, *Untitled*, 1962. Light cadmium red oil on wood with black enameled metal pipe, 48 × 33⅛ × 21¾" (121.9 × 84 × 54.6 cm). Kunstmuseum Basel.

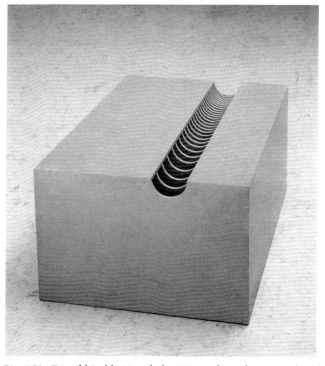

Fig. 131. Donald Judd, *Untitled*, 1963. Light cadmium red oil on wood, 19½ × 45 × 30½" (49.5 × 114.3 × 77.5 cm). The National Gallery of Canada, Ottawa.

Fig. 132. Dan Flavin, *Africa (to seventy-two negroes)*, 1960. Crushed can, oil, pencil, on masonite and balsa, 19 × 22 × 1⅞" (48.3 × 55.9 × 4.8 cm). Collection of the artist.

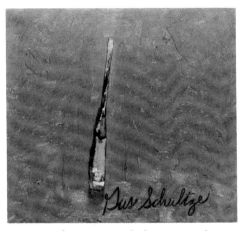

Fig. 133. Dan Flavin, *Gus Schultze's screwdriver (to Dick Bellamy)*, 1960. Screwdriver, oil, pencil, on masonite, and acrylic on balsa, 15⅜ × 17½ × 1¾" (39.1 × 44.5 × 4.5 cm). Collection of the artist.

Fig. 134. Dan Flavin, *Barbara Roses*, 1962–64. Terracotta flower pot, porcelain receptacle with pull chain, and Aerolux Flowerlite, 8½" (21.6 cm) tall. Collection of Barbara Rose.

transformed character of Flavin's sculptural materials linked his work to that of Brecht and the Pop artists. In each case, commercial materials appeared in their hard-edged, industrially reproduced form, unmediated by the personality of the artist. Because Flavin, like Judd, was interested in the power of simple geometries, he exploited the idea of the ready-made for structural rather than narrative ends.[170] Still, the common, public nature of his component materials, like the pedestrian subjects of the Pop artists, undermined the conception of art as a rarefied domain. Since Flavin's sculptures could theoretically be reproduced by anyone with access to a hardware store, they, even more than Pop, confounded the distinction between art and life. A light tube attached diagonally on a wall looks more like an ordinary object than like anything previously known as sculpture (Fig. 136). Flavin viewed the change of context his industrial materials underwent as a change of character. His assertion that "a common lamp becomes a common industrial fetish, as utterly reproducible as ever but somehow strikingly unfamiliar now" sounds remarkably like the Fluxus artists' implicit affirmation of the fundamental worth to be found

Fig. 135. Dan Flavin, *icon V (Coran's Broadway Flesh)*, 1962. Oil on masonite, porcelain receptacles, clear incandescent candle bulbs, 42⅛ × 42⅛ × 9⅞" (107 × 107 × 25.1 cm). Collection of Heiner Friedrich.

Fig. 136. Installation view of Dan Flavin's one-artist exhibition at the Green Gallery, New York, 1964.

Fig. 137. Walter De Maria, *Walk Around the Box*, 1961. Wood box: 15 × 13 × 13″ (38.1 × 33 × 33 cm); oil painting: 49½ × 24″ (125.7 × 61 cm). Collection of the artist.

Fig. 138. Walter De Maria, *Boxes for Meaningless Work*, 1961. Wood box: 9⅝ × 13³⁄₁₆ × 18″ (24.4 × 33.5 × 45.7 cm); wood base: 4⅛ × 4 × 24″ (10.5 × 10.2 × 61 cm); Inscribed in pencil on base: BOXES FOR MEANINGLESS WORK. TRANSFER THINGS FROM ONE BOX TO THE NEXT BOX BACK AND FORTH, BACK AND FORTH ETC. BE AWARE THAT WHAT YOU ARE DOING IS MEANINGLESS. Collection of the artist.

> BOXES for MEANINGLESS WORK
>
> I will have built two small boxes. I put small things in the boxes, A sign explains the boxes to anyone who should approach them. It says "Meaningless work boxes." Throw all of the things into one box, then throw all of the things into the other. Back and forth, back and forth. Do this for as long as you like. What do you feel? Yourself? The Box? The Things? Remember this doesn't mean anything.
>
> March, 1960

Fig. 139. Walter De Maria, "Project for Boxes; Boxes for Meaningless Work," originally printed in *An Anthology*, 1962.

in the seeming triviality of everyday experience.[171]

The interconnections between Minimalism, Fluxus, and dance were even more explicit in the case of Walter De Maria and Robert Morris. Their close friendships and collaborations with the performing artists they had known in San Francisco grew stronger after their arrival in New York in the fall of 1960 (p. 53). When La Monte Young began to assemble material for what became *An Anthology*, he asked Morris and De Maria to submit pieces. The entries of both artists anticipated much of their later sculpture. De Maria's text, "Meaningless Work," concerned "pure" activities having no connection with utilitarian function. Such activities were intentionally neither objects nor events that could be bought, sold, or exhibited: their value lay solely in the pleasure derived from performing the task. The conflation of art and performance became an essential dimension of De Maria's early sculpture. Implicit in pieces such as *Walk Around the Box* (1961), in which viewers walked around, stacked, or arranged boxes, or *Boxes for Meaningless Work* (1961), which instructed them to move a ball from one place to another, was the demand for the audience's active participation (Figs. 137–39). These pieces resembled Brecht's "game sculpture" of the same period (p. 51), although De Maria preferred a more severe and holistic compositional format than that found in Brecht's assemblages. The fundamental event orientation of De Maria's sculpture related as well to Yoko Ono's 1960–62 "instruction" pieces such as *Painting to Be Stepped On* or *Painting to Hammer a Nail In*.

De Maria's exploitation of simple directives stripped of all ornamentation or extraneous gesture referred also to the dances of Simone Forti and the single-gesture Events of the Fluxus artists. In all cases, the assignment of uncomplicated, isolated tasks structured the action—De Maria merely transferred the imperative to act from the designated performers to the audience. To accomplish this, instructions were written and incorporated into the sculpture as key elements. The public, comprehensible character of these words should theoretically have destroyed any residual private significance and made his art accessible to everyone. In practice, however, the introduction of words, which seemed so foreign to sculpture, made De Maria's work difficult for most observers; his word pieces were not publicly exhibited in New York until 1963, when he opened the 9 Great Jones Street Gallery with Robert Whitman.[172]

The literary-performance aspect of De Maria's work was not its only connection to the reductivist vocabulary of Fluxus. His unpainted plywood boxes of 1960–61, 8 by 4 by 4 feet, pared form down to its most elemental (Fig. 140). These sculptures were first exhibited in conjunction with a lecture-demonstration De Maria gave at Maciunas' AG Gallery in July 1961. While structurally similar to his game sculptures, the bare simplicity and lack of even a literary component imbued these plywood rectangles with a monumentality analogous to Young's musical compositions in which sequences of single notes were sustained for long durations without expressive variation of pitch or rhythm.

The other sculptor who belonged to the coterie around Young and the transplanted San Francisco dancers was Robert Morris. Morris' experiments with reductive forms were no doubt encouraged by his construction of the dance props used by his wife, Simone—for example, the inclined panel in *Slant Board* (Fig. 64) or the knotted ropes, suspended from the ceiling, in *Hangers* (1961). Equally important, however, was Morris' translation into sculpture of Simone's strategy of generating movement through task assignments. By adapting her device of determining the structure of a composition and then letting the process dictate its details, Morris could leave certain decisions to chance. Thus in *Box with the Sound of Its Own Making* (1961), Morris conceived the concept of taping con-

Fig. 140. Walter De Maria, *4' × 8' Box*, 1961. Plywood, 96 × 48 × 48" (243.8 × 122 × 122 cm). Collection of the artist.

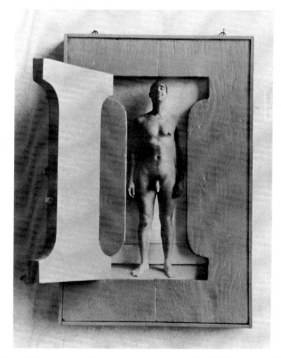

Fig. 141. Robert Morris, *I-Box* (open), 1962. Mixed media construction, 19 × 12¾ × 1⅜" (48.3 × 32.4 × 3.5 cm). Collection of Mr. and Mrs. Leo Castelli.

Fig. 142. Robert Morris, *Metered Bulb*, 1963.
Mixed media construction, 24 × 12″ (61 × 30.5
cm). Collection of Jasper Johns.

Fig. 143. Robert Morris, *Fountain*, 1963. Mixed media construction, 35½ × 13 × 14½″ (90.2 × 33 × 36.8 cm). Frank-
furter Kunstverein.

struction sounds, but allowed the sounds to be
those that arose naturally in the course of making
the box. His involvement with process and with
the witty, Duchampian language puns that were
popular among the Fluxus group can be seen in
works such as *I-Box*, *Metered Bulb*, and *Fountain*
(Figs. 141–43).

"Blank Form," one of the four word pieces Morris
prepared for *An Anthology*, served as a virtual
manifesto of his reductivist sculpture and of his
involvement with perceptual questions concerning
the nature of the art object and its relation to the
viewer. After suggesting three possible manifestations of "blank form" (one of which was "a column
with perfectly smooth, rectangular surfaces, 2 feet
by 2 feet by 8 feet, painted gray"), Morris put forth a
definition of art that hinged on the relationship
between the viewer and the subject:

So long as the form (in the broadest possible
sense: situation) is not reduced beyond percep-

tion, so long as it perpetuates and upholds itself
as being object in the subject's field of perception, the subject reacts to it in many particular
ways when I call it art. He reacts in other ways
when I do not call it art. Art is primarily a situation in which one assumes an attitude of reacting to some of one's awareness as art.[173]

Although these ideas informed much of Morris'
subsequent thinking about sculpture, they were
never made public. As one of Young's close friends
during this period, Morris had stored the loose
pages of *An Anthology* at his loft while they were
waiting to be bound. Thus, when he became disen-
chanted with Fluxus after Maciunas launched the
first series of Fluxus concerts (p. 55), it was easy for
him to remove his contributions.[174] As a result, his
word pieces were not bound with the rest of the
assembled material (Fig. 144).

Morris pursued the interconnection between
sculpture and perception in the piece he created for

Young's concert series at Yoko Ono's loft on Chambers Street in June 1961. *Passageway* was a 60-foot-long semicircular plywood passageway whose walls converged at the end so that viewers who walked into it were forced to turn around at some point and retrace their steps (Fig. 145). While the object itself was static, viewers' experiences of it varied, depending on whether they were walking into it for the first time—and therefore unaware of what to expect—or were walking out. Thus, instead of being an ideal, self-contained, unchanging entity, the work of art constituted an ever-changing relationship between the spectator-participant and the object; it had no meaning apart from this interaction.

Morris elaborated the concept of interdependence the following January in his dance performance *Column*, which he gave at The Living Theatre as part of an attempt to help Young finance the binding of *An Anthology*. Morris' piece featured a light gray plywood rectangle 8 feet tall, 2 feet wide, and 2 feet deep—a three-dimensional realization of what he had earlier called "Blank Form" (Fig. 146). The column stood vertically in the center of the stage for three and a half minutes, after which Morris pulled it by a string to the floor, where it rested horizontally for an equal period of time. In *Passageway*, the object had remained stationary while the viewer's position changed; in *Column*, the relationship was reversed. Morris remained concerned with the effect of position or orientation on our understanding of sculpture: *L-Beams* of 1965, for example, is predicated on the different meanings elicited by units of the same shape and size placed in varied positions. By suggesting that the art experience had three components—the object, the audience, and the environment—Morris challenged the notion of art as something that could be separated from the dynamics of viewing.

The "performer" in *Column* reappeared in Morris' work as freestanding sculpture in 1963, when he began making what he later termed "unitary forms"—gray painted plywood polyhedrons of such simple configurations that their totalities or "gestalts" were immediately apprehensible from any position (Fig. 147).[175] Between *Column* and these uninflected sculptures—exhibited in 1963 at Morris' first one-artist show at the Green Gallery—had been a group of less refined works, constructed out

BLANK FORM

From the subjective point of view there is no such thing as nothing - Blank Form shows this, as well as might any other situation of deprivation.

So long as the form (in the broadest possible sense: situation) is not reduced beyond perception, so long as it perpetuates and upholds itself as being object in the subject's field of perception, the subject reacts to it in many particular ways when I call it art. He reacts in other ways when I do not call it art. Art is primarily a situation in which one assumes an attitude of reacting to some of one's awareness as art.

Blank Form is still in the great tradition of artistic weakness-taste. That is to say I prefer it - especially the content (as opposed to "anti-form" for the attempt to contradict one's taste). Blank form is like life, essentially empty, allowing plenty of room for disquisitions on its nature and mocking each in its turn.

Blank Form slowly waves a large gray flag and laughs about how close it got to the second law of thermodynamics.

Some examples of Blank Form sculpture:
1. A column with perfectly smooth, rectangular surfaces, 2 feet by 2 feet by 8 feet, painted gray.
2. A wall, perfectly smooth and painted gray, measuring 2 feet by 8 feet by 8 feet.
3. A cabinet with simple construction, painted gray and measuring 1 foot by 2 feet by 6 feet - that is, a cabinet just large enough to enter.

Make an object to be lost.

Put something inside that makes a noise and give it to a friend with the instructions:

"To be deposited in the street with a toss."

1961

Fig. 144. Robert Morris, word pieces written in 1960–61 for *An Anthology* (1963), deleted by the author prior to publication.

of unpainted timbers (Fig. 148). Morris never exhibited these formative works and they have since been destroyed.

The concern for non-illusionistic and non-metaphoric concreteness epitomized by the Minimalist sculptors found a parallel expression in painting. As argued by Clement Greenberg, the goal of the modern artist was to eliminate those characteristics from each medium that were not exclusive to it. In this view, the three-dimensional implications in painting caused by modeling and value contrast were in direct conflict with painting's essentially flat nature. Following this reasoning, a number of painters in the early sixties,

Fig. 145. Installation views of Robert Morris' *Passageway* at Yoko Ono's Chambers Street loft, New York, 1961. Painted plywood, 96 × 600" (243.8 × 1524 cm). Destroyed.

Larry Poons and Jo Baer among them, began to eliminate noticeable brushstrokes from their work and to adopt simplified, easily read formats. The results were textureless, two-dimensional paintings whose unambiguous forms, large scale, and often bold color provided an unequivocal immediacy of impact.

Yet the appearance of such reductivist, flat paintings did not still the debate about whether painting could ever be fully non-illusionistic. As Lucy Lippard wrote, "This is a very literal period. Sculpture, existing in real space and physically autonomous, is *realer* than painting."[176] This attitude implied that painting was somehow not as "advanced" as sculpture, and it put a number of painters on the defensive.[177]

It was perhaps no accident that in these years many artists adopted a self-conscious, theoretical stance, for they had received a different education from that of their predecessors. Artists in the past had learned their craft either through imitation of a teacher or by trial and error in the studio. In the late fifties, however, large numbers of artists began attending college—often to avoid the draft. Whereas only one in ten Abstract Expressionists held college degrees, most of the artists of the late fifties generation did. The conceptual and polemical origin of sixties art may, in part, be due to the academic setting in which these artists were educated. As Kaprow said when comparing his generation with that of the Abstract Expressionists: "[We] went to school. . . . [The fifties] was a time of silent alienation and a growing resentment against the environment and against the glibness that seemed to bring success to everyone else. Muteness was seen as proof of one's determination to find another solution to the problem of self-realization. My generation, which is post-war, had the G.I. Bill, where everyone went to school for free. To get through it, you had to learn how to speak up."[178]

This new educational pattern nurtured an aes-

Fig. 146. Robert Morris, *Column*, 1961. Painted plywood, 96 × 24 × 24" (243.8 × 61 × 61 cm). Original destroyed. Photograph from a reconstruction at Ace Los Angeles gallery, 1973.

Fig. 147. Installation view of Robert Morris' one-artist exhibition at the Green Gallery, New York, 1963.

thetic intellectualism which was mirrored in the critical community by strong formalist rhetoric. Both Pop Art and Minimalism fell prey to this mode of critical interpretation. Critics such as Robert Rosenblum and Irving Sandler early on had recognized the formal similarities between Pop Art and Minimalist painting.[179] By the late sixties, Pop Art had come increasingly to be described, not in terms of its subject matter, but in terms of its formal properties—single-image format, hard edges, and a heightened sense of visual immediacy. Indeed it was the mutual possession of these formal characteristics among the various art forms of the sixties that served to give the decade its appearance of homogeneity.[180]

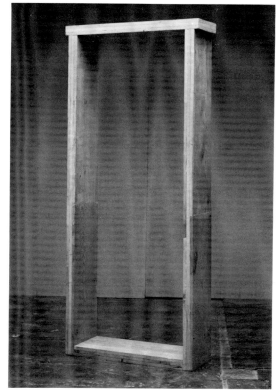

Fig. 148. Robert Morris, *Pine Portal*, c. 1961. Wood, 96 × 48 × 12" (243.8 × 121.9 × 30.5 cm). Destroyed.

Fig. 149. Claes Oldenburg, *Light Switches—Hard Version*, 1964. Painted wood, formica, metal, 47¾ × 47¾ × 11¾″ (121.3 × 121.3 × 29.8 cm). Private collection.

Epilogue

By the beginning of 1964, the evolution of this new sensibility was complete. In the six preceding years, the issues that were to mobilize artists for the next two decades were formulated in an intense and frenetic atmosphere. During this time the new art had fought with, and ultimately supplanted, the old. In the first stage of change, the work of the challengers remained stylistically, if not emotionally, linked to that of their ancestors: junk assemblage, Happenings, and the expressive phase of Pop Art initially retained the spontaneity and surface gestures of Abstract Expressionism. Even the Minimalists and Pop Art media painters produced work during this formative period which, in retrospect, seems tentative and handmade.

But by the end of 1963, a new aesthetic could be clearly perceived, an aesthetic that encompassed both Pop and Minimalism. As Minimalism came to the forefront of public attention with the exhibitions of Judd, Morris, and Flavin, Pop Art became more cool and detached, with sharply edged forms and non-textured surfaces. At the end of 1963, for example, in preparation for a show with Sidney Janis, Oldenburg exchanged the lumpy, paint-splattered commodities from *The Store* for objects having hard surfaces and clean contours (Figs. 149, 150). His concurrent decision to replace plaster and canvas with synthetic vinyl further heightened the contrast with his earlier, painterly style (Fig. 151). Warhol became preoccupied at this time with films such as *Sleep*, in which single events occurred in real time.[181]

In 1963, Wesselmann moved from collaging two-dimensional magazine reproductions to incorporating full-scale, complete objects into his work (Fig. 94). In keeping with the requirements of a more assertive scale, his painted images became larger and their edges crisper. By 1964, he, too, had brought a greater degree of restraint to his previously sensuous compositions (Fig. 152). In Rosenquist's paintings, there was a gradual but steady evolution from the dark tones and heavy paint surface of early works to the graduated tones and definitive contours of those after 1963 (Fig. 153). And Lichtenstein, for his part, purchased an opaque projector in late 1963 which allowed him to work with

Fig. 150. Claes Oldenburg's installation *Bedroom Ensemble*, first presented in "Four Environments by Four New Realists" at the Sidney Janis Gallery, New York, 1964. Wood, vinyl, metal, fake fur, and other materials in room, 204 × 252" (518.2 × 640.1 cm). The National Gallery of Canada, Ottawa.

Fig. 151. Claes Oldenburg, *Soft Pay-Telephone*, 1963. Vinyl filled with kapok mounted on painted wood panel, 46½ × 19 × 9″ (118.1 × 48.3 × 22.9 cm). The Solomon R. Guggenheim Museum, New York; Gift of Ruth and Philip Zierler in memory of their dear departed son, William S. Zierler.

Fig. 152. Tom Wesselmann, *Interior #4*, 1964. Acrylic, polished metal, and assemblage (including working fluorescent light, clock, and radio) on board, 66 × 54 × 9″ (167.6 × 137.2 × 22.9 cm). Private collection.

preparatory sketches, projecting finished images onto the canvas rather than sketching them in freehand. His adoption in late 1963 of a Ben-Day dot screen meant that the uneven and varied quality of his earlier, hand-drawn dots was supplanted by regularly spaced ones which gave his paintings a mechanical and commercial aspect only simulated earlier (Fig. 154). Because the dots were larger, they assumed greater prominence as abstract patterns—a feature Lichtenstein exploited by juxtaposing areas of them with areas of flat paint. In the process, his compositions became more stylized and complex. Eventually he drifted away from popular images; after 1964 he imposed a comic-book style on more traditionally "fine art" subjects—landscapes, architecture, and historic art styles (Fig. 156). Minimalism too became crisper, its execution more impersonal after 1964, as Judd, Morris, and De Maria began to have their designs executed by a fabricator, thereby eliminating the handmade look and soft-wood surface of their earlier achievements (Fig. 155).

As the decade wore on, Minimalism was to exert an even more profound influence on contemporary aesthetics. After 1964, a host of other artists—Sol LeWitt, Ronald Bladen, and Robert Grosvenor, among them—began to simplify their Constructivist-derived sculptures into modular or unitary forms. By the time Kynaston McShine's "Primary Structures" exhibition opened at The Jewish Museum in 1966, Minimalist sculpture had become a firmly established mode of expression. The same held true for painting. By 1965, Robert Mangold had replaced his biomorphic vocabulary with more hard-edged, geometric forms, while Robert Ryman had substituted flatly painted surfaces containing little inflection for the gestural brushstrokes of earlier years. Their reductivist style became the decade's dominant aesthetic.

Finally, by the beginning of 1964, the impetus that had brought the performing art groups together began to change. Just as college students move in different directions after graduation, the artists who had made up Fluxus and the Judson

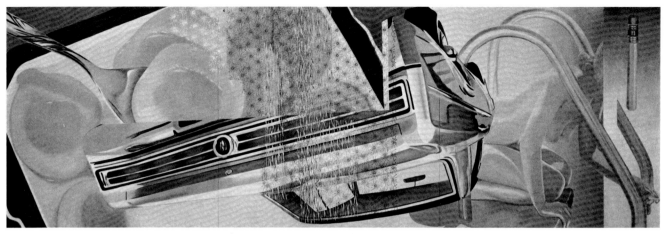

Fig. 153. James Rosenquist, *Lanai*, 1964. Oil on canvas, 62 × 186″ (157.5 × 472.4 cm). Collection of Kimiko and John Powers.

Fig. 154. Roy Lichtenstein, *Blonde Waiting*, 1964. Magna on canvas, 48 × 48″ (121.9 × 121.9 cm). Private collection.

Fig. 155. Donald Judd, *To Susan Buckwalter*, 1964. Blue lacquer on aluminum and galvanized iron, 30 × 141 × 30″ (76.2 × 358.2 × 76.2 cm). Collection of the artist.

Dance Theater began to cultivate more individual mannerisms. Rauschenberg's entry into the dance scene in late 1963 had brought with it an entirely new and expanded audience. With the prospect of fame, petty jealousies and competitiveness came to the surface. Individual dancers started to splinter off and perform on their own, in the process severing the group's cohesion.

Fluxus' first official United States concert in 1964, under Maciunas' implicit leadership, signaled the departure of artists from the organization and the end of the open camaraderie of earlier days (p. 53). As Fluxus artist Tomas Schmit later noted of the years before 1964: "those were the days. days, in which artists gathered instead of separating themselves from each other. . . . soon after Maciunas left for New York again, it started to fade away. . . ."[182]

In 1958, all the artists involved with Happenings, Fluxus, Pop Art, the New American Dance, and Minimalism had been unknown. By 1964, with the exception of those exclusively in Fluxus, they had attained international renown. The approbation which attended the Rauschenberg and Johns retrospectives at The Jewish Museum in 1963 and 1964, and the 1964 Venice Biennale's award of first prize to Rauschenberg were but a few signs that the new aesthetic was firmly established. It had already become the place from which another generation would extend and against which, ultimately, it would react.

Fig. 156. Roy Lichtenstein, *Kiss with Cloud*, 1964. Oil and magna on canvas, 60 × 60″ (152.4 × 152.4 cm). Collection of Irving Blum.

NOTES

1. Yvonne Rainer, *Work 1961–73* (Halifax: The Press of the Nova Scotia College of Art and Design, and New York: New York University Press, 1974), p. 8.

2. Alan Solomon's *New York: The Second Breakthrough, 1959–1964*, exhibition catalogue (Irvine, California: Art Gallery, University of California, Irvine, 1969) covered these years but dealt with only ten artists. Solomon excluded Minimalism (with the exception of Stella) and the performance arts.

3. The essay excludes artists active during this period who entered the art scene after these years as well as those who entered before, as did Ellsworth Kelly and Kenneth Noland. It also excludes the art of certain other major American artists—for the most part figurative painters and California Pop and assemblage artists—whose work came to maturity at this time but who did not significantly contribute to the development of the vanguard aesthetic which came to dominate the later 1960s. For example, California assemblagists Ed Kienholz and George Herms, and Pop artists Ed Ruscha and Joe Goode remained linked to the Surrealist tradition; their work, therefore, while outstanding on its own terms, did not break radically from the past. This was true as well for the figurative artists. Although painters such as Philip Pearlstein and Alex Katz shared a desire to invigorate art with references to everyday life, they accomplished this primarily by relying on earlier pictorial conventions rather than on those that came to be identified with sixties modernism.

4. See Donald Judd, "Local History," in *Arts Yearbook 7: New York: The Art World*, ed. James R. Mellow (New York: The Art Digest, 1964), p. 26.

5. E. M. Forster, *Howards End* (New York: Vintage Books, 1921), p. 106.

6. Harold Rosenberg, "The American Action Painters," *Art News*, 51 (December 1952), p. 23.

7. Walter De Maria, conversation with the author, June 30, 1983.

8. Irving H. Sandler, "Is There a New Academy?," *Art News*, 58 (Summer 1959), pp. 34–37, 58–59; "Is There a New Academy? Part II," ibid. (September 1959), pp. 36–39, 58–60.

9. Quoted in Sandler, "Is There a New Academy? Part II," p. 37.

10. Quoted in John Rublowsky, *Pop Art* (New York: Basic Books, 1965), p. 136; and Tom Wesselmann, conversation with the author, September 30, 1983.

11. John Coplans, "An Interview with Roy Lichtenstein," *Artforum*, 2 (October 1963), p. 31.

12. Quoted in Sandler, "Is There a New Academy? Part II," p. 60.

13. George Segal, conversation with the author, July 7, 1983.

14. The word "assemblage" was coined by Jean Dubuffet in 1953 to refer to his new pasted constructions. For a history of assemblage, see William C. Seitz, *The Art of Assemblage*, exhibition catalogue (New York: The Museum of Modern Art, 1961).

15. For a more complete discussion of Rauschenberg and his work, see Calvin Tomkins, *Off the Wall: Robert Rauschenberg and the Art World of Our Time* (Garden City, New York: Doubleday, 1980); and Lawrence Alloway, "Rauschenberg's Development," in *Robert Rauschenberg*, exhibition catalogue (Washington, D.C.: National Collection of Fine Arts, Smithsonian Institution, 1976), pp. 3–23.

16. Ivan Karp, conversation with the author, June 23, 1983.

17. Allan Kaprow, "The Legacy of Jackson Pollock," *Art News*, 57 (October 1958), pp. 24–26, 55–57.

18. Kaprow, ibid., pp. 56–57.

19. It was Kaprow's interest in electronic music that led him to enroll in John Cage's class on composition at the New School for Social Research, an experience that was to have a great influence on his work.

20. "Trend to the 'Anti-Art,' " *Newsweek*, 51 (March 31, 1958), pp. 94, 96.

21. "New Talent in the U.S.A. 1959," *Art in America*, 47, no. 1 (1959).

22. Quoted in Jan Van der Marck, *George Segal* (New York: Harry N. Abrams, 1975), p. 21.

23. That the Hansa Gallery's three youngest members—Kaprow, Whitman, and Segal—were later involved with Happenings underscores the direct evolution from assemblage to Happenings; from "found-object" to "found-movement" art. The subsequent transition to Pop or "found-image" art is exemplified by Segal's career and the fact that Karp and Bellamy moved from supporting assemblage to supporting Pop Art—Karp through his directorship of the Leo Castelli Gallery and Bellamy through his Green Gallery, which showcased Pop and Minimalist art during its five years of existence from 1960 to 1965.

24. The Hansa Gallery numbered between ten and fifteen artists, all of whom paid dues ranging from ten dollars to thirty dollars a month. Originally located in a third-floor walk-up on Twelfth Street in Greenwich Village, it moved to a brownstone on Central Park South in 1954. For a further history of the Hansa Gallery, see Joellen Bard, *Tenth Street Days: The Co-ops of the 50's*, exhibition catalogue (New York: Pleiades Gallery and The Association of Artist-Run Galleries, 1977); and Amy Goldin, "Requiem for a Gallery," *Arts Magazine*, 40 (January 1966), pp. 25–29.

25. Karp, conversation with the author, June 23, 1983.

26. Ibid.

27. The Judson Memorial Church had begun including artists in its program in 1957, under the influence of Reverend Howard Moody, who had become minister of the church the year before. After informal discussions with local artists, Moody and Bud Scott determined that the best service the church could render to the local artistic community would be to make gallery space available free of charge. The first show, which presented the work of Helen Shulik, took place in November 1958 in what was then called the Judson Studio. The studio was located in the basement, below the church's student housing. The name changed to the Judson Gallery in February 1959. For a year, beginning in December 1959, Kaprow served as the unofficial gallery director. After Al Carmines succeeded Scott as assistant minister in 1960, other features were added to the art, music, and film program: the literary magazine *Exodus*, the Hall of Issues, the Judson Poet's Theater, and the Judson Dance Theater.

28. For a discussion of the Reuben Gallery, see Lawrence Alloway, "The Reuben Gallery: A Chronology" (1965), reprinted in Alloway, *Topics in American Art Since 1945* (New York: W. W. Norton, 1975), pp. 151–54.

29. From an interview with Robert Pincus-Witten in 1963; quoted in Barbara Rose, *Claes Oldenburg*, exhibition catalogue (New York: The Museum of Modern Art, and Greenwich, Connecticut: New York Graphic Society, 1970), p. 37.

30. Red Grooms, conversation with the author, June 30, 1983; and Walter De Maria, conversation with the author, June 30, 1983.

31. For a discussion of the relationship between Beat poets and assemblagists, see Robert M. Murdock, "Assemblage: Anything and Everything, Late 50s," in *Poets of the Cities: New York and San Francisco 1950–1965*, ed. Neil A. Chassman, exhibition catalogue (Dallas Museum of Fine Arts and Southern Methodist University, and New York: E. P. Dutton, 1974), pp. 32–38.

32. Solomon, *The Second Breakthrough*, p. 7.

33. Oldenburg intended the exhibition to be a collaborative endeavor involving many artists. He later recalled that he imposed his ideas for the show on Dine, who was "something less than an enthusiastic collaborator"; quoted in Ellen H. Johnson, *Claes Oldenburg* (Baltimore: Penguin Books, 1971), p. 59, n. 14.

34. *Time* described this environment as "a shocking-pink and green affair with bedsprings hanging from the ceiling and an umbrella protruding from the wall, with cardboard signs reading, 'Breakfast Is Ready,' 'Go to Work,' and 'Why Can't We Be Friends?' Dine calls these 'phrases you hear around any household. I wanted to show the violence of a home.' " "Up-Beats," *Time*, 75 (March 14, 1960), p. 80.

35. Claes Oldenburg, conversation with the author, January 25, 1984.

36. From the Judson Gallery *Calendar of Events* of the 1960 season, Judson Memorial Church Archives, New York.

37. Transcript from panel entitled "New Uses of the Human Image in Painting" held at the Judson Gallery, December 2, 1959, Judson Memorial Church Archives, New York.

38. The other artists who produced comic books were Robert Whitman, Dick Higgins, Dick Tyler, and Red Grooms.

39. The analogy between the assemblagists and the Ashcan School was first noted by Irving H. Sandler, "Ash Can Revisited, a New York Letter," *Art International*, 4 (October 1960), pp. 28–30.

40. Hilton Kramer, "Month in Review," *Arts*, 35 (November 1960), p. 50. The first exhibition, entitled "New Media—New Forms: In Painting and Sculpture," opened in June 1960. It was so successful that a second version, entitled "New Media—New Forms: In Painting and Sculpture, Version II," was presented in September 1960. In October 1960, a catalogue for the *first* exhibition was published. In contrast to the exhibitions, the catalogue was entitled *New Forms—New Media I*.

41. See, for example, the review by John Canaday, "Art: A Wild, but Curious, End-of-Season Treat," *The New York Times*, June 7, 1960, section 5, p. 32.

42. Kaprow later explained why he joined Cage's class:

> It was purely accidental. Although I had known Cage's work and met him once or twice in the years before that, and although I was very interested in what he was doing, I wasn't especially interested in studying music. I was working on Environments in the mid-fifties. I was using, along with odors, many sounds. However, I wanted a richer source of sounds than gimmicked-up mechanical toys could give me. I had no background in sound whatsoever, and I didn't want to use or make music. I wanted *noise*, which had always interested me more. . . . So, I went to Cage to find out how to use tape-machines. . . .

Quoted in Richard Kostelanetz, *The Theatre of Mixed Means: An Introduction to Happenings, Kinetic Environments, and Other Mixed-Means Performances* (New York: The Dial Press, 1968), p. 105.

43. Quoted in Tomkins, *Off the Wall*, p. 149.

44. John Cage, "Experimental Music," in *Silence: Lectures and Writings* (Middletown, Connecticut: Wesleyan University Press, 1961), p. 12. For a general study of Cage, from which the present discussion is drawn, see Calvin Tomkins, *The Bride & The Bachelors: The Heretical Courtship in Modern Art* (New York: The Viking Press, 1965), pp. 69–144; Kostelanetz, *Theatre of Mixed Means*; and Michael Kirby, ed., *Happenings: An Illustrated Anthology* (New York: E. P. Dutton, 1966), pp. 31–32, 36–38.

45. For further information on Black Mountain College, which closed in 1956, see Martin Duberman, *Black Mountain: An Exploration in Community* (New York: E. P. Dutton, 1972).

46. While the audience faced the center of the room, holding white cups which had been placed on their chairs, Cage read, from a raised lectern at the side of the room, excerpts from the medieval German mystic Meister Eckhart, after which he performed a composition with radio; Richards read poetry; Rauschenberg, whose white paintings hung above the heads of the spectators, played old records on a hand-wound gramophone; Tudor played a "prepared piano," while Merce Cunningham improvised a dance through the aisles. Later, Tudor poured water from one bucket to another while Rauschenberg projected abstract slides and film clips onto the ceiling. The composer Jay Watt played exotic musical instruments in the corner, and coffee was served by four boys dressed in white. See Kirby, *Happenings*, pp. 31–32.

47. See Tomkins, *Off the Wall*, pp. 151–52, for a description of Kaprow's Happening at Segal's farm. Kaprow had earlier staged similar Happenings while attending Cage's class at the New School during 1958 and 1959. These classroom exercises were followed by an informal Happening presented at Douglass College, Rutgers University, in April 1958 and then by the Hansa picnic at Segal's. Kaprow's first official public Happening, *18 Happenings in Six Parts*, was presented at the Reuben Gallery in October 1959.

48. See Allan Kaprow, "Something to Take Place: A Happening," in Kirby, *Happenings*, pp. 53–66.

49. *18 Happenings in Six Parts* took place on October 4, 6, 7, 8, 9, 10. Kaprow assigned members of the audience to each of the three rooms. They did not remain in these rooms for the duration of the piece, however, but changed rooms at specific times. As the event began, the three rooms were flooded with bright light—pink, deep blue, and pale blue. The reverberating note of a bell was heard while loud electronic sounds issued simultaneously from loudspeakers in each corner of the gallery. The performers walked expressionlessly down the narrow corridors into the makeshift rooms and began to perform simple quasi-gymnastic moves. Among the activities that followed, one man stood with his hands on his hips for sixteen seconds, then bent forward and extended his arms like wings for five seconds; two men in suits walked formally down the side corridor, each carrying a small stick in front of him; from placards, two men read such things as "it is said that time is essence . . . we here know time . . . 'spiritually' "; a man played a record which asked, "Are the gentlemen ready?"; lights went off and on in a carefully programmed sequence; slides were shown; one girl bounced a ball and another did uncomplicated moves while kneeling in the center of the room. After ninety minutes of such activities, the performance was over. See Kaprow, "18 Happenings in 6 Parts," in Kirby, *Happenings*, pp. 67–83.

50. Given the distinct stylistic and intentional differences among the various artists who performed and created Happenings, the generic application of the word raised understandable objections. Even Kaprow voiced reservations, especially since the word's euphonious resemblance to happenstance erroneously connoted something unplanned or trite (Kirby, *Happenings*, pp. 47–48). Other labels were suggested, such as "Intermedia" (Dick Higgins), "Theater Events" (Whitman), "Plays" (Grooms), and "Theatre of Mixed Means" (Richard Kostelanetz).

51. Some writers have felt that this audience-actor relationship was basic to the concept of Happenings. Susan Sontag, for example, saw the intimacy as abusive and regarded this treatment as a central characteristic. Kirby, who played such an impressive early role in defining Happenings, disagreed, maintaining that jamming the audience together had more to do with limited space resources than with philosophy; that a Happening presented on a proscenium stage would still be a Happening. Kirby's analysis is accurate, but does not mitigate the fact that the involvement necessitated by these cramped spaces became a major component of Happenings. See Susan Sontag, "Happenings: An Art of Radical Juxtaposition," in *Against Interpretation and Other Essays* (New York: Dell, 1966), pp. 263–74; and Kirby, *Happenings*, p. 11.

52. *18 Happenings in Six Parts* was a scrupulously annotated work in which timing and details were orchestrated with meticulous precision. Two weeks were spent in rehearsal, during which time performers had to memorize stick drawings and time scores so that each movement and sequence could be carefully monitored; see also Fig. 24.

53. See Kirby, *Happenings*, p. 38; and Robert Whitman, conversation with the author, June 21, 1983.

54. See Allan Kaprow, "A Statement," in Kirby, *Happenings*, pp. 49–50.

55. The contrast between Kaprow's and Grooms's Happenings was first made by Oldenburg; see Kostelanetz, *Theatre of Mixed Means*, p. 135.

56. Kirby describes the event: "When he [Mathieu] re-enacted the thirteenth-century Battle of Bouvines on canvas, he wore a costume made up of black trousers, a black silk jacket, white cross-leggings, and a white helmet that tied under his chin. . . . The creation of the painting, which was based upon detailed historical research and executed during the same hours of the day that the battle itself was fought, was filmed." See Kirby, *Happenings*, p. 28.

57. See Kirby, *Happenings*, pp. 28–29. *The New York Times* report of the Gutai group's performances influenced Oldenburg; see Rose, *Oldenburg*, p. 25.

58. Grooms, conversation with the author, June 30, 1983.

59. Grooms, "A Statement," in Kirby, *Happenings*, p. 118.

60. Grooms, conversation with the author, June 30, 1983.

61. Grooms' *The Big Leap* was originally intended to have been presented as well.

62. Dine later recalled that his decision to do a Happening had been taken during a conversation with Oldenburg. Oldenburg said, "We're going to have these Happenings," and Dine responded, "O.K. I'd like to do one." Jim Dine, "A Statement," in Kirby, *Happenings*, p. 185.

63. Coosje van Bruggen, *Claes Oldenburg: Mouse Museum/Ray Gun Wing*, exhibition catalogue (Cologne: Museum Ludwig, 1979), p. 13.

64. See Kostelanetz, *Theatre of Mixed Means*, pp. 137–38.

65. Oldenburg's cast included himself and his wife, Pat, as well as Lucas Samaras, then studying acting with Stella Adler. For a more detailed exposition of Oldenburg's characters and scripts, see Rose, *Oldenburg*, p. 184.

66. Quoted in van Bruggen, *Claes Oldenburg*, p. 27. Oldenburg later presented many of the handmade stage props used in his Happenings as sculpture; for example, *Freighter and Sailboat*, held by Pat Oldenburg in *Store Days, II*.

67. Dine, "A Statement," in Kirby, *Happenings*, p. 188.

68. Ibid.

69. Segal, conversation with the author, July 7, 1983.

70. Kaprow's reputation in particular was adversely affected by the fugitive nature of Happenings. While other artists went on from Happenings to produce static objects which won them fame, Kaprow did not. His contribution to the formulation of the aesthetic of the early 1960s is thus often undervalued. In fact, he played a dominant role in the avant-garde community during this period, exerting incalculable influence not only on Happenings but on Pop Art as well.

71. Allan Kaprow, *Assemblage, Environments & Happenings* (New York: Harry N. Abrams, 1966), p. 184. Oldenburg reiterated this attitude by describing the series of Happenings he presented in connection with *The Store* as presenting "in events what the store presents in objects . . . a theater of real events (a newsreel)." Claes Oldenburg and Emmett Williams, *Store Days: Documents from The Store (1961) and Ray Gun Theater (1962)* (New York: Something Else Press, 1967), p. 80

72. Quoted in Rose, *Oldenburg*, p. 183.

73. This observation about the compartmentalized character of Happenings, as well as their relationship to assemblage, was first noted by Kirby, *Happenings*, pp. 13–21.

74. See Kaprow, "Jackson Pollock," pp. 56–57, and " 'Happenings' in the New York Scene," *Art News*, 60 (May 1961), pp. 36–39, 58–62.

75. Quoted in Rose, *Oldenburg*, p. 183.

76. Grooms, conversation with the author, June 30, 1983.

77. Rosenberg, "The American Action Painters," pp. 22–23, 48–50.

78. Since Happenings relied on chance and the acceptance of the unforeseen, they carried the same existentialist charge that fueled Abstract Expressionist painting. Chance implied risk—and potential failure. By hazarding failure, Happenings reinvested art with a sense of emotional tension that had all but vanished with the academic mannerisms of second-generation Abstract Expressionists.

79. Kaprow, " 'Happenings,' " pp. 60–62.

80. Ibid.

81. In a conversation between Allan Kaprow and Howard Moody at the Judson Gallery in December 1959, Kaprow admonished the gallery to "keep away from *Time* and *Life* and all attempts to sensationalize"; notes from the conversation preserved in the Judson Memorial Church Archives, New York.

82. Kaprow, " 'Happenings,' " pp. 60–62.

83. Quoted in Tomkins, *Off the Wall*, p. 154. The commercialism of art alluded to by Oldenburg was a fate suffered by much of the American avant-garde in the sixties.

84. "There's no moment in life that's not musical"; quoted in Irmeline Lebeer, "An Interview with George Brecht," in *An Introduction to George Brecht's Book of the Tumbler on Fire*, ed. Henry Martin (Milan: Multhipla Edizioni, 1978), p. 82.

85. Tristan Tzara, "Seven Dada Manifestoes," in *The Dada Painters and Poets: An Anthology*, ed. Robert Motherwell (New York: Wittenborn, Schultz), pp. 96–97.

86. This notice appeared on most of the Chambers Street concerts organized by La Monte Young and held at Yoko Ono's loft on Chambers Street from December 1960 to June 1961.

87. Brecht's "Towards Events" exhibition at the Reuben Gallery was subtitled "An Arrangement." According to Michael Nyman, Brecht "used this word in the sense 'of a musical arrangement, and also in the sense that things are arranged rather than made. The poster for the show was also made in a musical way. That is, you

had the text running over most of the left hand side, and down the right hand side you had a time notation, so that each line of the poster was to be read over a certain period of time.' " Michael Nyman, "An Interview with George Brecht," in Martin, *Introduction to Tumbler on Fire*, p. 119, n. 9.

88. It was through David Tudor, in attendance at the workshop recording some of Cage's music, that Young became more familiar with Cage's ideas.

89. La Monte Young, conversation with the author, July 7, 1983.

90. James Waring, letter to La Monte Young, December 1960. La Monte Young Archives, New York.

91. Simone Forti was known as Simone Morris when she first moved to New York. After her divorce from Robert Morris and her marriage to Robert Whitman, she became Simone Whitman. She is now known by her maiden name, Simone Forti.

92. Maciunas had opened the gallery along with a fellow Lithuanian, Almus Salcius, in the spring of 1961. Called the AG Gallery (the initials of their first names), it was devoted initially to literary readings, ancient music, and Abstract Expressionist art. See Jackson Mac Low, "Wie George Maciunas die New Yorker Avantgarde kennenlernte," in *1962 Wiesbaden Fluxus 1982: Eine kleine Geschichte von Fluxus in drei Teilen*, exhibition catalogue (Wiesbaden: Museum Wiesbaden, 1982), p. 110.

93. Included in *An Anthology* were pieces by Young, Brecht, Jackson Mac Low, James Waring, Nam June Paik, Simone Forti, Dick Higgins, Walter De Maria, Yoko Ono, John Cage, Richard Maxfield, Terry Riley, Earle Brown, Joseph Byrd, Toshi Ichiyanagi, Terry Jennings, Emmett Williams, Christian Wolff, and others. One of the items was an article entitled "Concept Art" by Henry Flynt—an unacknowledged precursor of the Conceptual art movement of the late 1960s.

94. There are various interpretations of what the word "Fluxus" meant. According to the most accepted version, it was a name Maciunas chose when he and a group of Lithuanians met and decided to start a Lithuanian magazine, a project that never materialized. See Mats B., "Birth of Fluxus—the Ultimate Version," in *George F. Maciunas*, exhibition catalogue (Berlings, Arlöv, Sweden: Kalejdoskop, 1981), unpaginated. The first time Maciunas used the name—in an announcement of a concert for early music at the AG Gallery—it referred to a proposed publication, now no longer Lithuanian. Beginning in the fall of 1962, Fluxus was used as an umbrella name for a series of concerts, rather than for a publication. Some disagreement exists about what constituted the first European Fluxus concert. While at least two concerts that included Fluxus artists took place prior to the Wiesbaden concert in September, these were billed as "neo-Dada" rather than as "Fluxus."

95. The Yam Festival included a month-long program of activities, among which were Al Hansen's performance *Auction*, an exhibition of "décollages" by the European Wolf Vostell, Alison Knowles' *Yam Hat Show* (for which more than two hundred artists were invited to bring their own hat creations), and a ping-pong tournament held on the rooftop of the Kornblee Gallery. The climax of the festival was a daylong event organized by Kaprow at Segal's farm on May 19, 1963, which included pieces by Young, Higgins, Yvonne Rainer, Trisha Brown, Kaprow, Vostell, and Charles Ginnever.

96. The New York Audio-Visual group met at the Epitome Café, run by Larry Poons. One of the typical pieces produced at these gatherings was Poons' *Tennessee*, created with a motorcycle, an electric guitar, and a basketball.

97. Letter from Robert Morris to George Maciunas, April 4, 1964, in the Maciunas Estate, New York; photocopy courtesy of Barbara Moore, New York. Asked in 1980 what Fluxus was, Morris replied, "I'm not informed about Fluxus"; see *Fluxus Etc.: The Gilbert and*

Lila Silverman Collection, exhibition catalogue (Bloomfield Hills, Michigan: Cranbrook Academy of Art Museum, 1981), p. 39.

98. "The group, with few exceptions, that associates itself with Fluxus is irresponsible," Kaprow complained. "It is my impression that many people just simply goof-off and pretend in a kind of very very nasty way, socially speaking, and certainly socially with respect to other artists, that they have certain superiority in their seemingly indifferent little activities such as sneeze tomorrow or a finger is as good as a hole in a wall, or any of these little directives which if acted out are somehow to me important rather than unimportant so far as its effect is to say to me and others— 'You guys are doing important things, but look, we are even more important doing unimportant things' "; quoted in Harry Ruhé, *Fluxus, The Most Radical and Experimental Art Movement of the Sixties* (Amsterdam: 'A,' 1979), unpaginated.

99. Stockhausen had reportedly said that all good music was based on the European tradition, a comment at which Flynt, who was involved with African and other forms of ethnic music, took particular umbrage. Conversation with Flynt and Barbara Moore, February 18, 1982.

100. For a more complete analysis of Maciunas' typographic style, see Barbara Moore, "George Maciunas: A Finger in Fluxus," *Artforum*, 21 (October 1982), pp. 38–45.

101. For some artists, such as Joe Jones, Maciunas was the total embodiment of Fluxus; when asked later what Fluxus was, he responded: "Fluxus was one man named George F. Maciunas"; quoted in *Fluxus Etc.*, p. 27. For others, Maciunas remained simply an organizer. As the French artist Ben Vautier later recalled: "If you ask me who was George Maciunas, I would say a classifier. I think his great job was classifying everything and everybody"; quoted in Emmett Williams, "Happy Birthday, Everybody!" in *Wiesbaden Fluxus*, p. 87.

102. That Maciunas capriciously included and excluded artists from the "organization" only exacerbated Fluxus' amorphous character. Emmett Williams, for example, the concrete poet, was expelled for failing to label a concert "Fluxus" that included what Maciunas had designated as the requisite percentage of Fluxus artists.

103. I am indebted, in the discussion of dance, to Jill Johnston's "A Criticism of Outrage," in *Judson Dance Theater: 1962–1966*, eds. Wendy Perron and Daniel J. Cameron, exhibition catalogue (Bennington, Vermont: Bennington College Judson Project, 1981), pp. 10–13, and "The New American Modern Dance," *Art and Literature*, 5 (Summer 1965), pp. 118–33; and Sally Banes' *Terpsichore in Sneakers: Post-Modern Dance* (Boston: Houghton Mifflin Company, 1980).

104. Cunningham's professional involvement with Cage had actually commenced in 1944 with a joint recital, in which Cunningham had selected a time structure for his dance and asked Cage to independently compose music of the same duration.

105. Cunningham's break with the modern dance practices of Martha Graham was particularly dramatic because he had trained under Graham and had been the company's principal dancer until 1945.

106. On July 6, 1962, three hundred people attended a three-hour program of twenty-three dances. The event was greeted with critical acclaim. For Jill Johnston, dance critic for *The Village Voice*, the performance marked the "beginning of the definitive end of the modern dance establishment"; Johnston, "New American Modern Dance," p. 118. For the dance historian Sally Banes, it was the "beginning of an historic process that changed the shape of dance history"; Banes, "Judson Dance Theatre: Democracy's Body 1962–1964" (Ph.D. dissertation, New York University, 1980), p. 1.

107. Johnston, "New American Modern Dance," p. 130.

108. Johnston, "A Criticism of Outrage," p. 12.

109. Yvonne Rainer, "A Quasi Survey of Some 'Minimalist' Tendencies in the Quantitatively Minimal Dance Activity Midst the Plethora, or an Analysis of Trio A," in *Minimal Art: A Critical Anthology*, ed. Gregory Battcock (New York: E. P. Dutton, 1968), pp. 263–73.

110. Quoted in Rose, *Oldenburg*, pp. 51–52.

111. The equation in *World's Fair, II* between the characters and the contents of their pockets was perceived by van Bruggen, *Claes Oldenburg*, p. 30.

112. Quoted in Rose, *Oldenburg*, p. 46.

113. Sidney Tillim, "Month in Review," *Arts Magazine*, 37 (November 1962), p. 38.

114. Though various critics had seen humor in *The Smiling Workman* (Fig. 40), Dine repudiated this assessment: "What I was doing was not a humorous situation. I think it was funny to see it, but I do not think obsession is funny or that not being able to stop one's intensity is funny. If I had performed it for an hour with that sort of intensity, I do not think it would have been funny. It took the form of a blackout or a vaudeville act. The nature of the medium did that, not the intent"; Dine, "A Statement," in Kirby, *Happenings*, p. 186.

115. Quoted in Oldenburg and Williams, *Store Days*, p. 13.

116. Quoted in G. R. Swensen, "What Is Pop Art?" *Art News*, 62 (November 1963), p. 25.

117. Segal later said that Happenings had given him license to deal more directly with mundane events; conversation with the author, July 7, 1983.

118. Lichtenstein's use of parody was noted as early as 1953 in Fairfield Porter, "Reviews and Previews," *Art News*, 51 (February 1953), p. 74:

> He pretends at first to be interested in the illustrations in grammar-school history books, he pretends to be copying them—but what is he thinking of, how did it turn out this way? The surprise is very funny, that what he is really thinking of is painting, and that he is an extremely sophisticated young man. He hides his wit, he hides his comment, butter wouldn't melt in his mouth. It is the reverse of putting a moustache on the Mona Lisa; he dresses innocent, dull provinciality in fashionable city clothes, because, after all, innocence and provinciality are just as interesting as the acceptable still-life. And so he kids also the city. And while he does this he shows that he understands the essential nature of painting. He gets it down in one spontaneous layer, and he gets it down right.

119. Coplans, "An Interview with Roy Lichtenstein," p. 31.

120. Television interview with Roy Lichtenstein and Allan Kaprow by Joan W. Konner and Selden Rodman; part of the series "Artists of New Jersey," telecast on WNET/Channel 13, September 23, 1964. Tape in The Museum of Modern Art Film Study Center, Television Archives of the Arts.

121. Under Kaprow's leadership, Rutgers University, during this period, was a seedbed for experimentation in the arts. Kaprow, Robert Watts, and Lichtenstein taught there; Robert Whitman and Lucas Samaras were Kaprow's students. George Segal, who lived near the campus, and George Brecht, who worked in the nearby Johnson & Johnson plant, were all members of this extended Rutgers community. For further information on the Rutgers group, see *Ten from Rutgers University*, exhibition catalogue (New York: Bianchini Gallery, 1965); and *Twelve from Rutgers*, exhibition catalogue (New Brunswick, New Jersey: University Art Gallery, 1977).

122. Quoted in Bruce Glaser, "Lichtenstein, Oldenburg, Warhol: A Discussion," *Artforum*, 4 (February 1966), p. 21.

123. Quoted in Jean Stein, *Edie: An American Biography*, ed. George Plimpton (New York: Dell, 1982), p. 192.

124. These aspects of Johns' work were first articulated by Leo Steinberg in "Jasper Johns: The First Seven Years of His Art" (1962), revised in *Other Criteria: Confrontations with Twentieth-Century Art* (New York: Oxford University Press, 1972), pp. 17–54, and Alan R. Solomon in *Jasper Johns*, exhibition catalogue (New York: The Jewish Museum, 1964).

125. John Coplans, "Talking with Roy Lichtenstein," *Artforum*, 5 (May 1967), p. 34.

126. Quoted in Swenson, "What Is Pop Art?," p. 26.

127. "I think that the reaction to the painting of the last generation, which is generally believed to have been a highly subjective generation, is impersonality"; Oldenburg, quoted in Glaser, "Lichtenstein, Oldenburg, Warhol," p. 22.

128. John Ashbery was the first to write about the relationship between Robbe-Grillet and the Pop artists; see his "The New Realism," in *New Realists*, exhibition catalogue (New York: Sidney Janis Gallery, 1962), unpaginated.

129. See Sontag, "Against Interpretation," in *Against Interpretation*, pp. 3–14.

130. Quoted in Morris Dickstein, *Gates of Eden: American Culture in the Sixties* (New York: Basic Books, 1977), p. 9.

131. Quoted in Rose, *Oldenburg*, p. 11.

132. Discussion of media became increasingly pronounced in these years. It can be argued, for example, that Marshall McLuhan's *Understanding Media*, published in 1965, was successful not because it precipitated an awareness of contemporary media, but because it articulated already accepted and widespread views.

133. See Swenson, "What Is Pop Art?," p. 25.

134. For a full catalogue of Oldenburg's Mouse Museum and Ray Gun Museum, see van Bruggen, *Claes Oldenburg*.

135. See Sontag, "Notes on 'Camp,'" in *Against Interpretation*, pp. 275–92.

136. Warhol began painting Marilyn Monroe's portrait after her death in 1962, and Elizabeth Taylor's portrait in response to her near-fatal illness in the early 1960s; see Swenson, "What Is Pop Art?," p. 60.

137. See Max Kozloff, " 'Pop' Culture, Metaphysical Disgust, and the New Vulgarians," *Art International*, 6 (March 1962), pp. 34–36.

138. Tillim, "Month in Review," p. 36.

139. The term "Pop Art" was not applied to the works until the spring of 1963. It had initially been used by Lawrence Alloway in England to describe industrialized, urban media of mass communication. The term had evolved in the 1950s in discussions among a group of English artists, writers, and architects, known as the Independent Group, who were interested in expanding their aesthetic awareness so that it encompassed all aspects of the manmade environment and popular culture. See Alloway, "Pop Art: The Words," in *Topics in American Art*, pp. 119–22; and Jasia Reichardt, "Pop Art and After," *Art International*, 7 (February 1963), pp. 42–47.

Certain problems attended the grouping of artists on the basis of subject matter alone. Particularly for Oldenburg and Dine, it ignored their gestural style and the more figurative way objects functioned in their work. Similarly confusing was the occasional though inconsistent addition of Johns and Rauschenberg to this category. The definition of Pop Art, and of those who qualified as Pop artists, thus remained nebulous. George Brecht, for example, was included in many of the early Pop shows, but Oldenburg frequently was not. Nor did Oldenburg consider any of his work before the end of 1963 to be Pop. Whether Segal was or was not Pop remained a question as late as 1970, when Lawrence Alloway curated the show "Pop Art" at the Whitney Museum: he included Rauschenberg and Johns but not Segal. Even Leo Castelli, one of the primary Pop Art dealers, categorized Warhol solely on the basis of subject matter, considering Warhol's Campbell's Soup Can paintings Pop, but not his portraits or disaster series. See Suzi Gablik, "Protagonists of Pop," *Studio International*, 178 (July-August 1969), p. 10.

140. Sidney Janis, "On the Theme of the Exhibition," in *New Realists*, unpaginated.

141. Harold Rosenberg, "The Art Galleries: The Game of Illusion," *The New Yorker*, 38 (November 24, 1962), pp. 162, 167.

142. Thomas B. Hess, "Reviews and Previews," *Art News*, 61 (December 1962), p. 12.

143. Grooms, conversation with the author, June 30, 1983.

144. Hess, "Reviews and Previews," p. 12.

145. Sidney Janis, conversation with the author, July 20, 1983.

146. George Segal, "On Whitman and Things," *Arts Magazine*, 47 (November 1972), p. 55.

147. Max Kozloff, Clement Greenberg, John Canaday, Dore Ashton, Irving Sandler, Hilton Kramer, and Thomas Hess were all initially hostile to Pop Art. Even Barbara Rose, a later advocate, was suspicious. In answer to the question whether Pop Art was really art, she replied: "I am willing to say that if it is in the Guggenheim, it is art"; see Rose, "Pop Art at the Guggenheim," *Art International*, 7 (May 1963), p. 22.

148. Peter Selz, "Pop Goes the Artist," *Partisan Review*, 30 (Summer 1963), p. 314.

149. Quoted in Swenson, "What Is Pop Art?," p. 25.

150. Clement Greenberg, "Avant-Garde and Kitsch" (1936) in *Art and Culture: Critical Essays* (Boston: Beacon Press, 1961), p. 10.

151. Kozloff, "The New Vulgarians," p. 36.

152. The relationship between the development of Abstract Expressionism and the growing disenchantment with politics in the 1930s and 1940s has been forcefully articulated by Serge Guilbaut, *How New York Stole the Idea of Modern Art: Abstract Expressionism, Freedom, and the Cold War* (Chicago: The University of Chicago Press, 1983). His analysis fulfills Clement Greenberg's prophecy that "Some day it will have to be told how anti-Stalinism which started out more or less as Trotskyism turned into art for art's sake, and thereby cleared the way, heroically, for what was to come" (ibid., p. 17).

153. Adolph Gottlieb and Mark Rothko, "Statement," in *Theories of Modern Art: A Source Book by Artists and Critics*, ed. Herschel B. Chipp (Berkeley: University of California Press, 1968), p. 545.

154. Barnett Newman's exhibition at French and Co. in 1959, arranged by Clement Greenberg, was a revelation to many artists and encouraged the exploration of single-image formats based on color.

155. A typical comment about the tedium of Stella's work was made by Brian O'Doherty in 1964 when he called Stella "the Oblomov of art, the Cézanne of nihilism, the master of *ennui*"; quoted in Robert Rosenblum, *Frank Stella* (Baltimore: Penguin Books, 1971), p. 26. Irving Sandler, in "The New Cool-Art," *Art in America*, 1 (February 1965), pp. 96–101, later compared the boring quality he found in Stella to that of the Pop artists.

156. William Rubin, "Younger American Painters," *Art International*, 4 (January 1960), p. 24.

157. The special character of the Black paintings and their relationship to Stella's mood were meticulously documented by Brenda Richardson and Mary Martha Ward in *Frank Stella: The Black Paintings*, exhibition catalogue (Baltimore: The Baltimore Museum of Art, 1976).

158. Quoted in William S. Rubin, *Frank Stella*, exhibition catalogue (New York: The Museum of Modern Art, 1970), p. 37.

159. As paraphrased in Sandler, "The New Cool-Art," p. 96.

160. Quoted in Rubin, *Frank Stella*, p. 44.

161. Quoted in Bruce Glaser, "Questions to Stella and Judd," *Art News*, 65 (September 1966), pp. 58–59.

162. Stella did not agree with the Minimalist sculptors' comprehension of his work. "It was to the detriment of sculpture that it picked up the simplest things that were going on in painting. The sculptors just scanned the organization of painting and made sculpture out of it. It was a bad reading of painting; they really didn't get much of what the painting was about"; quoted in Rubin, *Frank Stella*, p. 70.

163. This relationship between Judd's and Stella's work was noted by Rosalind E. Krauss, *Passages in Modern Sculpture* (New York: The Viking Press, 1977), pp. 243–88.

164. *Arts Yearbook 7: New York: The Artworld*, ed. James R. Mellow (New York: The Art Digest, 1964) and *Arts Yearbook 8: Contemporary Sculpture*, ed. William Seitz (New York: The Art Digest, 1965), respectively.

165. Judd, "Specific Objects," *Arts Yearbook 8*, p. 78.

166. Quoted in John Coplans, "An Interview with Don Judd," *Artforum*, 9 (June 1971), p. 44.

167. For a discussion of the relationship between Pop Art and Minimalism in this regard, see Barbara Rose, "Problems of Criticism V: The Politics of Art, Part II," *Artforum*, 7 (January 1969), pp. 44–49.

168. Quoted in Tomkins, *The Bride & the Bachelors*, p. 193. Kaprow reiterated this desire in describing his move from Abstract Expressionism to assemblage: "I wanted more tangible reality than it was possible to suggest through painting alone"; quoted in Kostelanetz, *Theatre of Mixed Means*, p. 107.

169. Quoted in Swenson, "What Is Pop Art?," p. 63.

170. See Krauss, *Passages*, p. 250.

171. Quoted in *Dan Flavin, Fluorescent Light, Etc. from Dan Flavin*, exhibition catalogue (Ottawa: The National Gallery of Canada, 1969), p. 168. Fluxus' emphasis on the trivial can be seen in Brecht's statement, "the occurrence that would be of most interest to me would be the little occurrences on the street"; quoted in Ruhé, *Fluxus*, unpaginated.

172. De Maria had shown his game sculptures before this at the Ergo Suits Festival in Woodstock, August 1962. They traveled with the festival to East Hampton, Long Island, the following week.

173. Excerpt from Robert Morris, "Blank Form," which had been scheduled for publication in *An Anthology*, but later withdrawn; see p. 100 and n. 174 below.

174. Morris removed his contributions from *An Anthology* but not his title page, which backed Simone Morris' entry. For the second edition, published in 1970, even his title page was removed.

175. See Robert Morris, "Notes on Sculpture," *Artforum*, 4 (February 1966), pp. 43–44.

176. Lucy R. Lippard, "As Painting Is to Sculpture: A Changing Ratio," in *American Sculpture of the Sixties*, ed. Maurice Tuchman, exhibition catalogue (California: Los Angeles County Museum of Art, 1967), p. 32.

177. Judd's remark, "It looks like painting is finished," exemplified the kind of pressure exerted on painters; quoted in Dan Flavin, "An Autobiographical Sketch," *Artforum*, 4 (December 1965), p. 21.

178. Quoted in Kostelanetz, *Theatre of Mixed Means*, p. 121. Artists even began claiming art history and philosophy as plausible fields of study: Kaprow was a trained art historian, earning an M.A. from Columbia; Morris received an M.A. in art history from Hunter College; and Judd, who held a B.A. from Columbia University, had studied there with art historian Meyer Schapiro.

179. See Sandler, "The New Cool-Art" and Robert Rosenblum, "Pop Art and Non-Pop: An Essay in Distinction," *Canadian Art*, 23 (January 1966), pp. 50–54.

180. The aesthetic unity of the decade was noted by a number of critics. For example, see Hilton Kramer, "Episodes from the Sixties," *Art in America*, 58 (January-February 1970), pp. 56–61. Barbara Rose, in *American Art Since 1900* (New York: Holt, Rinehart and Winston, 1975), p. 204, wrote: "From the present vantage point, sixties' painting reveals a definite stylistic unity, linking flat and three-dimensional, abstract and representational, pop and 'minimal' art." See also Rose and Irving Sandler, "Sensibility of the Sixties," *Art in America*, 55 (January-February 1967), pp. 44–57.

181. Although *Sleep* logically extended painting into a temporal dimension—"moving" pictures, as it were—it also echoed concerns found among certain of the Fluxus group, particularly La Monte Young. Jonas Mekas connected Warhol and Fluxus more directly by ascribing the impetus for Warhol's first films to a narrative piece by Jackson Mac Low, in which the camera holds the image of a tree for the duration of the film; see Mac Low, "George Maciunas," in *Wiesbaden Fluxus*, p. 124.

182. Quoted in *Fluxus Etc.*, p. 49.

The American Independent Cinema 1958–1964

JOHN G. HANHARDT

Imagine an eye unruled by man-made laws of perspective, an eye unprejudiced by compositional logic, an eye which does not respond to the name of everything but which must know each object encountered in life through an adventure of perception.[1]
—Stan Brakhage

But it's so easy to make movies, you can just shoot and every picture comes out right.[2]
—Andy Warhol

The everyday world is the most astonishing inspiration conceivable. A walk down 14th Street is more amazing than any masterpiece of art. If reality makes any sense at all, it is here. Endless, unpredictable, infinitely rich, it proclaims THE MOMENT as man's sole means of grasping the nature of ALL TIME. . . . Thus, one grasps, dimly at first, later more clearly, that all events are available, are at least potentially equivalent in value, and none would be out of place in art.[3]
—Allan Kaprow

The years 1958 to 1964 constitute a formative period in the history of the American independent film. It was a time of transition, during which major changes occurred involving both aesthetic issues and such practical matters as how and where films should be distributed and exhibited. One outcome of these controversies was that the film-maker and filmmaker-run organizations took on an activist role, as a result of which independent film fashioned a new presence for itself in American culture and received greater public attention. As had happened in American jazz and the Off-Broadway theater, the independent filmmaker established an indigenous, new art form which expressed radical changes taking place in American culture. The films being produced and distributed in these turbulent years did not comprise a single school of filmmaking whose progress and influence are easily charted; rather, the film community was a competitive and vociferous group of individuals joined by friendships and loose affiliations to meet specific needs or voice particular ideological and aesthetic goals.

During these years, the fundamental changes in the filmmakers' relationship to the medium centered on subject matter, style, and form. This essay will not map out all the participants in or vicissitudes of these developments. It will identify critical moments in filmmaking that mark an attempt to refashion the cinematic image and re-form the cinematic apparatus through the employment of new aesthetic strategies.

Between 1958 and 1964 the relationship of the film image to the cinematic apparatus (camera, film, projection system) shifted: instead of projecting a symbolic, hallucinatory dream state representing the unconscious along narrative lines, filmmakers focused on the direct acknowledgment of the material properties of film and of the artifice of the production process. The art of film confronted and ultimately dismantled a cinema predicated on Surrealist aesthetic models and replaced it with an eclectic and distinctly American film culture.

In addition, filmmakers discarded the taboos defining what should and should not be seen on film as judged by the defenders of public morality. The independent film, like the Off-Broadway theater, gained in notoriety as more work was produced and exhibited. Controversy—caused on the one hand by censorship, on the other by the outraged response that often greeted new forms of cinematic representation—abounded both within and outside the film community. Thus the American independent film stood poised against the dominant morality of its time and the public's expectation of what a film was as entertainment and art. The independent cinema achieved a cultural celebrity that was to give the filmmaker a new prominence in the 1960s and 1970s.

Opposite: Robert Indiana in Andy Warhol's *Eat*, 1963 (see Fig. 175).

119

The Emergence of the American Independent Film

The tradition confronting the independent film-maker in the late 1950s was that formed by the films of the preceding decade, especially the commercial entertainment cinema. Filmmaking had been dominated by Hollywood's large-format 35mm film production industry. The movies were a business and, as in any business, the product's success in the marketplace was determined by a manipulation of public awareness and an understanding of consumer trends. The producer, distributor, and theater owner offered the viewer films that were readily perceived as familiar commodities, affirmed popularly held perceptions or beliefs, and provided easy-to-understand entertainment. The Hollywood studio was a "dream factory." It produced films for the public imagination, spectacles shared by the majority of people and embraced by the consumer culture to which they were distributed and for whom they were made. Hollywood was an industry of mass-produced entertainments that made moviegoing a ritual of fulfilled expectations. The possibilities for an alternative cinema were opened up by a technical development that enabled the filmmaker to work without a large staff or expensive, cumbersome equipment. In the early 1940s a portable motion picture camera was introduced. The Bolex 16mm camera was sturdy and easy to use, with flexible focal lengths that permitted the filmmaker to shift quickly from close-ups to long shots and to manipulate the film image by altering the camera's speed—the rate at which images were being recorded.

The 16mm camera heralds the beginning of an alternative cinema in America, which can be traced to the film *Meshes of the Afternoon* (1943) by Maya Deren in collaboration with Alexander Hammid. This film was to become emblematic of the first decade of the independent cinema, a period shaped by Deren and filmmakers Sidney Peterson, James Broughton, Kenneth Anger, Willard Maas, Marie Menken, Douglas Crockwell, Gregory Markopoulos, and others. P. Adams Sitney opens his book *Visionary Film*, a history of the American independent cinema, with a discussion of *Meshes*

Fig. 157. Maya Deren in Maya Deren and Alexander Hammid's *Meshes of the Afternoon*, 1943. Black and white, silent, 18 minutes. Still courtesy of Anthology Film Archives, New York.

of the Afternoon. He locates its aesthetic in European twentieth-century modernism and the avant-garde art movements of Constructivism, Surrealism, and Expressionism. The often reproduced still (Fig. 157) of Deren from the film stands as a symbol of her position in the history of independent film. We see her hands pressed against a membrane of window glass that reflects the outside world; as she stares through that reflecting surface, as if into the camera's lens or through a film screen out into the world, she becomes a reflection of herself mediated by the projected film image. It is the relation of the artist to the projected dreamworld of film that dominated the first ten years of the independent cinema. As Deren describes *Meshes of the Afternoon*, it "is concerned with the interior experiences of an individual. It does not record an event which will be witnessed by other persons. Rather, it reproduces the way in which the sub-conscious of an individual will develop, interpret and elaborate an apparently simple and casual incident into a critical emotional experience."[4]

The film depicts a woman moving through the interior spaces of a house, an action repeated in a silent dreamlike scenario. *Meshes of the Afternoon*, as Deren notes, "is still based on a strong literary-dramatic line as a core, and rests heavily upon the symbolic value of objects and situations."[5] In Deren's film, a formation of the artistic self is articulated in the expression of the dream state, a dream narrative within a dream film, in which a psychological presence is created within the illusionistic film space. This attitude—the articulation of subconscious experience along a narrative line—became a powerful focus for early avant-garde film and continues to function today as a genre within independent filmmaking.

Many terms have been used to identify the cinema of Maya Deren and what followed: avant-garde, experimental, vanguard, underground, New American Cinema, independent. I have chosen to use the term "independent" because it best and most simply expresses what this cinema was, namely, independent of the production formulas and corporate control of the dominant commercial film industry.

During the period from 1958 to 1964, independent cinema participated in a cultural and social upheaval that began to break through the conventional boundaries in the arts between genres and forms. These changes did not emerge as a single, linear development but occurred in a dialectical space of social and political events, art world happenings, and public demonstrations. Independent filmmakers did not live or work in a vacuum; they interacted with other filmmakers and were deeply involved with what was happening in all of the arts and in society at large.

Stan Brakhage and Bruce Conner

The radical developments in independent cinema at the end of the 1950s can be represented by the work of two filmmakers from different parts of the country and with dissimilar backgrounds. Stan Brakhage, having lived in New York City and San Francisco, then settled down to spend most of his creative life in Colorado. Although physically removed from the centers of the art world, his presence looms large in the history of the American independent cinema. His prolific oeuvre, with its protean range of expression, articulated an observational and subjective stance that was in part shared by the psychological dramas characteristic of the independent film of the 1950s. However, Brakhage evolved a distinctive aesthetic significantly influenced by his interest in the modernist vision of such authentic American poets as Charles Olson, Edward Dorn, Robert Creeley, and Robert Duncan. The work of these poets was deeply personal and expressive of the American landscape and culture.

The literary critic Sherman Paul, discussing these poets' relationship to American art, characterized their work as being "freer in its attitudes toward the medium, seeing in the random or accidental the beginning of an order."[6] As these poets shaped texts out of the vernacular of American speech and experience, so Brakhage made films drawn from his domestic life. The result was Brakhage's *Anticipa-*

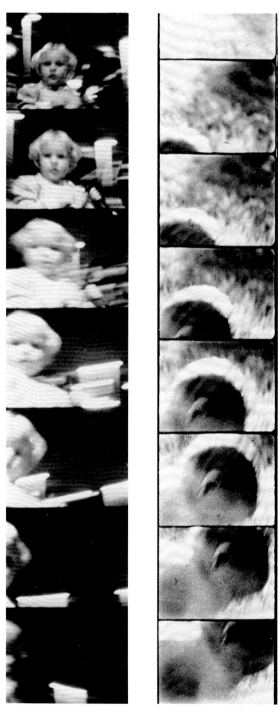

Figs. 158, 159. Stan Brakhage, *Anticipation of the Night*, 1958. Color, silent, 42 minutes. Frames courtesy of The American Federation of Arts, New York.

tion of the Night (1958; Figs. 158, 159), an important achievement which represented a critical break and change in the perception of filmmaking. *Anticipation of the Night* rejects drama and the notion of a narrative that represents a coherent and stable point of view. Brakhage loosens the camera as cascading, fragmentary images of color and light filter through scenes from the artist's life: children, flowers, lawns, home, night and day. The editing movement forms a constant inquiry into images, liberating the film from the narrative constraints of shot-to-shot continuity and vantage point.

Brakhage's own words convey the shifting imagery of the film:

> The daylight shadow of a man in its movement evokes lights in the night. A rose bowl, held in hand, reflects both sun and moon-like illuminations. The opening of a doorway onto trees anticipates the twilight into the night. A child is born on the lawn, born of water, with promissory rainbow, and the wild rose. It becomes the moon and the source of all night light. Lights of the night become young children playing a circular game. The moon moves over a pillared temple to which all lights return. There is seen the sleep of the innocents and their animal dreams, becoming their amusement, their circular game, becoming the morning. The trees change color and lose their leaves for the morn, become the complexity of branches on which the shadow man hangs himself.[7]

Brakhage is not denying the self of the artist as a presence in his films, but instead represents that self through a new and radical appropriation of filmic space—abstraction and a breaking down of the perspectival coordinates of the frame. He urges the liberation of the camera from the linear language of narrative to an intense, personal space of evolving forms created from light and color and mediated by "metaphors on vision," the title of his manifesto published in 1963 by the journal *Film Culture*. The camera lens refines and distorts reality, collapsing the perspective into an abstract two-dimensional plane and then opening it up into an illusionistic space; the film frame becomes a single space as foreground and background are joined into a continually shifting field of action. Variations in camera speed, from eight, to sixteen, to twenty-four frames per second, and the use of different film stocks create subtle changes and modulations in the image.

The aesthetic stance in *Anticipation of the Night* prefigures many later developments in independent film. In his interplay of camera movement with editing, even scratching directly on the film surface, Brakhage manipulated the tensions between the recognizable photographic image and the abstraction of the film frame. He strove to erase the surface and boundaries of illusion and create a new language of filmmaking. *Anticipation of the Night* was a controversial work that challenged views of filmmaking even within the independent film community. Cinema 16, then the leading showcase

Fig. 160. Bruce Conner, *A Movie*, 1958. Black and white, sound, 12 minutes. Still courtesy of The American Federation of Arts, New York.

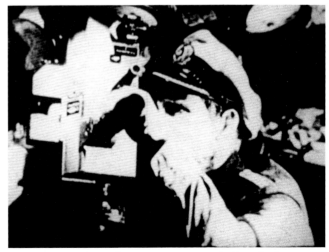

Fig. 161. Bruce Conner, *A Movie*, 1958. Black and white, sound, 12 minutes. Still courtesy of The American Federation of Arts, New York.

for independent film in New York, refused to show the film in its program (p. 129).

Another film released in 1958 was *A Movie* by Bruce Conner (Figs. 160, 161). Conner, a leading figure in the assemblage art movement, lived in San Francisco, which was also the center of the new Beat movement. The hip vernacular of American speech became the province of the Beats. As they appropriated language, Bruce Conner appropriated found footage to articulate a new mode of filmmaking. In *A Movie*, as in his assemblage sculpture, Conner picked up the debris of a consumer society—the detritus of the Hollywood dream factory.

Bruce Conner's films constitute another important and highly distinct development within the independent film movement. His filmmaking was directly influenced by his work as an assemblage artist. *A Movie*, his first film, was originally presented as part of an assemblage environment. The found footage is drawn from entertainment features, television, and educational and scientific films. These sequences are edited together to form a playful new language of visual puns. Conner juxtaposes the actions in unrelated shots in an associative montage which achieves its own narrative continuity and creates a radically different and ironic meaning: in a shot from a World War II action film, a submarine captain peers through a periscope; this is followed by a shot of Marilyn Monroe in a pornographic short; then a shot of torpedoes being fired from a submarine; the sequence ends with an atomic bomb blast.

A Movie shares the aesthetic strategy of assemblage art—found objects are removed from their everyday contexts and assembled into new sequences to create new constellations of meanings. In Conner's films, each shot differs according to the production qualities of the original film and the kind of film stocks used. Conner establishes a rhythm as he edits the shots together by adding a contrapuntal sound track of pop and classical music that lends further irony to the remade narrative.

Although *Anticipation of the Night* and *A Movie* posit divergent approaches, each constitutes a filmmaking practice liberated from the traditional conventions of the medium. In Brakhage's film, the camera is freed from the constraints of narrative representation. His intensely personal iconography still transcends its specificity, rendering the screen as a canvas of moving images. Conner acknowledges the mythic properties of the cinema as he appropriates all of its languages and iconographies and transforms them in a cinematic assemblage of associative references.

The New American Cinema Group and Cinema 16

The independent cinema in 1959 was coalescing along two lines: the personal cinema of short works identified with Brakhage, Bruce Baillie, Ed Emshwiller, Jordan Belson, Carmen D'Avino, Len Lye, and Joseph Cornell; and another cinema, including Conner, Robert Breer, Stan VanDerBeek, and Harry Smith, that was appropriating forms from the other arts, popular culture, and the materials of everyday life to be cinematically reused in innovative ways. This second group of artists transformed our perception and understanding of quotidian materials and, in the process, infused the found object's iconographic powers with new meanings. This cinema included the graphic cutout animation of Harry Smith's hermetic *No. 12* (*Heaven and Earth Magic, The Magic Feature*) (1958–61; Fig. 162), Stan VanDerBeek's ironic commentary on Cold War politics in *Science Friction* (1959; Fig. 163), and the free graphic line animation of abstraction and figuration in Robert Breer's films. Breer was strongly influenced by the currents of modernism in Europe, where he had lived and worked as a painter before returning to New York in the late 1950s, and by his collaborations and friendships with Jean Tinguely and Claes Oldenburg. As Brecr moved between painting, sculpture, and film, he discovered that "films were very liberating. . . . I wanted to see some things I'd never seen before. . . . For me, film was another medium that permitted mixing of all this extraneous stuff, ideas and words and configurative elements that I couldn't justify putting in paintings anymore."[8]

Independent filmmakers were engaging in an aesthetic discourse for film that emphasized its participation in contemporary art-making. Many filmmakers crossed over to other art forms to borrow imagery and translate ideas into their own me-

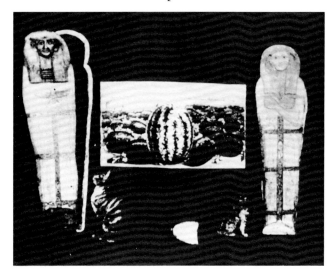

Fig. 162. Harry Smith, *No. 12 (Heaven and Earth Magic, The Magic Feature)*, 1958–61. Black and white, silent, 66 minutes. Still courtesy of Anthology Film Archives, New York.

Fig. 163. Stan VanDerBeek, *Science Friction*, 1959. Color, sound, 9 minutes. Still courtesy of The American Federation of Arts, New York.

dium, imbuing film with a remarkable range of styles, forms, and ideas—just as assemblage, Minimalism, and Pop Art were redefining Off-Broadway theater, dance, music, painting, sculpture, and literature, and being redefined in turn. Ed Emshwiller, for example, in *Dance Chromatic* (1959) filmed the movements of a dance and then painted abstractions on the film frames. Here the gestures of dance informed another layer of imagery. Dance was transformed within a cinematic space of time, movement, and superimposition.

In this rich period of artistic expansion and interdisciplinary cross-fertilization, new voices arose to champion the American independent cinema. One of the most articulate was that of Jonas Mekas, a Lithuanian immigrant and filmmaker who was to

become the leading figure in the American independent cinema during the 1960s and 1970s. Mekas' role as a spokesman for independent film began in 1955 when he founded *Film Culture* magazine. In this journal, one can follow Mekas' shift from a preference for the European art film to a growing appreciation and advocacy of American independent films. In 1958 Mekas also began to publish "Movie Journal," a weekly film column in *The Village Voice*. A highly personal, poetic, and diaristic commentary on the independent film scene in New York, it soon became the most influential criticism in the field.

In 1959 Mekas established *Film Culture*'s Independent Film Award to "point out original and unique American contributors to the cinema."[9] The recipient of the first award was John Cassavetes' *Shadows* (1959; Figs. 164, 166). The loosely structured narrative follows a group of young people through New York's nightlife and jazz clubs. The freewheeling action is focused on a light-skinned black woman and her darker-skinned brothers. In one scene her white boyfriend meets her brother and confronts the realization that she is black. Mekas presented the award to *Shadows* because in it

> Cassavetes . . . was able to break out of conventional molds and traps and retain original freshness. The improvisation, spontaneity, and free inspiration that are almost entirely lost in most films from an excess of professionalism are fully used in this film. The situations and atmosphere of New York night life are vividly, cinematically, and truly caught in *Shadows*. It breathes an immediacy that the cinema of today vitally needs if it is to be a living and contemporary art.[10]

Shadows marked the emergence of a new narrative cinema, which, although often scripted, conveyed a sense of the real world. The narratives—frequently improvised and recorded on location in apartments, streets, and alleyways with hand-held cameras—achieved a sense of spontaneity, as if the story had been captured on film just as it happened. This semi-documentary fictional style, where actors were filmed on location, outside of the studio, reflected stylistic developments taking place in contemporary *cinéma-vérité* documentary filmmaking. These documentaries employed the tech-

Fig. 164. John Cassavetes (right) and camera crew shooting scenes for his film *Shadows*, 1959. Black and white, sound, 81 minutes. Photograph courtesy of Anthology Film Archives, New York.

Fig. 165. Ricky Leacock filming *Primary*, 1960. Black and white, sound, 53 minutes. Photograph courtesy of Anthology Film Archives, New York.

nology of the portable camera and the portable sound-recording system to convey immediacy: filmmakers directly responded to the world's events by taking their cameras "on location." In 1961 *Film Culture* gave its third Independent Film Award to *Primary* (1960; Fig. 165), a film produced by Ricky Leacock, Don Pennebaker, Robert Drew,

Fig. 166. Hugh Hurd (left), Lelia Goldoni, and Anthony Ray in John Cassavetes' *Shadows*, 1959. Black and white, sound, 81 minutes. Still courtesy of Anthology Film Archives, New York.

and Al Maysles. Mekas cites *Primary*, a documentary film about primary elections that focuses on politicians angling for votes, for its

> new cinematic techniques of recording life on film. [The filmmakers] have caught scenes of real life with unprecedented authenticity, immediacy, and truth. . . . *Shadows* . . . indicated new cinematic approaches stylistically and formally. *Primary* goes one step further: By exploring new camera, sound, and lighting methods, it enables the filmmaker to pierce deeper into the area of new content as well. . . . The techniques of *Primary* indicate that we are entering a long-awaited era, when the budget for a sound film is the same as that of a book of poems, and when a filmmaker can shoot his film with sound, alone and by himself and unobtrusively, almost the same way as a poet observing a scene. . . . There is a feeling in the air that cinema is only just beginning.[11]

The juxtaposition of *Shadows* and *Primary* in a single statement captures something essential about this period. A fictional narrative feature film about an interracial family, two brothers and a sister moving through the netherworld of New York jazz clubs, is compared *cinematically* to a documentary film about the American political system.

Mekas' choice of award-winning films signals the breakdown of the traditional barriers of genre.

Cassavetes, however, sought a wider audience and greater commercial success for his narrative cinema: later in 1959 he re-edited *Shadows* and rereleased the film in a different version. To Mekas, "the second version of *Shadows* is just another Hollywood film—however inspired, at moments— [whereas] the first version is the most frontier-breaking American feature film in at least a decade."[12] Cassavetes' repudiation of his first version as "too arty" reflected his ambivalent feelings about the rawness of its style and the deep division that existed between different forms of filmmaking and the audiences they spoke to. Cassavetes soon moved to Hollywood and achieved success within the commercial film world. This same path was later followed by other filmmakers, such as Brian De Palma, who explored new forms in independent cinema before going on to become directors of entertainment films, thus carrying the techniques of the new cinema to Hollywood.

Shadows and such productions as Shirley Clarke's *The Connection* (1961) and *The Cool World* (1963), Lionel Rogosin's *Come Back Africa* (1958), Morris Engels' *Weddings and Babies* (1958), *The Savage Eye* (1959) by Ben Maddow, Joseph Strick, and Sidney Meyers, and *Pull My Daisy* (1959) by Robert Frank and Alfred Leslie sparked the formation on September 28, 1960, of the New American Cinema Group. The first meeting included twenty-three independent filmmakers brought together by Lewis Allen (producer of *The Connection*) and Jonas Mekas; a temporary executive board was elected that included Shirley Clarke, Emile De Antonio, Edward Bland, Mekas, and Allen. The New American Cinema Group did not identify itself with any "aesthetic" school and was open to anyone. Its manifesto outlined a number of goals, among them:

1. We believe that cinema is indivisibly a personal expression. We, therefore, reject the interference of producers, distributors, and investors until our work is ready to be projected on the screen.
2. We reject censorship. . . .
3. We are seeking new forms of financing, working toward a reorganization of film investing methods, setting up the basis for a free film industry. . . .
4. The New American Cinema is abolishing the Budget Myth. . . . The low budget is not a purely commercial consideration. It goes with our ethical and aesthetic beliefs. . . .
5. We'll take a stand against the present distribution-exhibition policies. . . .
6. We plan to establish our own cooperative distribution center. . . .
7. It's about time the East Coast had its own film festival. . . .
8. We shall meet with the unions to work out more reasonable [requirements for smaller-budget films], similar to those existing Off-Broadway—a system based on the size and the nature of the production.
9. We pledge to put aside a certain percentage of our film profits, so as to build up a fund that would be used to help our members finish films or stand as a guarantor for the laboratories.[13]

This manifesto of the New American Cinema Group laid out for the first time a set of goals that was to serve as a model for future generations of independent filmmakers. It extended the purview of independent filmmaking into all areas of production, distribution, and exhibition. These ambitions were encouraged by the considerable media attention given to the new films; film critics recognized a freshness and immediacy in these works that had not been seen before in commercial cinema.

Fig. 167. Peter Orlovsky, Gregory Corso, and Allen Ginsberg in Robert Frank and Alfred Leslie's *Pull My Daisy*, 1959. Black and white, sound, 29 minutes. Still courtesy of the Walker Art Center, Minneapolis.

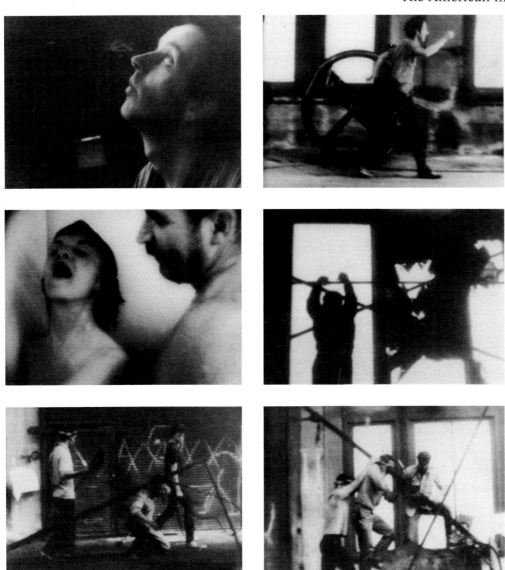

Fig. 168. Ron Rice, *The Flower Thief*, 1960. Black and white, sound, 75 minutes. Frames courtesy of Anthology Film Archives.

There were a number of important interdisciplinary collaborations within this group of filmmakers, including that between the painter Alfred Leslie and the photographer Robert Frank. Frank's collection of photographs, *The Americans*, published in 1959, was to revolutionize the art of photography as it conveyed an immediate and vibrant impression of the edges of daily life. Frank and Leslie co-directed *Pull My Daisy* (Fig. 167), the key Beat film of its generation. This film featured Jack Kerouac, Allen Ginsberg, Gregory Corso, Peter Orlovsky, and Alice Neel in a story loosely constructed from improvisational antics and spontaneous scenes. It creates a disjointed narrative around a couple and the poets and artists who drift in and out of their loft and lives. The Beat sensibility of anarchic fun and self-parody inspires the lively action of *Pull My Daisy*. In awarding the work *Film Culture*'s second Independent Film Award, Mekas links the attitude of the film to the look of the film itself, citing its

> modernity and its honesty, its sincerity and its humility, its imagination and its humor, its youth, its freshness, and its truth [which are] without comparison in our last year's pompous cinematic production. In its camera work, it effectively breaks with the accepted and 1000-year-old official rules of slick polished Alton Y Co. cinematographic schmaltz. It breathes an immediacy that the cinema of today vitally needs if it is to be a living and contemporary art.[14]

The spirit of anarchy in these films reflected their production process. Ron Rice's *The Flower*

Thief (1960; Fig. 168) follows actor Taylor Mead as he moves through assorted landscapes and improvises encounters with a variety of people and objects. Such films were largely derived from the unscripted experience of the production itself—an ongoing dialogue between the filmmaker and actor that was guided only by the framework of a location and the sketchy idea of a gag or story. This same attitude is found in *Hallelujah the Hills* (1963), by Adolfas Mekas, Jonas' brother, in which a band of intrepid New Yorkers cavorts through the countryside in an improvised love triangle that parodies the then fashionable high seriousness of European art films.

In these independent films actors are not directed; rather, they creatively collaborate with the filmmaker. This practice of collaboration extended to other disciplines as well. Shirley Clarke's *The Connection* (Figs. 169, 170) is based on Jack Gelber's revolutionary Off-Broadway play and voiced an underground sensibility of protest against the hypocrisy of the time. Clarke translated Gelber's play into a powerful film *about the filming* of a documentary. We follow the actions of a group of drug addicts waiting in a room for their fix—as they are being filmed by a documentary film unit which, in order to film them, has given the junkies the money they need for their drugs. The claustrophobic environment and the hostility of the addicts, often directed to the camera, are startlingly real. By opening up the film to include the filmmaker, Clarke achieved a dramatic realism. In this compelling re-creation of the drug world, the language of the playwright and the vision of the filmmaker merge into a synthesis of drama and filmmaking.

The New American Cinema eventually floundered as a movement—by 1962 the filmmakers went their separate ways, pursuing individual projects and interests in different parts of the country. In addition to their landmark films, however, the Group could claim some success in establishing new outlets for all forms of independent film. As the Group's initial manifesto had declared, distribution and exhibition were integrally related to continued efforts to produce new work; since theatrical distribution was dominated by the major commercial conglomerates, the independents were forced to seek other outlets to reach audiences,

Fig. 169. Shirley Clarke, *The Connection*, 1961. Black and white, sound, 100 minutes. Still courtesy of Anthology Film Archives.

maintain dialogues with other artists, and remain financially solvent.

During this period, the leading exhibition program in New York City devoted to the independent cinema was Cinema 16. From 1949 to 1963, this independent showcase, under the direction of Amos Vogel, exhibited regularly scheduled film programs every Sunday and Wednesday. Included in its programs were many of the films associated with the New American Cinema Group. The programs were varied and eclectic, often focusing on such topics as censorship and racism and organizing features and short-length films—narrative, avant-garde, scientific, and documentary works—into one-artist, group, and thematic programs. One program on the elevated trains included documentaries as well as Stan Brakhage's *The Wonder Ring* (1955), a lyrical meditation on the light and spaces of the el.

Cinema 16, a nonprofit organization, attracted a large and loyal following who supported the programs and carefully prepared program notes through donations and memberships; Cinema 16 also held symposia, panel discussions, and lectures on independent film. It received considerable press attention and was recognized as the key public outlet for independent and foreign films. But by 1963, unable to maintain its operation at increased costs, Cinema 16 was forced to close. There was, moreover, additional competition in New York from television and from the growing number of other showcases for alternative film programming, which

Fig. 170. Shirley Clarke, *The Connection*, 1961. Black and white, sound, 100 minutes. Still courtesy of Anthology Film Archives.

attracted a new generation of viewers and film-makers. In 1963 Vogel helped to establish the first New York Film Festival at Lincoln Center; he continued to distribute the Cinema 16 film catalogue until he sold it to Grove Press in 1966.

As the New American Cinema Group had stated in its manifesto, there was a great need for alternative systems of distribution and exhibition. In 1960 Bruce Baillie had formed the Canyon Cinema in San Francisco to screen independent films. In New York, Jonas Mekas became involved with the weekend midnight screenings at the Charles Theater, established by Walter Langford and Sol Stein in 1961. These programs featured independent work, including the premieres of films by Ron Rice, Stan VanDerBeek, Robert Breer, Harry Smith, Marie Menken, Brian De Palma, and Ed Emshwiller. Jazz concerts and art exhibitions in the lobby complemented the films and added an air of openness that reflected the interdisciplinary interests of avant-garde artists. Mekas suggested to the theater owners that they hold monthly open screenings to which filmmakers could bring their latest titles; the advocacy of open screenings—the spirit of tolerance for the new—was the major legacy of the Charles Theater, which closed for financial reasons in 1962. The often vociferous ambience of these screenings expressed the fluidity of this period in film history, when artists, film-makers, poets, painters, and musicians mingled, argued, and learned from one another's efforts and attitudes.

In 1962 Jonas Mekas played an instrumental role in establishing the Film-Makers' Cooperative in New York, a profit-sharing, nonexclusive national distribution system which accepted all filmmakers who sought an outlet for their films. The Charles Theater experience became a model for the Film-Makers' Cinematheque program, which was also established in 1962 and first showed programs at the Charles Theater before it closed. Every Monday night, "independent, dependent, abstract, neodada, collage, decollage, home, absurd, zen, etc. movies" were shown.[15] The programs included one-artist retrospectives of filmmakers from New York and the West Coast and premieres of Brakhage's *Dog Star Man: Part I* (1962) and *The Sin of Jesus* (1961) by Robert Frank. After the close of the Charles Theater, the Cinematheque organized Monday night exhibitions at the Bleecker Street Theater, from which its members were eventually barred in 1963 because the theater owners did not want to be associated with its "controversial" programs.

The history of alternative film screenings in New York reflects the nomadic life of the independent film exhibition and its lack of permanence. The press, drawn to the novelty and controversy of these works, covered many of the Cinematheque festivals and recognized a newly emerging, low-budget independent feature cinema. However, there was also controversy and debate within the independent film community itself. The establishment of the Film-Makers' Cinematheque not only reflected the original goals of the New American Cinema Group—to promote new outlets for independent film—but stemmed in part from a falling-out between Mekas and Vogel over Vogel's failure to screen Brakhage's *Anticipation of the Night* at Cinema 16. Jonas Mekas' greater emphasis on non-narrative films—the work of Stan Brakhage and others—and his open screening approach were opposed to Amos Vogel's programming policy. Moreover, the abstract imagery and nonlinear form of *Anticipation of the Night*—made more provocative by its forty-minute running time—were problematic for a showcase that emphasized subject matter in film. The new aesthetic articulated in *Anticipation of the Night* posed a challenge for distribution and exhibition outlets accustomed to narratives with identifiable subjects.[16]

Kenneth Anger and Jack Smith

The major achievement of independent cinema in this period was its realization of new forms, styles, and contents for filmmaking. These independent films are notable for their variety, extending from Brakhage's lyrical cinema to Conner's transformation of found footage to new narrative genres related to avant-garde theater and literature.

Kenneth Anger grew up in Hollywood and as a child acted in Max Reinhardt's Hollywood production of *A Midsummer Night's Dream*. In 1960 Anger published *Hollywood Babylon*, a scandalous history of the underworld of the "movie capital." Three years later, Anger produced *Scorpio Rising*

Fig. 171. Kenneth Anger, *Scorpio Rising*, 1963. Color, sound, 29 minutes. Still courtesy of The American Federation of Arts.

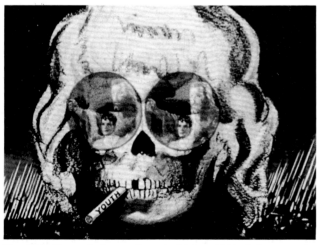

Fig. 172. Kenneth Anger, *Scorpio Rising*, 1963. Color, sound, 29 minutes. Still courtesy of The American Federation of Arts.

(Figs. 171, 172), one of the best-known and most influential films of the independent cinema. A sound track of thirteen pop songs is heard over a montage of the private and public rituals of a motorcycle gang. Although *Scorpio Rising* was not the first independent film to unite pop hits with visuals (Bruce Conner's *Cosmic Ray* of 1961 has that honor), it is a singular work which weaves the private actions and paraphernalia of a leather-jacketed motorcycle gang with images of public mythology such as Western movies, Jesus Christ from a Hollywood epic, and Marlon Brando in *The Wild One*. "Slowly, without hurrying, in poisonously sensuous colors, Anger shows, or more truly lets the subject reveal itself, bit by bit, motion by motion, detail by detail, belts, knobs, chrome, chests, pedals, rings, boots, leather jackets, rituals and mysteries of the motorcycle youth, steel and chrome perversions."[17] The underlying theme is sexual violence. The perverse appropriation of the icons of popular culture and history—James Dean, Marlon Brando, Hitler, Stalin—is also found in the work of the Beat poets (Ginsberg, Corso), playwrights (Gelber), and visual artists (Oldenburg, Kaprow). It is a strategy designed to expose the hidden messages in the images and conventions of the mass media. "A conjuration of the Presiding Princes, Angels, and spirits of the Sphere of MARS, formed as a 'high' view of the Myth of the American Motorcyclist. The Power Machine seen as a tribal totem, from toy to terror. Thanatos in chrome and black leather and bursting jeans."[18]

Controversy surrounded both *Scorpio Rising* and Jack Smith's *Flaming Creatures* (1963). The public viewed them as obscene "underground films"; they revealed an outrageous world which, unlike the "movies," did not present the conventional narratives offered in such current films as *Lawrence of Arabia* (1962) or *Cleopatra* (1963). This issue of censorship was topical and highly public in the arts of this period. Jonas Mekas reported on June 18, 1964:

A verdict was passed in the New York Criminal Court last Friday that Jack Smith's film *Flaming Creatures* is obscene. A similar decision was passed by the Los Angeles court on Kenneth Anger's film *Scorpio Rising*. In practical terms, what this means is this: From now on, at least in these two cities, it will be a crime to show either

Fig. 173. Jack Smith, *Flaming Creatures*, 1963. Black and white, sound, 45 minutes.

Fig. 174. Jack Smith, *Flaming Creatures*, 1963. Black and white, sound, 45 minutes.

Flaming Creatures or *Scorpio Rising*, either publicly or privately. . . .

During the trial, we had offered—through ourselves and through Lewis Allen, Willard van Dyke, Herman G. Weinberg, Susan Sontag, Shirley Clarke, Joseph Kaster, Allen Ginsberg, Dr. E. Hornick, and Dr. John Thompson—to explain some of the meanings of *Flaming Creatures* and to give some insight into the meaning of art in general. The court chose to ignore us; it preferred to judge the film by what it called "the community standards."[19]

In its confrontation with the censorship laws and its proclamation of a liberated cinema of outrageous images, Jack Smith's *Flaming Creatures* (Figs. 173, 174) became the *cause célèbre* of independent cinema. Unlike *Scorpio Rising*, it is not constructed as a complex intellectual montage of symbols and iconography. Susan Sontag described the film:

> In *Flaming Creatures*, a couple of women and a much larger number of men, most of them clad in flamboyant thrift-shop women's clothes, frolic about, pose and posture, dance with one another, enact various scenes of voluptuousness, sexual frenzy, romance, and vampirism . . . the group rape of a bosomy young woman, rape happily cavorting itself into an orgy. Of course *Flaming Creatures* is outrageous, and intends to be. The very title tells us that.[20]

Jack Smith stands as a major figure who, with his collaborator Ken Jacobs in *Blonde Cobra* (1959–63) and *Little Stabs at Happiness* (1958–63) and in his own *Flaming Creatures*, created a cinema that deliberately destroyed conventional narrative plots and structures. Using costumes and imaginary scenes drawn from such cult Hollywood figures as Maria Montez and Marlene Dietrich, Smith and his performers stripped away the narrative of the movie myths to reveal the visual texture and erotic subtext of the "dream factory," a *mise-en-scène* roughened by Smith's use of old (and cheap) film stocks, faded celluloid that produced ghostlike penumbras around the images of his imaginary Hollywood.

The fascination that Jack Smith had for Hollywood mythology extended beyond the movie stories and plots. These narratives masked the real intrigue on the screen. Smith looked to the sets, lighting, makeup, and costumes as distinctive elements in the vision of the director. The movies and their stars were to Jack Smith a mythopoeic world of desires expressing the extravagant wishes of their directors. Smith's perception of Hollywood films, a view which defines his aesthetic, is perhaps best expressed in his description of von Sternberg directing Marlene Dietrich.[21] It also reveals how Smith viewed himself directing his own films, the world he saw in his imagination and through his camera.

[Von Sternberg's] expression was of the erotic realm—the neurotic gothic deviated sex-colored world and it was a turning inside out of himself and magnificent. You had to use your eyes to know this tho because the sound track babbled inanities—it alleged Dietrich was an honest jewel thief, noble floosie, fallen woman, etc. to cover up the visuals. In the visuals she was none of those. She was V.S. himself. A flaming neurotic—nothing more or less—no need to know she was rich, poor, innocent, guilty, etc. Your eye if you could use it told you more interesting things (facts?) than those. Dietrich was his visual projection—a brilliant transvestite in a world of delirious unreal adventures. Thrilled by his/her own movement—by superb taste in light, costumery, textures, movement, subject and camera, subject camera/revealing faces—in fact all revelation but *visual* revelation.[22]

The extravagant sensibility of Smith's cinema offers a new vision of American myth as re-enacted by a troupe of transvestites, male and female personae shuffled and reshuffled within the stage of the screen. Smith's mercurial character and cinema of sexual ambiguities made him a unique figure in the independent cinema and an influence on Andy Warhol's development as a filmmaker. Warhol and other artists—among them, Claes Oldenburg and Ken Jacobs—were attracted to the "on the edge" sensibility, the problematic procedures of production and performance, the energy of the unknown. Smith's sets were like the Happenings of Kaprow, only more perverse. The exchange between theater and film resulted from the mixed group of artists who acted in the films and the scenarios they frequently contributed to the films' production.

Andy Warhol

Andy Warhol's entry into film was shaped by his friendships and encounters in the society of the art world, especially the Off-Broadway theater. At Ronald Tavel's Theater of the Ridiculous he met the actor Taylor Mead, who had performed in Ron Rice's films and later traveled with Warhol to California. Warhol also developed friendships with filmmakers such as Emile De Antonio and Jack Smith. Smith was the subject of one of Warhol's first films (*Andy Warhol Films Jack Smith Filming "Normal Love,"* 1963) and acted in Warhol's 1964 *Batman Dracula*.

Andy Warhol, in addition to following the improvisational and outrageous cinema of Ron Rice and Jack Smith, was intensely interested in other aspects of the independent film world. He regularly attended screenings at the Film-Makers' Cinematheque, where his first films were premiered by Jonas Mekas. However, the films that Warhol began to produce in 1963 were distinctly his own. Warhol turned his camera onto the world around him and remade it on film by destroying the conventions of filmmaking and expectations of filmgoing. Warhol's cinema, unlike that of other independent filmmakers, did not use complex editing strategies, seek out new locations and actors, refashion found footage together with sound tracks, construct elaborate narratives, or satirize other film styles and genres; neither did he trouble to explain his films in manifestos. Rather, in Warhol's studio, The Factory, he fabricated a myth around a life-style exemplified by Baudelairean remove, his cool detachment from the world around him. Warhol transformed himself and his art into a single aesthetic social presence, which became the work of art. In his films he extended Duchamp's strategy of isolating the found object as art by placing within the camera's frame whatever chanced to occur before it and turning this found imagery into cinema. The hangers-on who assembled in his studio became the players in his films. Warhol's 16mm Bolex was a silent eye recording a culture of styles and gestures, "superstars" and "scenes"—the "cool" lifestyle of the 1960s. It was a new cinema which in its raw and naive energy became a powerful presence in the independent film.

In his films and in his art, Warhol was fascinated with the borders between the real and the reproduced worlds. As he simply painted a Campbell's soup can, so he simply placed the camera on a tripod in The Factory, recording at the push of a button individuals and events as they chanced to happen. Because there were no planned scenarios, no directions, the camera—and by extension, the filmmaker—became passive spectators. People who visited The Factory were asked to sit for their portraits before the stationary camera; they were in

Fig. 175. Robert Indiana in Andy Warhol's *Eat*, 1963. Black and white, silent, 45 minutes. Frames courtesy of Anthology Film Archives.

quence of couples kissing in close-up, each couple lasting for one roll of film, and includes Warhol regulars Naomi Levine, Gerard Malanga, Baby Jane Holzer, and John Palmer, in addition to the artist Marisol, art critic Pierre Restany, and poet Ed Sanders. In November 1963, Warhol filmed *Eat* (Fig. 175), which showed Robert Indiana slowly eating one mushroom. Time figures strongly in this work: a simple action is repeated and slowed down by loop printing, frozen frames, and a retarded projection speed.

Warhol and his associates knew nothing of the technical requirements of filmmaking—editing, lighting, sound, camera movement. In a sense he pressed the lens against the real world and became fused with it. It is not what the film is about but that the film is. The action is refined through a new sense of cinematic time; real time is presented as a continuous presence. The 100-foot rolls of film that make up each title can be likened to serial

a sense appropriated by the camera and entered through it into Warhol's world.

The titles of Warhol's first films (*Kiss, Eat,* and *Sleep* in 1963 and *Couch, Empire,* and *Blow Job* in 1964) are in their conceptual simplicity Minimalist expressions of a direct cinema of representation. However, just as Warhol's silkscreens and paintings are not slick representations of soup cans and headlines, the films are not polished recordings of action. There is no sound track in *Kiss, Eat,* and *Sleep,* and the film is projected not at 24 frames per second but at silent speed—16 fps—thus further retarding the minimal action. There is a tension within these films between their structure, the method of filming, and the action. The six-hour film *Sleep* shows John Giorno on a couch in various positions of sleep. Warhol further elongates the action, recorded on 100-foot rolls of film, by repeating filmed segments through loop printing; the concluding image is a frozen still of the final shot. *Kiss,* originally shown as a serial, features a se-

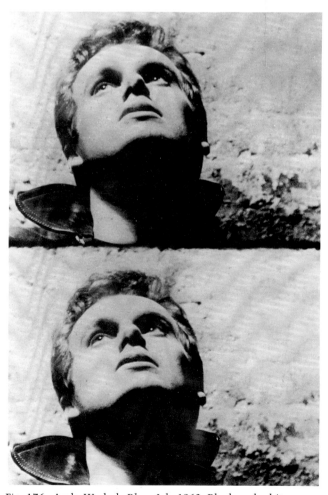

Fig. 176. Andy Warhol, *Blow Job*, 1963. Black and white, silent, 30 minutes. Frames courtesy of Anthology Film Archives.

imagery, each roll a piece of time separated by light flashes at the end and beginning, like Warhol's serial silkscreens with their rough edges and acknowledgment of process and materials. This dialogue between the camera and time reached an apotheosis in *Empire*, an eight-hour shot of the Empire State Building, from night to morning, filmed on June 25, 1964, from the forty-fourth floor of the Time-Life Building. In *Couch*, which "stars," among others, Gerard Malanga, Gregory Corso, Allen Ginsberg, Ondine, Jack Kerouac, and Taylor Mead, the camera framing the couch is stationary; it shows "a nude woman on a couch [trying] to get a man's attention. Later, there is much banana eating, and love-making attempts are seen, man to man, as other men sit in front of the couch, or walk around it."[23]

The cinema of Andy Warhol is a cinema of observation that shapes a discourse out of the geography of the human body. *Blow Job* (Fig. 176) presents a young man's face while someone, unseen by the camera, performs fellatio on him. Here the film represents the revelation of desire, an ecstatic response that was to become an emblem of a new cinema and life-style.

Warhol's cinema is a dialogue with the world, mediated through film in its rawest possible state. Just as Warhol transformed the fabricated world of consumer images by the style of his paintings and prints, so in his films he acknowledged the medium and the mirror of the camera's lens. In 1964 he received *Film Culture*'s sixth Independent Film Award for his films *Sleep, Eat, Haircut, Kiss,* and *Empire*. As Jonas Mekas wrote in the citation:

> Andy Warhol is taking cinema back to its origins, to the days of Lumière, for a rejuvenation and cleansing. In his work, he has abandoned all the "cinematic" form and subject adornments that cinema had gathered around itself until now.[24]

Mekas argues that Warhol offers an epistemology of seeing through film since

> we see it sharper than before. Not in dramatic, rearranged contexts and meanings, not in the service of something else (even Cinéma Vérité did not escape this subjection of the objective reality to ideas) but as pure as it is in itself: eating as eating, sleeping as sleeping, haircut as haircut.[25]

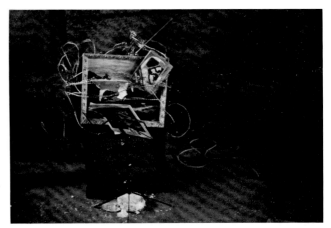

Fig. 177. Wolf Vostell, *TV-Dé-Collage*, 1963. South Brunswick, New Jersey. Photograph by Peter Moore.

This emphasis on an "unadorned" cinema echoes Mekas' citations in his awards to Cassavetes' *Shadows* and Leacock's *Primary*. Warhol opened the lens of his camera in a direct observation of the culture of his decade.

Fig. 178. Wolf Vostell, *TV-Dé-Collage*, 1963. Smolin Gallery, New York. Photograph by Peter Moore.

Independent Film and the Arrival of Video

The history of the independent film from 1958 to 1964 represents an extraordinary period of creative achievement that had a lasting influence on the American film. The efforts of filmmakers to organize the distribution and exhibition of their films set a model for the future of independent film. The period encompasses an enormous range of genres—narrative, nonnarrative, documentary, animation—and of styles—abstract, representational, and minimal—in films that ran from three minutes to eight hours. The structural cinema that was to dominate the avant-garde of the 1970s had its origins in Warhol's static camera and limitless stare, perhaps best articulated in his monumental *Empire*.

In the years following 1964, independent filmmakers would also see enormous increases in the support they received on state, federal, and private levels. The Ford Foundation in 1964 awarded its first grants to filmmakers, signaling the growing recognition of these films by established institutions. However, controversy continued, as witnessed by the arrest of Jonas Mekas for the public showing of *Flaming Creatures* in 1964. It was such individual efforts on behalf of fellow artists that solidified the community of filmmakers and guaranteed its future.

During this same period a new medium was introduced into art-making. Television, then beginning to challenge the dominance of the commercial film industry, was appropriated by two Fluxus artists, Wolf Vostell and Nam June Paik. In 1963 Paik had his first one-artist exhibition, which included thirteen transformed television sets, at the Galerie Parnass in Wuppertal, West Germany. In that same year the Yam Festival, organized by Robert Watts, George Brecht, and Allan Kaprow, included Vostell's destroyed and buried televisions at George Segal's farm in New Jersey (Fig. 177; and p. 56) and a roomful of altered televisions at the Smolin Gallery in New York (Fig. 178). This latter installation marked the first time in America that televisions were incorporated into an art installation. Each of the televisions, altered electronically, was decorated with barbed wire, and its surface covered with a framed painting, thus transforming the television into a new object and radically altering our perception of its uses. In 1964 Paik moved to New York City and the following year acquired the newly developed portable videotape recorder which, like the 16mm Bolex in the 1940s, revolutionized the medium by making it accessible to artists. Paik, over the next twenty years, became the leading advocate of this new art form.

Thus at the close of the period 1958–64 a new moving image medium entered the culture; the aesthetics of independent film, Fluxus, Happenings, and Pop had helped to make that crossover possible. But the open interchange of media was shortlived: in the late 1960s and 1970s film and video went their separate ways. It was not until the 1980s that artists in both media would look at and learn from each other's work, creating a dialogue that cut across traditional boundaries. As this dialogue between artists and art forms is developing, as the aesthetics of film and video respond to the pressures of changing technologies, it may be useful to recall that the openness of film culture in the years 1958 to 1964 released an extraordinary body of work.

NOTES

1. Stan Brakhage, quoted in P. Adams Sitney, *Visionary Film: The American Avant-Garde* (New York: Oxford University Press, 1974), p. 183.

2. Andy Warhol, quoted in Jonas Mekas, "Notes after Reseeing the Movies of Andy Warhol," in *Andy Warhol*, ed. John Coplans (Greenwich, Connecticut: New York Graphic Society, 1970), p. 139.

3. Allan Kaprow, "The Principles of Modern Art," *It Is*, 4 (Autumn 1959), p. 51.

4. Maya Deren, quoted in Sitney, *Visionary Film*, p. 9.

5. Ibid.

6. Sherman Paul, *The Lost America of Love: Rereading Robert Creeley, Edward Dorn, and Robert Duncan* (Baton Rouge: Louisiana State University Press, 1981), p. xiii.

7. Stan Brakhage, quoted in Sitney, *Visionary Film*, p. 181.

8. Robert Breer, quoted in Stuart Liebman, "Program 2," in *A History of the American Avant-Garde Cinema*, exhibition catalogue (New York: The American Federation of Arts, 1976), p. 93.

9. Jonas Mekas, "Appendix: The Independent Film Award," in *Film Culture Reader*, ed. P. Adams Sitney (New York: Praeger Publishers, 1970), p. 423.

10. Ibid., pp. 423–24.

11. Ibid., pp. 424–25.

12. Jonas Mekas, *Movie Journal: The Rise of the New American Cinema, 1959–1971* (New York: Collier Books, 1972), p. 10.

13. "The First Statement of the New American Cinema Group," in *Film Culture Reader*, pp. 81–82.

14. Mekas, "Appendix: The Independent Film Award," p. 424.

15. Quoted from Film-Makers' Showcase program note at the Bleecker Street Cinema.

16. Even though Vogel did not exhibit Brakhage's new film, he eventually did distribute *Anticipation of the Night* through the Cinema 16 catalogue.

17. Mekas, *Movie Journal*, pp. 108–9.

18. Kenneth Anger, quoted in Sitney, *Visionary Film*, p. 116.

19. Mekas, *Movie Journal*, pp. 141–42.

20. Susan Sontag, quoted in Carel Rowe, *The Baudelairean Cinema: A Trend within the American Avant-Garde* (Ann Arbor, Michigan: UMI Research Press, 1982), p. 127.

21. "Nowhere has Jack Smith spoken as well about himself," wrote Sitney, *Visionary Film*, p. 391.

22. Jack Smith, quoted in ibid.

23. Jonas Mekas, "The Filmography of Andy Warhol," in *Andy Warhol*, p. 148.

24. Mekas, "Appendix: The Independent Film Award," p. 427.

25. Ibid.

CHRONOLOGY

Compiled by Susan J. Cooke

A listing of selected exhibitions and selected Happenings/Performances is followed by a filmography of independent films presented during the years 1958 to 1964. Catalogues and reviews published after 1964 are included in the Bibliography section.

Selected Exhibitions and Reviews

1958

Leo Castelli Gallery, New York. "Jasper Johns" (paintings of flags and targets). January 20–February 8, 1958.

> P[orter], F[airfield]. "Reviews and Previews: Jasper Johns." *Art News*, 56 (January 1958), p. 20.

> R[osenblum], R[obert]. "In the Galleries: Jasper Johns." *Arts*, 32 (January 1958), pp. 54–55.

Hansa Gallery, New York. "George Segal" (paintings and pastels). February 17–March 8, 1958.

> A[shbery], J[ohn]. "Reviews and Previews: George Segal." *Art News*, 56 (February 1958), p. 5.

> D[ash], R. W[arren]. "In the Galleries: George Segal." *Arts*, 32 (February 1958), pp. 57–58.

Leo Castelli Gallery, New York. "Robert Rauschenberg" (combine-paintings). March 4–29, 1958.

> A[shbery], J[ohn]. "Five Shows Out of the Ordinary: Robert Rauschenberg." *Art News*, 57 (March 1958), pp. 40, 56, 57.

> Rice, Dustin. "Art: Enfant Terrible." *The Village Voice*, March 12, 1958, p. 12.

Hansa Gallery, New York. "Allan Kaprow" (environment with sound and light). March 10–29, 1958.

> P[arker], T[yler]. "Reviews and Previews: Allan Kaprow." *Art News*, 57 (May 1958), p. 14.

Hansa Gallery, New York. "Allan Kaprow" (environment with sound, light, and odors). November 25–December 13, 1958. Brochure with essay by the artist.

> Kramer, Hilton. "Month in Review." *Arts*, 33 (January 1959), p. 50.

> P[orter], F[airfield]. "Reviews and Previews: Allan Kaprow." *Art News*, 57 (January 1959), pp. 11–12.

1959

Hansa Gallery, New York. "Robert Whitman" (three-dimensional multimedia constructions). January 12–30, 1959.

> P[orter], F[airfield]. "Reviews and Previews: New Names This Month—Robert Whitman." *Art News*, 57 (January 1959), p. 18.

> T[illim], S[idney]. "In the Galleries: Robert Whitman." *Arts*, 33 (March 1959), p. 63.

Hansa Gallery, New York. "George Segal" (paintings, life-size plaster figures, drawings). February 2–21, 1959.

> S[chuyler], J[ames]. "Reviews and Previews: George Segal." *Art News*, 57 (February 1959), p. 16.

> T[illim], S[idney]. "In the Galleries: George Segal." *Arts*, 33 (February 1959), pp. 57–58.

City Gallery, New York. "Jay Milder and Red Grooms" (figurative paintings in an expressionist style). February 6–March 1, 1959.

> H[ale], H[erbert] D. "Reviews and Previews: New Names This Month—Milder and Grooms." *Art News*, 57 (February 1959), p. 18.

Judson Gallery, Judson Memorial Church, New York. "Jim Dine, Marc Ratliff, Tom Wesselmann" (paintings, drawings, and collages). February 14–March 7, 1959.

Judson Gallery, Judson Memorial Church, New York. "Drawings, Sculptures, Poems by Claes Oldenburg" (*papier-mâché* figurative constructions and sketches of the nude). May 22–June 10, 1959.

> Dunsterville, Harriet. "Art Reviews." *The Villager*, June 4, 1959, p. 10.

Condon Riley Gallery, New York. "Roy Lichtenstein" (paintings in an Abstract Expressionist style). June 2–27, 1959.

> D[e] M[ott], H[elen]. "In the Galleries: Roy Lichtenstein." *Arts*, 33 (June 1959), p. 66.

Reuben Gallery, New York. "George Brecht: Towards Events—An Arrangement" (assemblage objects with instructions for performances). October 16–November 5, 1959.

> D[ennison], G[eorge]. "In the Galleries: George Brecht." *Arts*, 34 (December 1959), pp. 69–70.

> H[ayes], R[ichard]. "Reviews and Previews: George Brecht." *Art News*, 58 (December 1959), p. 22.

Reuben Gallery, New York. "Lucas Samaras" (paintings and pastels). November 6–26, 1959.

> M[eyer], A[rline] J. "Reviews and Previews: Lucas Samaras." *Art News*, 58 (November 1959), p. 65.

> V[entura], A[nita]. "In the Galleries: Lucas Samaras." *Arts*, 34 (December 1959), p. 59.

Judson Gallery, Judson Memorial Church, New York. "Dine/Oldenburg" (two-artist exhibition, paintings and drawings). November 13–December 3, 1959.

> V[entura], A[nita]. "In the Galleries: Claes Oldenburg, James Dine." *Arts*, 34 (December 1959), p. 59.

Reuben Gallery, New York. "Robert Whitman" (multimedia constructions and collage paintings). November 27–December 7, 1959.

> D[ennison], G[eorge]. "In the Galleries: Robert Whitman." *Arts*, 34 (December 1959), p. 69.

H[ayes], R[ichard]. "Reviews and Previews: Robert Whitman." *Art News*, 58 (December 1959), p. 20.

Bodley Gallery, New York. "Wild Raspberries by Andy Warhol" (drawings of food). December 1–24, 1959.

Preston, Stuart. "Art: North of the Border." *The New York Times*, December 5, 1959, p. 20.

The Museum of Modern Art, New York. "Sixteen Americans" (group exhibition, including Jasper Johns, Robert Rauschenberg, and Frank Stella). December 16, 1959–February 14, 1960. Catalogue, with statements by the artists.

"Art: The Higher Criticism." *Time*, 75 (January 11, 1960), p. 59.

Genauer, Emily. "Art." *New York Herald Tribune*, December 20, 1959, section 4, p. 8.

———. "16-Artist Show Is on Today at Museum of Modern Art." *New York Herald Tribune*, December 16, 1959, p. 26.

Preston, Stuart. "Art: 'Sixteen Americans.' " *The New York Times*, December 16, 1959, p. 50.

———. "The Shape of Things to Come?" *The New York Times*, December 20, 1959, section 2, p. 11.

Rubin, William. "Younger American Painters." *Art International*, 4, no. 1 (1960), pp. 24–31.

Stella, Frank. "An Artist Writes to Correct and Explain." *New York Herald Tribune*, December 27, 1959, section 4, p. 7.

Reuben Gallery, New York. "Below Zero" (group exhibition: Yvonne Anderson, George Brecht, Jim Dine, Martha Edelheit, Jean Follett, Bruce Gilchrist, Red Grooms, Al Hansen, Ray Johnson, Allan Kaprow, Renee Miller, Claes Oldenburg, Robert Rauschenberg, George Segal, Richard Stankiewicz, James Waring, Robert Whitman). December 18, 1959–January 5, 1960.

1960

Reuben Gallery, New York. "Red Grooms" (paintings, collages, and constructions for stage sets). January 9–28, 1960.

S[eelye], A[nne]. "Reviews and Previews: New Names This Month—Red Grooms." *Art News*, 58 (February 1960), p. 18.

V[entura], A[nita]. "In the Galleries: Red Grooms." *Arts*, 34 (February 1960), p. 67.

Reuben Gallery, New York. "Paintings" (group exhibition: Herb Brown, Jim Dine, Red Grooms, Al Jensen, Lester Johnson, Allan Kaprow, Nicholas Krushenick, Claes Oldenburg, Patricia Passloff, Renee Rubin, Lucas Samaras, George Segal, Robert Whitman). January 29–February 18, 1960.

Judson Gallery, Judson Memorial Church, New York. "Ray-Gun" (two-artist exhibition: Jim Dine, *The House*; Claes Oldenburg, *The Street*). January 30–March 17, 1960.

Kiplinger, Suzanne. "Art: Ray-Gun." *The Village Voice*, February 17, 1960, p. 11.

Leo Castelli Gallery, New York. "Jasper Johns" (paintings with stenciled words, collage elements). February 15–March 5, 1960.

J[udd], D[onald]. "In the Galleries: Jasper Johns." *Arts*, 34 (March 1960), pp. 57–58.

S[andler], I[rving] H. "Reviews and Previews: Jasper Johns." *Art News*, 58 (February 1960), p. 15.

Leo Castelli Gallery, New York. "Robert Rauschenberg" (combine-paintings). March 29–April 16, 1960.

Ashton, Dore. "Art: Derivation of Dada." *The New York Times*, March 30, 1960, p. 42.

Genauer, Emily. "Art: Two Shows Contrasted—Dada's the Disease, Geometry a Cure?" *New York Herald Tribune*, April 3, 1960, section 4, p. 7.

S[andler], I[rving] H. "Reviews and Previews: Robert Rauschenberg." *Art News*, 59 (April 1960), p. 14.

T[illim], S[idney]. "In the Galleries: Robert Rauschenberg." *Arts*, 34 (May 1960), pp. 58–59.

Reuben Gallery, New York. "Jim Dine" (paintings, drawings, and sculptures). April 1–14, 1960.

S[andler], I[rving] H. "Reviews and Previews: New Names This Month—Jim Dine." *Art News*, 59 (April 1960), p. 17.

V[entura], A[nita]. "In the Galleries: James Dine." *Arts*, 34 (April 1960), p. 73.

Reuben Gallery, New York. "Claes Oldenburg: *The Street*" (drawings, sculptures, and constructions; revised version of installation at Judson Gallery, Judson Memorial Church, January–March 1960). May 6–19, 1960.

S[andler], I[rving] H. "Reviews and Previews: Claes Oldenburg." *Art News*, 59 (Summer 1960), p. 16.

T[illim], S[idney]. "In the Galleries: Claes Oldenburg." *Arts*, 34 (June 1960), p. 53.

Judson Gallery, Judson Memorial Church, New York. "Tom Wesselmann and Marc Ratliff" (two-artist exhibition, paintings and collages). May 6–27, 1960.

C[rehan], H[ubert]. "Reviews and Previews: New Names This Month—Wesselmann and Ratliff." *Art News*, 59 (May 1960), p. 58.

D[e] M[ott], H[elen]. "In the Galleries: Marc Ratliff, Tom Wesselmann." *Arts*, 34 (May 1960), p. 69.

Martha Jackson Gallery, New York. "New Media—New Forms: In Painting and Sculpture" (group exhibition: 71 artists, including George Brecht, Jim Dine, Dan Flavin, Red Grooms, Jasper Johns, Allan Kaprow, Claes Oldenburg, Robert Rauschenberg, Robert Whitman). June 6–24, 1960. Catalogue entitled *New Forms—New Media I*, with essays by Lawrence Alloway and Allan Kaprow, photographs by Rudolph Burckhardt.

"Art: Here Today . . ." *Time*, 75 (June 20, 1960), p. 62.

B[urrows], C[lyde]. "New Media, Forms." *New York Herald Tribune*, June 12, 1960, section 4, p. 7.

Canaday, John. "Art: A Wild, but Curious, End-of-Season Treat." *The New York Times*, June 7, 1960, section 5, p. 32.

Hess, Thomas B. "Mixed Mediums for a Soft Revolution." *Art News*, 59 (Summer 1960), pp. 45, 62.

Morse, John D. "The Artist in America: He Returns to Dada." *Art in America*, 48, no. 3 (1960), pp. 76–78.

Sandler, Irving H. "Ash Can Revisited, a New York Letter." *Art International*, 4 (October 1960), pp. 28–30.

Leo Castelli Gallery, New York. "Frank Stella" (paintings from the Aluminum series). September 27–October 15, 1960.

D[e] M[ott], H[elen]. "In the Galleries: Frank Stella." *Arts*, 35 (October 1960), p. 64.

P[etersen], V[alerie]. "Reviews and Previews: Frank Stella." *Art News*, 59 (November 1960), p. 17.

Preston, Stuart. "Housing in Art's Many Mansions." *The New York Times*, October 2, 1960, section 2, p. 21.

Sandler, Irving H. "New York Letter." *Art International*, 4 (December 1960), p. 25.

Martha Jackson Gallery and David Anderson Gallery, New York. "New Media—New Forms: In Painting and Sculpture, Version II" (group exhibition: 72 artists, including George Brecht, Jim Dine, Dan Flavin, Jasper Johns, Allan Kaprow, Claes Oldenburg, Robert Rauschenberg, Lucas Samaras, Robert Whitman). September 28–October 22, 1960.

Canaday, John. "The Blind Artist—In a Crucial Time He Plays at Games." *The New York Times*, October 2, 1960, section 2, p. 21.

Kramer, Hilton. "Month in Review." *Arts*, 35 (November 1960), pp. 50–51.

Green Gallery, New York. "George Segal" (paintings and sculptures). November 15–December 10, 1960.

B[eck], J[ames] H. "Reviews and Previews: George Segal." *Art News*, 59 (November 1960), p. 14.

T[illim], S[idney]. "In the Galleries: George Segal." *Arts*, 35 (December 1960), p. 54.

Judson Gallery, Judson Memorial Church, New York. "Allan Kaprow: An Apple Shrine" (environment). November 30–December 24, 1960.

P[etersen], V[alerie]. "Reviews and Previews: Allan Kaprow." *Art News*, 59 (January 1961), p. 12.

Tucker, Theodore. "Art: Kaprow's 'Apple Shrine.' " *The Village Voice*, January 12, 1961, p. 7.

Judson Gallery, Judson Memorial Church, New York. "Jim Dine: Rainbow Thoughts" (environment). January 1961.

J[ohnston], J[ill]. "Reviews and Previews: Jim Dine." *Art News*, 59 (February 1961), p. 15.

1961

Leo Castelli Gallery, New York. "Jasper Johns: Drawings and Sculpture." January 31–February 25, 1961.

Judson Gallery, Judson Memorial Church, New York. "dn flavin: constructions and watercolors." May 8–June 5, 1961.

J[ohnston], J[ill]. "Reviews and Previews: New Names This Month—Dan Flavin." *Art News*, 60 (May 1961), pp. 20–21.

Martha Jackson Gallery and David Anderson Gallery, New York. "Environments, Situations, Spaces" (group exhibition: George Brecht, *Iced Dice*; Jim Dine, *Spring Cabinet*; Walter Gaudnek, *Unlimited Dimensions*; Allan Kaprow, *Yard*; Claes Oldenburg, *The Store*; Robert Whitman, *Untitled*). May 25–June 23, 1961. Catalogue, with statements by the artists.

"Art: Jumping on Tires." *Newsweek*, 57 (June 12, 1961), p. 92.

K[roll], J[ack]. "Reviews and Previews: Situations and Environments." *Art News*, 60 (September 1961), p. 16.

O'Doherty, Brian. "Art: 3 Displays Run Gamut of Styles." *The New York Times*, June 6, 1961, p. 43.

The Museum of Modern Art, New York. "The Art of Assemblage" (group exhibition: 142 artists, including George Brecht, Jasper Johns, Robert Rauschenberg, and Lucas Samaras). October 2–November 12, 1961. Catalogue, with essay by William C. Seitz. Unpublished transcript, in The Museum of Modern Art Library files, of a symposium presented in conjunction with the exhibition, October 19: William C. Seitz, moderator, Roger Shattuck, Charles R. Huelsenbeck, Marcel Duchamp, Robert Rauschenberg, and Lawrence Alloway, participants.

Ashton, Dore. "But, But, But . . . An Assemblage of Wayward Opinion on the Art of Assemblage." *Arts and Architecture*, 79 (January 1962), pp. 4–5, 32–33.

Canaday, John. "Art Out of Anything." *The New York Times Magazine*, October 1, 1961, p. 52.

———. "Art: Spectacular Show—New 'Assemblage' Display at Modern Museum Is Called a 'Dazzler.' " *The New York Times*, October 4, 1961, p. 42.

———. "A Mixed-Up Show—'Art of Assemblage' Leaves a Little Something to Be Desired." *The New York Times*, October 8, 1961, section 2, p. 19.

Coplans, John. "Review: San Francisco—The Art of Assemblage." *Artforum*, 1 (June 1962), p. 35.

Hess, Thomas B. "Collage as an Historical Method." *Art News*, 60 (November 1961), pp. 30–32, 69–71.

Kiplinger, Suzanne. "Art: Assemblage." *The Village Voice*, October 26, 1961, p. 8.

Raynor, Vivien. "The Current Scene: The Art of Assemblage." *Arts Magazine*, 36 (November 1961), pp. 18–19.

Seitz, William C. "Assemblage: Problems and Issues." *Art International*, 6 (February 1962), pp. 26–34.

———. "Problems of 'New Directions' Exhibitions." *Artforum*, 2 (September 1963), pp. 23–25.

Leo Castelli Gallery, New York. "Robert Rauschenberg" (combine-paintings). November 7–December 5, 1961.

J[udd], D[onald]. "New York Exhibitions: In the Galleries—Robert Rauschenberg." *Arts Magazine*, 36 (January 1962), pp. 39–40.

K[roll], J[ack]. "Reviews and Previews: Robert Rauschenberg." *Art News*, 60 (December 1961), p. 12.

Ray Gun Mfg. Co., 107 East Second Street, New York, in cooperation with Green Gallery, New York. "Claes Oldenburg: The Store" (expanded version of the installation of reliefs at Martha Jackson Gallery, May 1961). December 1, 1961–January 1962.

J[ohnston], J[ill]. "Exhibitions for 1961–62: Claes Oldenburg." *Art News*, 60 (January 1962), pp. 46–47, 60.

Tillim, Sidney. "New York Exhibitions: Month in Review." *Arts Magazine*, 36 (February 1962), pp. 34–37.

Green Gallery, New York. "Lucas Samaras: Pastels—Plasters—Boxes—Etcetera." December 5–23, 1961.

J[ohnston], J[ill]. "Reviews and Previews: Lucas Samaras." *Art News*, 60 (December 1961), p. 14.

J[udd], D[onald]. "In the Galleries: Lucas Samaras." *Arts Magazine*, 36 (February 1962), p. 44.

Tanager Gallery, New York. "Tom Wesselmann: Great American Nude" (collages). December 8–30, 1961.

E[dgar], N[atalie]. "Reviews and Previews: Tom Wesselmann." *Art News*, 60 (December 1961), p. 56.

R[aynor], V[ivien]. "New York Exhibitions: In the Galleries—Tom Wesselmann." *Arts Magazine*, 36 (February 1962), p. 47.

1962

Martha Jackson Gallery with David Anderson Gallery, New York. "Jim Dine: New Works" (paintings of articles of clothing, with three-dimensional collage elements). January 9–February 3, 1962. Catalogue, with essay by Lawrence Alloway.

"Art: The Smiling Workman." *Time*, 79 (February 2, 1962), p. 44.

Ashton, Dore. "New York Commentary." *The Studio*, 163 (April 1962), p. 157.

J[ohnston], J[ill]. "Reviews and Previews: James Dine." *Art News*, 60 (January 1962), pp. 12–13.

Kozloff, Max. "Art." *The Nation*, 194 (January 27, 1962), p. 88.

T[illim], S[idney]. "New York Exhibitions: In the Galleries—Jim Dine." *Arts Magazine*, 36 (March 1962), pp. 46–47.

Green Gallery, New York. "James Rosenquist" (paintings). January 30–February 17, 1962.

Sandler, Irving H. "In the Art Galleries." *New York Post*, February 18, 1962, section 2, p. 12.

S[wenson], G[ene] R. "Reviews and Previews: New Names This Month—James Rosenquist." *Art News*, 60 (February 1962), p. 20.

T[illim], S[idney]. "New York Exhibitions: In the Galleries—James Rosenquist." *Arts Magazine*, 36 (March 1962), pp. 46–47.

Leo Castelli Gallery, New York. "Roy Lichtenstein" (paintings). February 10–March 3, 1962.

E[dgar], N[atalie]. "Reviews and Previews: Roy Lichtenstein." *Art News*, 61 (March 1962), p. 14.

J[udd], D[onald]. "New York Exhibitions: In the Galleries—Roy Lichtenstein." *Arts Magazine*, 36 (April 1962), pp. 52–53.

Dallas Museum for Contemporary Arts. "1961" (group exhibition: 36 artists, including Jim Dine, Jasper Johns, Roy Lichtenstein, Claes Oldenburg, Robert Rauschenberg, and James Rosenquist; Oldenburg presented a partial re-creation of *The Store*). April 3–May 13, 1962. Catalogue, with essay by Douglas MacAgy.

Leo Castelli Gallery, New York. "Frank Stella" (paintings from the Copper series). April 28–May 19, 1962.

C[ampbell], L[awrence]. "Reviews and Previews: Frank Stella." *Art News*, 61 (Summer 1962), p. 17.

J[udd], D[onald]. "New York Exhibits: In the Galleries—Frank Stella." *Arts Magazine*, 36 (September 1962), p. 51.

Green Gallery, New York. "George Segal" (paintings and life-size plaster figures in environmental settings). May 8–June 2, 1962.

J[ohnston], J[ill]. "Reviews and Previews: George Segal." *Art News*, 61 (May 1962), p. 16.

J[udd], D[onald]. "New York Reports: In the Galleries—George Segal." *Arts Magazine*, 36 (September 1962), p. 55.

Ferus Gallery, Los Angeles. "Andy Warhol" (paintings of Campbell's soup cans). July 9–August 4, 1962.

H[opkins], H[enry] T. "Reviews: Los Angeles—Andy Warhol." *Artforum*, 1 (September 1962), p. 15.

Smolin Gallery, New York. "Allan Kaprow: *Words*" (environment). September 11–12, 1962.

C[ampbell], L[awrence]. "Reviews and Previews: Allan Kaprow." *Art News*, 61 (October 1962), pp. 13–14.

M[cDarrah], F[red]. "Art." *The Village Voice*, September 6, 1962, p. 9.

O'Doherty, Brian. "Art: 'Environment: Words' Exploits Law of Chance." *The New York Times*, September 15, 1962, p. 22.

Green Gallery, New York. "Claes Oldenburg" (large-scale "soft" sculptures). September 18–October 20, 1962.

Ashton, Dore. "New York Report." *Das Kunstwerk*, 16 (November-December 1962), pp. 69–72.

———. "New York Letter." *Das Kunstwerk*, 16 (January 1963), p. 32.

C[ampbell], L[awrence]. "Reviews and Previews: Claes Oldenburg." *Art News*, 61 (October 1962), pp. 13–14.

Fried, Michael. "New York Letter." *Art International*, 6 (October 1962), pp. 74–76.

J[ohnston], J[ill]. "Reviews and Previews: Claes Oldenburg." *Art News*, 61 (November 1962), p. 13.

Preston, Stuart. "Current and Forthcoming Exhibitions: New York." *Burlington Magazine*, 104 (November 1962), p. 508.

Rudikoff, Sonya. "New York Letter." *Art International*, 6 (November 1962), p. 62.

Tillim, Sidney. "New York Exhibitions: Month in Review—Claes Oldenburg." *Arts Magazine*, 37 (November 1962), pp. 36–38.

Leo Castelli Gallery, New York. "John Chamberlain/Frank Stella" (two-artist exhibition: sculptures/paintings). October 16–November 7, 1962.

Ashton, Dore. "New York Report." *Das Kunstwerk*, 16 (November-December 1962), pp. 69–72.

Fried, Michael. "New York Letter." *Art International*, 6 (November 1962), p. 54.

R[aynor], V[ivien]. "New York Exhibitions: In the Galleries—Frank Stella, John Chamberlain." *Arts Magazine*, 37 (December 1962), pp. 46–47.

S[andler], I[rving] H. "Reviews and Previews: John Chamberlain and Frank Stella." *Art News*, 61 (December 1962), p. 54.

Sidney Janis Gallery, New York. "The New Realists" (group exhibition: 29 artists, including Jim Dine, Roy Lichtenstein, Claes Oldenburg, James Rosenquist, George Segal, Andy Warhol, and Tom Wesselmann). October 31–December 1, 1962. Catalogue, with essays by John Ashbery and Pierre Restany.

Ashton, Dore. "New York Report." *Das Kunstwerk*, 16 (November-December 1962), pp. 69–72.

H[ess], T[homas] B. "Reviews and Previews: 'New Realists.' " *Art News*, 61 (December 1962), pp. 12–13.

Johnston, Jill. "The Artist in a Coca-Cola World." *The Village Voice*, January 31, 1963, pp. 7, 24.

Kramer, Hilton. "Art." *The Nation*, 195 (November 17, 1962), pp. 334–35.

O'Doherty, Brian. "Art: Avant-Garde Revolt—'New Realists' Mock U.S. Mass Culture in Exhibition at Sidney Janis Gallery." *The New York Times*, October 31, 1962, p. 41.

———. " 'Pop' Goes the New Art." *The New York Times*, November 4, 1962, section 2, p. 23.

Raol, Rosine. "New York Letter: Bang or Whimper?" *Apollo*, 76 (December 1962), p. 819.

Rosenberg, Harold. "The Art Galleries: The Game of Illusion." *The New Yorker*, 38 (November 24, 1962), pp. 161–67.

Rudikoff, Sonya. "New Realists in New York." *Art International*, 7 (January 1963), pp. 38–41.

Sandler, Irving. H. "In the Art Galleries." *New York Post*, November 18, 1962, section 2, p. 12.

———. "New York Letter." *Quadrum*, 14 (1963), pp. 115–24.

T[illim], S[idney]. "New York Exhibitions: In the Galleries—The New Realists." *Arts Magazine*, 37 (December 1962), pp. 43–44.

Stable Gallery, New York. "Andy Warhol" (silkscreen paintings of movie stars and commercial products). November 6–24, 1962. Catalogue, with essay by Suzy Stanton. Reprinted as "Warhol at Bennington." *Art Journal*, 22 (Summer 1963), pp. 237–39.

Ashton, Dore. "New York Report." *Das Kunstwerk*, 16 (November-December 1962), pp. 69–72.

Fried, Michael. "New York Letter." *Art International*, 6 (December 1962), p. 57.

J[udd], D[onald]. "New York Exhibitions: In the Galleries—Andy Warhol." *Arts Magazine*, 37 (January 1963), p. 49.

S[wenson], G[ene] R. "Reviews and Previews: Andy Warhol." *Art News*, 61 (November 1962), p. 15.

Green Gallery, New York. "Wesselmann: Collages/Great American Nude & Still Life." November 13–December 1, 1962.

J[ohnston], J[ill]. "Reviews and Previews: Tom Wesselmann." *Art News*, 61 (November 1962), p. 15.

O'Doherty, Brian. "Art: 'Pop' Show by Tom Wesselmann Is Revisited." *The New York Times*, November 28, 1962, p. 36.

R[aynor], V[ivien]. "In the Galleries: Tom Wesselmann." *Arts Magazine*, 37 (January 1963), p. 45.

Dwan Gallery, Los Angeles. "My Country 'Tis of Thee" (group exhibition: 13 artists, including Jasper Johns, Roy Lichtenstein, Claes Oldenburg, Robert Rauschenberg, James Rosenquist, Andy Warhol, and Tom Wesselmann). November 18–December 15, 1962. Catalogue, with essay by Gerald Nordland.

Langsner, Jules. "Los Angeles Letter." *Art International*, 7 (January 1963), pp. 81–83.

W[holden], R[osalind] G. "Reviews: My Country 'Tis of Thee." *Artforum*, 1 (February 1963), p. 20.

1963

9 Great Jones Street, New York. "An Interior of Sculpture: New Work by Robert Whitman" and "Walter de Maria" (boxes and plywood objects). January 5–February 2, 1963.

J[ohnston], J[ill]. "Reviews and Previews: Robert Whitman." *Art News*, 61 (February 1963), pp. 12–13.

———. "Reviews and Previews: New Names This Month—Walter De Maria." *Art News*, 61 (February 1963), p. 19.

Green Gallery, New York. "New Work Part I" (group exhibition: Milet Andrejevic, Dan Flavin, Donald Judd, Yayoi Kusama, Robert Morris, Larry Poons, Lucas Samaras, George Segal). January 8–February 2, 1963.

Fried, Michael. "New York Letter." *Art International*, 7 (February 1963), p. 64.

Flavin, Dan. "Editor's Letters." *Art News*, 62 (April 1963), p. 6.

J[ohnston], J[ill]. "Reviews and Previews: New Work." *Art News*, 62 (March 1963), p. 50.

Tillim, Sidney. "New York Exhibitions: Month in Review." *Arts Magazine*, 37 (March 1963), pp. 61–62.

Leo Castelli Gallery, New York. "Jasper Johns" (paintings with words and three-dimensional collage elements). January 12–February 7, 1963.

S[wenson], G[ene] R. "Reviews and Previews: Jasper Johns." *Art News*, 61 (February 1963), pp. 11–12.

Tillim, Sidney. "New York Exhibitions: Month in Review." *Arts Magazine*, 37 (March 1963), p. 62.

Sidney Janis Gallery, New York. "Jim Dine" (paintings with three-dimensional bathroom appurtenances as collage elements). February 4–March 2, 1963. Catalogue, with essay by Oyvind Fahlstrom.

Ashton, Dore. "Correspondents: Letter from New York." *Canadian Art*, 20 (May 1963), p. 189.

———. "Modern Symbolism and Strained 'Pop': New York Commentary—Sidney Janis." *Studio International*, 165 (May 1963), p. 198.

Fried, Michael. "New York Letter." *Art International*, 7 (March 1963), p. 51.

J[ohnston], J[ill]. "Reviews and Previews: Jim Dine." *Art News*, 62 (March 1963), p. 14.

O'Doherty, Brian. "Showing Jim Dine." *The New York Times*, February 11, 1963, p. 5.

Preston, Stuart. "Current and Forthcoming Exhibitions: New York." *Burlington Magazine*, 105 (March 1963), p. 140.

Tillim, Sidney. "New York Exhibitions: Month in Review." *Arts Magazine*, 37 (March 1963), pp. 61–62.

Ferus Gallery, Los Angeles. "Frank Stella" (paintings from Multi-colored Concentric Squares and Mitered Mazes series). February 18–March 31, 1963.

F[actor], D[onald]. "Reviews: Los Angeles—Frank Stella." *Artforum*, 1 (May 1963), p. 44.

Langsner, J[ules]. "Los Angeles Letter." *Art International*, 7 (March 1963), pp. 75–76.

The Solomon R. Guggenheim Museum, New York. "Six Painters and the Object" (group exhibition: Jim Dine, Jasper Johns, Roy Lichtenstein, Robert Rauschenberg, James Rosenquist, Andy Warhol). March 14–June 2, 1963. Catalogue, with essay by Lawrence Alloway.

"Art: Pop Pop." *Time*, 82 (August 30, 1963), p. 40.

F[actor], D[on]. "Six Painters and the Object and Six More, L.A. County Museum of Art." *Artforum*, 2 (September 1963), pp. 13–14.

Horowitz, Leonard. "Art: 6 Characters in Search of an Art Movement." *The Village Voice*, April 4, 1963, p. 11.

J[udd], D[onald]. "New York Exhibitions: In the Galleries—Six Painters and the Object." *Arts Magazine*, 37 (May-June 1963), pp. 108–9.

Preston, Stuart. "On Display: All-Out Series of Pop Art—'Six Painters and the Object' Exhibited at Guggenheim." *The New York Times*, March 21, 1963, p. 8.

Rose, Barbara. "Pop Art at the Guggenheim." *Art International*, 7 (May 1963), pp. 20–22.

The Jewish Museum, New York. "Robert Rauschenberg" (retrospective). March 31–May 12, 1963. Catalogue, with essay by Alan R. Solomon.

J[udd], D[onald]. "New York Exhibitions: Robert Rauschenberg." *Arts Magazine*, 37 (May-June 1963), pp. 103–4.

O'Doherty, Brian. "Robert Rauschenberg." *The New York Times*, April 28, 1963, section 2, p. 13.

Ferus Gallery, Los Angeles. "Roy Lichtenstein" (paintings). April 1–27, 1963.

M[cClellan], D[oug]. "Reviews: Los Angeles—Roy Lichtenstein." *Artforum*, 2 (July 1963), pp. 44–46.

Green Gallery, New York. "James Rosenquist" (paintings). April 15–May 25, 1963.

Washington Gallery of Modern Art, Washington, D.C. "The Popular Image" (group exhibition: George Brecht, Jim Dine, Jasper Johns, Roy Lichtenstein, Claes Oldenburg, Robert Rauschenberg, James Rosenquist, Andy Warhol, Robert Watts, John Wesley, Tom Wesselmann). April 18–June 2, 1963. Catalogue, with essay by Alan R. Solomon, accompanied by a 33 rpm phonograph record of interviews with the artists, edited by Billy Klüver. Solomon's essay reprinted as "The New Art." *Art International*, 7 (September 1963), pp. 37–43.

"Show Business: Happenings—Pop Culture." *Time*, 81 (May 3, 1963), p. 73.

Wesselmann, Tom. "Editor's Letters." *Art News*, 62 (Summer 1963), p. 6.

80 Jefferson Street, New York. "George Brecht" (object-Events). April 1963.

J[ohnston], J[ill]. "Reviews and Previews: George Brecht." *Art News*, 62 (May 1963), p. 63.

Oakland Art Museum and the California College of Arts & Crafts. "Pop Art USA" (group exhibition: 47 artists, including George Brecht, Jim Dine, Jasper Johns, Roy Lichtenstein, Claes Oldenburg, Robert Rauschenberg, James Rosenquist, Andy Warhol, Tom Wesselmann). September 7–29, 1963. Catalogue, with essay by John Coplans. Reprinted as "Pop Art, U.S.A." *Artforum*, 2, no. 4 (1963), pp. 27–30.

Coplans, John. "Pop Art—U.S.A." *Art in America*, 51 (October 1963), pp. 26–27.

Green Gallery, New York. "Group Show" (group exhibition: Milet Andrejevic, George Brecht, Leslie Kerr, Robert Morris, Lucas Samaras, George Segal, Sidney Tillim, Tom Wesselmann, H. C. Westermann). Opened September 24, 1963.

Fried, Michael. "New York Letter." *Art International*, 7 (December 1963), p. 68.

Leo Castelli Gallery, New York. "Roy Lichtenstein" (paintings). September 28–October 24, 1963.

C[ampbell], L[awrence]. "Reviews and Previews: Roy Lichtenstein." *Art News*, 62 (November 1963), pp. 12–13.

Fried, Michael. "New York Letter." *Art International*, 7 (December 1963), p. 66.

J[udd], D[onald]. "New York Exhibitions: In the Galleries—Roy Lichtenstein." *Arts Magazine*, 38 (November 1963), pp. 32–33.

O'Doherty, Brian. "Lichtenstein: Doubtful But Definite Triumph of the Banal." *The New York Times*, October 27, 1963, section 2, p. 21.

Ferus Gallery, Los Angeles. "Andy Warhol" (paintings of Elvis Presley). September 30–October 1963.

Dwan Gallery, Los Angeles. "Oldenburg" (large-scale "soft" sculptures of food and clothing). October 1–26, 1963.

Nordland, Gerald. "Marcel Duchamp and Common Object Art." *Art International*, 8 (February 1964), pp. 30–32.

Green Gallery, New York. "Robert Morris" (boxes and large-scale wooden geometric constructions). October 15–November 2, 1963.

J[ohnston], J[ill]. "Reviews and Previews: New Names This Month—Robert Morris." *Art News*, 62 (October 1963), pp. 14–15.

O'Doherty, Brian. "Art: Connoisseurs Face Busy Season—Robert Morris." *The New York Times*, October 19, 1963, p. 22.

Rose, Barbara. "New York Letter." *Art International*, 7 (December 1963), pp. 61–64.

T[illim], S[idney]. "In the Galleries: New York Exhibitions—Robert Morris." *Arts Magazine*, 38 (December 1963), pp. 61–62.

Tibor de Nagy Gallery, New York. "Red Grooms" (wood and *papier-mâché* figures, paintings, and painted relief constructions). October 15–November 2, 1963.

Hieronymus, Clara. "A Bright Occasion." *The Nashville Tennessean*, November 17, 1963, section C, pp. 1–2.

Preston, Stuart. "Art: Contemporary Galaxy." *The New York Times*, October 20, 1963, p. 16.

Rose, Barbara. "New York Letter." *Art International*, 7 (December 1963), p. 63.

Sandler, Irving H. "In the Art Galleries." *New York Post*, October 27, 1963, section 2, p. 14.

S[wenson], G[ene] R. "Reviews and Previews: New Names This Month—Red Grooms." *Art News*, 62 (October 1963), p. 14.

T[illim], S[idney]. "New York Exhibitions: In the Galleries—Red Grooms." *Arts Magazine*, 38 (December 1963), pp. 63–64.

Leo Castelli Gallery, New York. "Robert Rauschenberg" (black-and-white silkscreen paintings). October 26–November 21, 1963.

Kozloff, Max. "Art." *The Nation*, 197 (December 7, 1963), pp. 402–3.

The Buffalo Fine Arts Academy, Albright-Knox Art Gallery, Buffalo. "Mixed Media and Pop Art" (group exhibition: 66 artists, including George Brecht, Jim Dine, Jasper Johns, Roy Lichtenstein, Robert Morris, Robert Rauschenberg, James Rosenquist, Lucas Samaras, George Segal, Andy Warhol, Tom Wesselmann). November 19–December 15, 1963. Catalogue.

Green Gallery, New York. "Don Judd" (painted wooden wall reliefs and three-dimensional geometric constructions). December 17, 1963–January 11, 1964.

Fried, Michael. "New York Letter." *Art International*, 8 (February 1964), p. 26.

Kramer, Hilton. "Art Centers: New York—The Season Surveyed." *Art in America*, 52 (June 1964), p. 112.

Lippard, L[ucy] R. "New York: Don Judd." *Artforum*, 2 (March 1964), pp. 18–19.

O'Doherty, Brian. "Recent Openings." *The New York Times*, December 21, 1963, p. 20.

S[wenson], G[ene] R. "Reviews and Previews: New Names This Month—Donald Judd." *Art News*, 62 (February 1964), p. 20.

Tillim, Sidney. "New York Exhibitions: Month in Review—The New Avant-Garde." *Arts Magazine*, 38 (February 1964), pp. 20–21.

1964

Sidney Janis Gallery, New York. "Four Environments by Four New Realists" (group exhibition: Jim Dine, Claes Oldenburg, James Rosenquist, George Segal). January 3–February 1, 1964.

Ashton, D[ore]. "Four Environments: Exhibition at Janis Gallery." *Arts and Architecture*, 81 (February 1964), p. 9.

Genauer, Emily. "Art: Heard Any Good Paintings Lately?" *New York Herald Tribune*, January 26, 1964, p. 35.

Oeri, Georgine. "The Object of Art." *Quadrum*, 16 (1964), pp. 4–6.

Rose, Barbara. "New York Letter." *Art International*, 8 (April 1964), p. 53.

S[wenson], G[ene] R. "Reviews and Previews: Four Environments." *Art News*, 62 (February 1964), p. 8.

Leo Castelli Gallery, New York. "Frank Stella" (paintings from the Purple series). January 4–February 6, 1964.

Kozloff, Max. "New York Letter." *Art International*, 8 (April 1964), p. 64.

Lippard, L[ucy] R. "New York: Frank Stella." *Artforum*, 2 (March 1964), pp. 18–19.

O'Doherty, Brian. "Frank Stella and a Crisis of Nothingness." *The New York Times*, January 19, 1964, section 2, p. 21.

S[wenson], G[ene] R. "Reviews and Previews: Frank Stella." *Art News*, 62 (February 1964), p. 11.

Tillim, Sidney. "New York Exhibitions: Month in Review—The New Avant-Garde." *Arts Magazine*, 38 (February 1964), pp. 20–21.

Wadsworth Atheneum, Hartford, Connecticut. "Black, White and Gray" (group exhibition: 22 artists, including George Brecht, Jim Dine, Dan Flavin, Jasper Johns, Roy Lichtenstein, Robert Morris, Robert Rauschenberg, Frank Stella, Andy Warhol). January 9–February 9, 1964.

Judd, Donald. "Nationwide Reports: Hartford—Black, White and Gray." *Arts Magazine*, 38 (March 1964), pp. 36–38.

Wagstaff, Samuel J. "Paintings to Think About." *Art News*, 62 (January 1964), pp. 38, 62.

Green Gallery, New York. "James Rosenquist" (paintings and three-dimensional constructions). January 15–February 8, 1964.

Kozloff, Max. "New York Letter: Rosenquist." *Art International*, 8 (April 1964), p. 62.

Preston, Stuart. "Art: Pop Works Appear Everywhere." *The New York Times*, January 18, 1964, p. 20.

S[wenson], G[ene] R. "Reviews and Previews: James Rosenquist." *Art News*, 62 (February 1964), p. 8.

T[illim], S[idney]. "New York Exhibitions: In the Galleries." *Arts Magazine*, 38 (March 1964), p. 63.

Ebling Brewery, Bronx, New York. "Allan Kaprow: Eat" (environment, sponsored by Smolin Gallery). January 18, 19, 25, 26, 1964.

Green Gallery, New York. "Tom Wesselmann" (painting-collages, Great American Nude series). February 11–March 7, 1964.

Fried, Michael. "New York Letter." *Art International*, 8 (April 1964), p. 60.

H[arrison], J[ane]. "New York Exhibitions: In the Galleries—Tom Wesselmann." *Arts Magazine*, 38 (April 1964), pp. 32–33.

Horowitz, Leonard. "Art." *The Village Voice*, February 20, 1964.

J[ohnston], J[ill]. "Reviews and Previews: Tom Wesselmann." *Art News*, 63 (April 1964), p. 13.

The Jewish Museum, New York. "Jasper Johns" (retrospective). February 16–April 12, 1964. Catalogue, with essays by Alan R. Solomon and John Cage.

"Art: The Younger." *Newsweek*, 63 (February 24, 1964), pp. 82–83.

Ashton, Dore. "New York Commentary: Acceleration in Discovery and Consumption." *Studio International*, 167 (May 1964), pp. 212–13.

Kozloff, Max. "Johns and Duchamp." *Art International*, 8 (March 1964), pp. 42–45.

Porter, Fairfield. "The Education of Jasper Johns." *Art News*, 62 (February 1964), pp. 44–45, 61–62.

Preston, Stuart. "Art: Jasper Johns Retrospective Show." *The New York Times*, February 15, 1964, p. 20.

P[reston], S[tuart]. "Pop Hits the Big Time." *The New York Times*, February 16, 1964, section 2, p. 15.

Tillim, Sidney. "New York Exhibitions: Month in Review—Ten Years of Jasper Johns." *Arts Magazine*, 38 (April 1964), pp. 22–26.

Kaymar Gallery, New York. "Dan Flavin: some light" (constructions with electric lights). March 5–29, 1964.

J[udd], D[onald]. "New York Exhibitions: In the Galleries—Dan Flavin." *Arts Magazine*, 38 (April 1964), p. 31.

L[evin], K[im]. "Reviews and Previews: New Names This Month—Dan Flavin." *Art News*, 63 (March 1964), p. 14.

Lippard, L[ucy] R. "New York: Dan Flavin." *Artforum*, 2 (May 1964), p. 54.

Rose, Barbara. "New York Letter." *Art International*, 8 (Summer 1964), p. 80.

Green Gallery, New York. "George Segal" (life-size plaster figures in three-dimensional environments). March 11–April 4, 1964.

S[wenson], G[ene] R. "Reviews and Previews: George Segal." *Art News*, 63 (May 1964), pp. 10–11.

Sidney Janis Gallery, New York. "Recent Work by Claes Oldenburg" (large-scale "soft" sculptures of food, clothing, and household appliances). April 7–May 2, 1964. Catalogue.

Canaday, John. "Art: By Claes Oldenburg—An Exhibition of Food and Other Things at the Sidney Janis Gallery." *The New York Times*, April 7, 1964, p. 32.

———. "Maybe Hopeful—Symptoms in a New Pop Exhibition." *The New York Times*, April 12, 1964, section 2, p. 19.

Genauer, Emily. "The Large Oldenburgs and the Small van Goghs." *New York Herald Tribune*, April 12, 1964, p. 39.

J[ohnston], J[ill]. "Reviews and Previews: Claes Oldenburg." *Art News*, 63 (May 1964), p. 12.

J[udd], D[onald]. "In the Galleries: Claes Oldenburg." *Arts Magazine*, 38 (September 1964), p. 63.

Kozloff, Max. "Art: New Works by Oldenburg." *The Nation*, 198 (April 27, 1964), pp. 445–46.

Rose, Barbara. "New York Letter." *Art International*, 8 (Summer 1964), p. 80.

Green Gallery, New York. "New Work: Part III" (group exhibition: Dan Flavin, Donald Judd, Larry Poons, George Segal, Richard Smith, Neil Williams). April 8–May 2, 1964.

Stable Gallery, New York. "Andy Warhol" (facsimiles of grocery cartons). April 21–May 9, 1964.

C[ampbell], L[awrence]. "Reviews and Previews: Andy Warhol." *Art News*, 63 (Summer 1964), p. 16.

Glueck, Grace. "Art Notes: Boom?" *The New York Times*, May 10, 1964, section 2, p. 19.

Rose, Barbara. "New York Letter." *Art International*, 8 (Summer 1964), p. 80.

T[illim], S[idney]. "In the Galleries: Andy Warhol." *Arts Magazine*, 38 (September 1964), p. 62.

United States Pavilion, 32nd International Biennial Exhibition of Art, Venice. "Four Germinal Painters—Four Younger Artists" (group exhibition, two sections: Jasper Johns, Morris Louis, Kenneth Noland, Robert Rauschenberg; John Chamberlain, Jim Dine, Claes Oldenburg, Frank Stella). June 20–October 15, 1964. Catalogue, with essay by Alan R. Solomon.

"Art: Carnival in Venice." *Newsweek*, 64 (July 6, 1964), pp. 74–75.

Baro, Gene. "The Canal Goes 'Pop.' " *The New York Times*, June 28, 1964, section 2, p. 12.

———. "The Venice Biennale." *Arts Magazine*, 38 (September 1964), pp. 32–37.

Genauer, Emily. "Art: The Merchandise of Venice." *Sunday New York Herald Tribune Magazine*, July 12, 1964, p. 21.

Gendel, Milton. "Hugger-mugger at the Giardini." *Art News*, 63 (September 1964), pp. 32–35, 53.

"Vatican Newspaper Criticizes 'Pop Art.' " *The New York Times*, June 25, 1964, p. 30.

Zevi, Tullia. "Art: The Biennale—How Evil Is Pop Art?" *The New Republic*, 151 (September 19, 1964), pp. 32–34.

Green Gallery, New York. "Lucas Samaras" (re-creation of the artist's bedroom). September 16–October 10, 1964.

J[ohnston], J[ill]. "Reviews and Previews: Lucas Samaras." *Art News*, 63 (September 1964), p. 10.

R[aynor], V[ivien]. "In the Galleries: Lucas Samaras." *Arts Magazine*, 39 (October 1964), pp. 65–66.

Rose, Barbara. "New York Letter: Lucas Samaras—His Life in Art." *Art International*, 8 (November 1964), p. 54.

The Hudson River Museum, Yonkers, New York. "8 Young Artists" (group exhibition, including Carl Andre). October 11–25, 1964. Catalogue, with essay by E. C. Goossen.

Leo Castelli Gallery, New York. "Roy Lichtenstein: Landscapes." October 24–November 19, 1964.

J[ohnston], J[ill]. "Reviews and Previews: Roy Lichtenstein." *Art News*, 63 (December 1964), p. 15.

J[udd], D[onald]. "In the Galleries: Roy Lichtenstein." *Arts Magazine*, 39 (December 1964), p. 66.

Picard, Lil. "The New School of New York." *Das Kunstwerk*, 18 (December 1964), p. 26.

Preston, Stuart. "Rear and Advance Guard Marching." *The New York Times*, November 1, 1964, section 2, p. 25.

Rose, Barbara. "New York Letter: Pop Art Revisited." *Art International*, 8 (December 1964), pp. 48–49.

Sidney Janis Gallery, New York. "Jim Dine" (paintings of palettes, bathrobes, color charts). October 27–November 21, 1964. Catalogue.

G[ablik], S[uzi]. "Reviews and Previews: Jim Dine." *Art News*, 63 (November 1964), p. 12.

J[udd], D[onald]. "In the Galleries: Jim Dine." *Arts Magazine*, 39 (December 1964), p. 72.

Picard, Lil. "The New School of New York." *Das Kunst-werk*, 18 (December 1964), p. 26.

Preston, Stuart. "Rear and Advance Guard Marching." *The New York Times*, November 1, 1964, section 2, p. 25.

Rose, Barbara. "New York Letter: Pop Art Revisited." *Art International*, 8 (December 1964), pp. 48–49.

Dwan Gallery, Los Angeles. "Rosenquist" (paintings with assemblage elements). October 27–November 24, 1964.

W[ilson], W[illiam]. "Los Angeles: James Rosenquist." *Artforum*, 3 (December 1964), pp. 12–13.

Green Gallery, New York. "Dan Flavin: fluorescent light" (sculptures made of fluorescent tubing). November 18–December 12, 1964.

Bourdon, David. "Art: Dan Flavin." *The Village Voice*, November 26, 1964, p. 11.

G[rossberg], J[acob]. "In the Galleries: Dan Flavin." *Arts Magazine*, 39 (January 1965), p. 54.

J[ohnston], J[ill]. "Reviews and Previews: Dan Flavin." *Art News*, 63 (January 1965), p. 13.

Lippard, Lucy R. "New York Letter." *Art International*, 9 (February 1965), p. 37.

Leo Castelli Gallery, New York. "Andy Warhol: Flower Paintings." November 21–December 17, 1964.

Bourdon, David. "Andy Warhol." *The Village Voice*, December 3, 1964, p. 11.

H[ess], T[homas] B. "Reviews and Previews: Andy Warhol." *Art News*, 63 (January 1965), p. 11.

Ferus Gallery, Los Angeles. "Roy Lichtenstein" (paintings). November 24–December 1964.

D[anieli], F[idel] A. "Los Angeles: Roy Lichtenstein." *Artforum*, 3 (January 1965), p. 12.

Marmer, Nancy. "Los Angeles Letter." *Art International*, 9 (February 1965), pp. 31–32.

Dwan Gallery, Los Angeles. "Lucas Samaras" (pin- and glass-covered boxes, assemblage wall pieces, and multimedia "paper bags"). November 24, 1964–January 5, 1965.

Marmer, Nancy. "Los Angeles Letter." *Art International*, 9 (February 1965), p. 31.

———. "Los Angeles: Lucas Samaras." *Artforum*, 3 (January 1963), pp. 11–12.

Green Gallery, New York. "Robert Morris" (seven large plywood constructions). December 1964–January 9, 1965.

J[udd], D[onald]. "In the Galleries: Robert Morris." *Arts Magazine*, 39 (February 1965), p. 54.

Lippard, Lucy R. "New York Letter." *Art International*, 9 (May 1965), pp. 57–58.

Rose, Barbara. "Looking at American Sculpture." *Artforum*, 3 (February 1965), pp. 35–36.

Selected Happenings/Performances and Reviews

1958

Douglass College, Rutgers University, New Brunswick, New Jersey. Allan Kaprow, *Untitled* (Happening). April 15, 1958.

Sun Gallery, Provincetown, Massachusetts. Red Grooms, *A Play Called Fire* (Happening). August–September 1958.

1959

Reuben Gallery, New York. Allan Kaprow, *Intermission Piece* (sound Happening). June 11, 1959.

Sun Gallery, Provincetown, Massachusetts. Red Grooms, *The Walking Man* (Happening). September 1959.

Reuben Gallery, New York. Allan Kaprow, *18 Happenings in Six Parts*. October 4, 6–10, 1959.

Livingston, J[ane] H. "Miscellany: Mr. Kaprow's 18 Happenings." *The Village Voice*, October 7, 1959, p. 11.

M[eyer], A[rline] J. "Reviews and Previews: Allan Kaprow." *Art News*, 58 (November 1959), p. 14.

Delancey Street Museum, 148 Delancey Street, New York. Red Grooms, *The Burning Building* (Happening). December 4–11, 1959.

1960

Reuben Gallery, New York. *Four Evenings* (Happenings): Red Grooms, *The Magic Train Ride* (changed from *Fireman's Dream*); Allan Kaprow, *The Big Laugh* (changed from *January Happening*); Robert Whitman, *Small Cannon*. January 8–11, 1960.

Talmer, Jerry. "Theatre (?): Three New Happenings." *The Village Voice*, January 13, 1960, p. 9.

Judson Gallery, Judson Memorial Church, New York. "Ray Gun Spex" (Happenings): Claes Oldenburg, *Snapshots from the City* (performed in the environment of *The Street*); Jim Dine, *The Smiling Workman* (performed in the environment of *The House*); Dick Higgins, *Edifices, Cabarets & Einschlutz*; Al Hansen, *Projections*; Allan Kaprow, *Coca-Cola, Shirley Cannonball?*; Robert Whitman, *Duet for a Small Smell*. February 29, March 1–2, 1960.

"Art: 'Up-Beats.' " *Time*, 75 (March 14, 1960), p. 80.

The Living Theatre, New York. *A Concert of New Music* (program arranged by Nicola Cernovich and James Waring): works by George Brecht, John Cage, Al Hansen, Ray Johnson, Allan Kaprow, Richard Maxfield, John Herbert McDowell, Robert Rauschenberg, among others. March 14, 1960.

Memorial Hall, Pratt Institute, New York. *A Program of Happenings? Events! & Situations?* (directed by Al Hansen): music and performances by George Brecht, Al Hansen, Allan Kaprow, Jackson Mac Low, among others. May 2, 1960.

Reuben Gallery, New York. *An Evening of: Sound Theatre—Happenings*: Jim Dine, *The Vaudeville Show*; Allan Kaprow,

Intermission Piece; Robert Whitman, *E.G.*; George Brecht, *Gossoon*; and Richard Maxfield, *Electronic Music.* June 11, 1960.

Johnston, Jill. "Dance: New 'Happenings' at the Reuben." *The Village Voice*, June 23, 1960, p. 13.

Robinson, Jean. "New Happenings at the Reuben." *The Village Voice*, June 16, 1960, p. 13.

The Living Theatre, New York. New York Audiovisual Group, *New Music* (concert): works by Al Hansen, Dick Higgins, Ray Johnson, Larry Poons, Jackson Mac Low, among others. August 1, 1960.

Reuben Gallery, New York. Jim Dine, *Car Crash* (Happening). November 1–6, 1960.

Johnston, Jill. "Art: Car Crash." *The Village Voice*, November 10, 1960, p. 8.

P[etersen], V[alerie]. "Reviews and Previews: Jim Dine." *Art News*, 59 (December 1960), pp. 16–17.

Reuben Gallery, New York. Robert Whitman, *The American Moon* (theater piece). November 29–December 7, 1960.

P[etersen], V[alerie]. "Reviews and Previews: Robert Whitman." *Art News*, 59 (January 1961), p. 13.

S[chmidt], S[andra]. "Theatre: American Moon." *The Village Voice*, December 15, 1960, p. 10.

Reuben Gallery, New York. *Varieties* (Happenings): Jim Dine, *A Shining Bed*; Simone Morris (Forti), *See Saw* and *Rollers*; Claes Oldenburg, *Blackouts: Chimney Fire*; *Erasers*; *The Vitamin Man*; *Butter and Jam.* December 16–18, 1960.

P[etersen], V[alerie]. "Reviews and Previews: Varieties." *Art News*, 59 (February 1961), p. 16.

1961

112 Chambers Street, New York. Series of concerts organized by La Monte Young at Yoko Ono's loft; performances, dance, and music by Jackson Mac Low, Richard Maxfield, Robert Morris, Simone Morris (Forti), La Monte Young, among others. January-June 1961.

Reuben Gallery, New York. Claes Oldenburg, *Circus (Ironworks/Fotodeath)* (two-part Happening). February 1961.

P[etersen], V[alerie]. "Reviews and Previews: Varieties." *Art News*, 59 (February 1961), p. 16.

J[ohnston], J[ill]. "Art Without Walls: Claes Oldenburg." *Art News*, 60 (April 1961), pp. 36, 57.

Nichols, Robert. "Entertainment: Ironworks/Fotodeath." *The Village Voice*, March 2, 1961, p. 10.

AG Gallery, New York. Series of Literary Evenings and Musica Antiqua et Nova concerts: Festival of Electronic Music and Concert of New Sounds and Noises (sponsored by *Bread & literary* magazine and AG Gallery). Works by Trisha Brown, Joseph Byrd, John Cage, Walter De Maria, Henry Flynt, Dick Higgins, Toshi Ichiyanagi, Ray Johnson, Jackson Mac Low, Robert Morris, Simone Morris (Forti), Yvonne Rainer, among others. March-July 1961.

Reuben Gallery, New York. Allan Kaprow, *A Spring Happening.* March 22–27, 1961.

Johnston, Jill. "Ingenious Womb." *The Village Voice*, April 6, 1961, p. 13.

———. "Reviews and Previews: Allan Kaprow." *Art News*, 60 (Summer 1961), pp. 61–62.

Reuben Gallery, New York. Robert Whitman, *Mouth* (theater piece). April 18–23, 1961.

Carnegie Recital Hall, New York. Yoko Ono, *A Grapefruit in the World of Park*, *A Piece for Strawberries and Violin*, and *AOS—to David Tudor* (concert): with sound and movement by George Brecht, Philip Corner, Jackson Mac Low, Yvonne Rainer, La Monte Young, among others. November 24, 1961.

Green Gallery, New York. Robert Whitman, *Ball* (theater piece). December 29, 30, 1961, and January 2–6, 1962.

Johnston, Jill. "Dance: Environment, Uptown." *The Village Voice*, January 4, 1962, p. 6.

———. "Reviews and Previews: Robert Whitman." *Art News*, 60 (February 1962), p. 15.

1962

Henry Street Playhouse, New York. George Brecht, *Dithyramb* (music and objects, presented by James Waring and Dance Company). January 5, 1962.

The Living Theatre, New York. *An Anthology* and *An Anthology II* (concerts): sound, music, and performances by contributors to *An Anthology* to raise money for its printing and binding. January 8 and February 5, 1962.

Maidman Playhouse, New York. American Theater for Poets, Inc., Poets Festival: music by Joseph Byrd, Philip Corner, Richard Maxfield, La Monte Young; dances by Fred Herko, Yvonne Rainer (March 5), Trisha Brown and Fred Herko, Aileen Passloff, Yvonne Rainer, James Waring (March 13); Happenings by Allan Kaprow, *A Service for the Dead, I,* and Robert Whitman, *Movies with Sound, Movements, Song, Play* (March 22); films by Stan VanDerBeek and Nicola Cernovich.

Johnston, Jill. "Boiler Room." *The Village Voice*, March 29, 1962, p. 14.

———. "Fresh Winds." *The Village Voice*, March 15, 1962, p. 13.

Moore, Lillian. "Rainer-Herko Dance Recital." *New York Herald Tribune*, March 6, 1962, p. 12.

Ray Gun Mfg. Co., 107 East Second Street, New York. "Ray Gun Theater" (Happenings): *Store Days, I,* February 23, 24; *Store Days, II,* March 2, 3; *Nekropolis, I,* March 9–10; *Nekropolis, II,* March 16–17; *Injun, I,* April 20–21; *Injun, II,* April 27–28; *Voyages, I,* May 4–5; *Voyages, II,* May 11–12; *World's Fair, I,* May 18–19; *World's Fair, II,* May 25–26.

" 'In' Audience Sees Girls Doused: What Happened? A Happening." *The New York Times*, April 30, 1962, p. 1.

Johnston, Jill. "Off Off B'Way: 'Happenings' at Ray Gun Mfg. Co." *The Village Voice*, April 26, 1962, p. 10.

———. "Reviews and Previews: New Names This Month—Claes Oldenburg." *Art News*, 61 (May 1962), p. 55.

Dallas Museum of Contemporary Art. Claes Oldenburg, *Injun* (second version) (Happening, presented in conjunction with the exhibition entitled "1961"). April 6, 7, 1962.

80 Jefferson Street, New York. George Brecht, *Nectarine* (Event). June 12, 1962.

Judson Memorial Church, New York. Judson Dance Theater, *Concert of Dance*: works by William Davis, Judith Dunn, Robert Dunn, Ruth Emerson, David Gordon, Sally Gross, Alex Hay, Deborah Hay, Fred Herko, Gretchen MacLane, John Herbert McDowell, Steve Paxton, Rudy Perez, Yvonne Rainer, Charles Rotmil, Carol Scothorn and Elaine Summers. July 6, 1962.

Hughes, Allen. "Dance Program Seen at Church." *The New York Times*, July 2, 1962, p. 9.

Johnston, Jill. "Democracy." *The Village Voice*, August 23, 1962, p. 9.

Ergo Suits Festival (Happenings and performance pieces): Allan Kaprow, *Sweeping*, in the woods, Woodstock, New York; Al Hansen, *Car Bibbe*, East Hampton, New York; Allan Kaprow, *A Service for the Dead, II*, on the beach, Bridgehampton, New York; Alison Knowles, *Light House*, East Hampton, New York; Walter De Maria, *Boxes + Balls*, *The Ball Game*, East Hampton, New York; and La Monte Young, *Sopranino*, East Hampton, New York, among others. August 18–August 25, 1962.

Turnau Opera House, Woodstock, New York. Judson Dance Theater, *Concert of Dance 2* (organized by Elaine Summers): works by Laura De Freitas and June Ekman and Sally Gross, Ruth Emerson, Elizabeth Keen, Elaine Summers. August 31 (September 1?), 1962.

Johnston, Jill. "Central Park: At Woodstock." *The Village Voice*, September 20, 1962, p. 2.

Green Gallery, New York. Claes Oldenburg, *Sports* (Happening; presented during his one-artist show). September 18, 1962.

Mills Hotel, New York. Allan Kaprow, *The Courtyard* (Happening; sponsored by Smolin Gallery, New York). November 23–25, 1962.

1963

Judson Memorial Church, New York. Judson Dance Theater, *Concert of Dance 3 and 4*: works by Trisha Brown, Philip Corner, Lucinda Childs, William Davis, Judith Dunn, Ruth Emerson, Deborah Hay, Fred Herko, Bob Huot and Robert Morris, John Herbert McDowell, Steve Paxton, Steve Paxton and Yvonne Rainer, Yvonne Rainer, Arlene Rothlein, Carolee Schneemann, Carol Scothorn, Elaine Summers. January 29 and 30, 1963.

Johnston, Jill. "Judson Concerts #3, #4." *The Village Voice*, February 28, 1963, p. 9.

Lexington Hall, University of Chicago. Claes Oldenburg, *Gayety* (Happening). February 8–10, 1963.

9 Great Jones Street, New York. Robert Whitman, *Flower* (theater piece). Fridays and Saturdays, March 1963.

Benedikt, Michael. "Happening: Flower." *The Village Voice*, April 4, 1963, pp. 14, 16.

J[ohnston], J[ill]. "Reviews and Previews: Robert Whitman." *Art News*, 62 (May 1963), p. 62.

Washington Gallery of Modern Art, Washington, D.C. Claes Oldenburg, *Stars* (Happening; presented as part of the Pop Art Festival organized in conjunction with the exhibition entitled "The Popular Image"). April 24, 25, 1963.

Judson Memorial Church, New York. Judson Dance Theater, *An Evening of Dance*: Yvonne Rainer, *Terrain*. April 28, 29, 1963.

Johnston, Jill. "Yvonne Rainer: I." *The Village Voice*, May 23, 1963, p. 7.

———. "Yvonne Rainer: II." *The Village Voice*, June 6, 1963, pp. 11, 18.

Smolin Gallery, New York; George Segal's farm, South Brunswick, New Jersey; Hardware Poets Playhouse, New York. Yam Festival (Happenings, performances, dance, music, Events organized by George Brecht and Robert Watts): works by George Brecht, John Cage, Lucinda Childs, Philip Corner, Red Grooms, Al Hansen, Dick Higgins, Ray Johnson, Allan Kaprow, Alison Knowles, George Maciunas, Jackson Mac Low, Robert Morris, Yvonne Rainer, Robert Watts, La Monte Young, among others. May 1–31, 1963.

America on Wheels skating rink, Washington, D.C. Judson Dance Theater, *Concert of Dance 5* (sponsored by the Washington Gallery of Modern Art as part of the Pop Art Festival organized in conjunction with the exhibition entitled "The Popular Image"): works by Trisha Brown, William Davis, Judith Dunn, David Gordon, Steve Paxton, Yvonne Rainer, Yvonne Rainer and Steve Paxton, Robert Rauschenberg, Albert Reid. May 9, 1963.

9 Great Jones Street, New York. Robert Whitman, *Hole* (theatrical piece). May 27–June 1, 1963.

Judson Memorial Church, New York. Judson Dance Theater, *Concert of Dance 6, 7, 8*: works by Trisha Brown, Lucinda Childs, Philip Corner, Judith Dunn, Ruth Emerson, David Gordon, Deborah Hay, Fred Herko, Elizabeth Keen, John Herbert McDowell, Robert Morris, Rudy Perez, Arlene Rothlein, Joseph Schlichter, Sally Stackhouse and Joseph Schlichter, Elaine Summers. June 23, 24, 25, 1963.

Hughes, Allen. "Judson Dance Theater Seeks New Paths." *The New York Times*, June 26, 1963, section 2, p. 34.

Johnston, Jill. "From Lovely Confusion to Naked Breakfast." *The Village Voice*, July 18, 1963, p. 12.

———. "Judson Speedlimits." *The Village Voice*, July 25, 1963, p. 10.

Gramercy Arts Theater, New York. Judson Dance Theater, *Concert of Dance 9, 10, 11, 12*: works by Eddie Barton, Lucinda Childs, Philip Corner, Judith Dunn, Ruth Emerson, Sally Gross, Al Hansen, Deborah Hay and Fred Herko, Susan Kaufman, Elizabeth Keen, John Herbert McDowell, Aileen Passloff, Rudy Perez, Arlene Rothlein, Beverly Schmidt, Elaine Summers, James Tenney, James Waring. July 30, August 1, 6, 8, 1963.

Judson Memorial Church, New York. 1st Festival of the Avant Garde (music and performances organized by Charlotte Moorman). August 20–September 4, 1963.

521 N. La Cienega, Los Angeles. Robert Whitman, *Water* (theater piece). September 3, 4, 1963.

101 Appletree Lane, Berkeley Heights, New Jersey. Judson Dance Theater, *Afternoon (a Forest Concert)*: choreographed by Steve Paxton. October 6, 1963.

Johnston, Jill. "Fall Colors." *The Village Voice*, October 31, 1963, p. 7.

Judson Memorial Church, New York. Judson Dance Theater, *Concert of Dance 13*: collaborative event with environment by sculptor Charles Ross and works by Joan Baker, Carla Blank, Lucinda Childs, Philip Corner, Ruth Emerson, Alex Hay, Deborah Hay, Yvonne Rainer, Yvonne Rainer and Charles Ross, Arlene Rothlein, Carolee Schneemann. November 19, 20, 1963.

> Johnston, Jill. "Judson Collaboration." *The Village Voice,* November 28, 1963, p. 18.

American Institute of Aeronautics and Astronautics parking lot, Los Angeles. Claes Oldenburg, *Autobodys* (Happening). December 9, 10, 1963.

1964

Fluxhall, 359 Canal Street, New York. *12 Fluxus Concerts:* works by George Brecht, Philip Corner, Walter De Maria, Robert Filliou, Dick Higgins, Toshi Ichiyanagi, Joe Jones, Allan Kaprow, Alison Knowles, Shigeko Kubota, Jackson Mac Low, George Maciunas, Jonas Mekas, Robert Morris, Nam June Paik, Ben Vautier, Robert Watts, Emmett Williams, La Monte Young, among others. March–May 1964.

Judson Memorial Church, New York. Judson Dance Theater, *Concert of Dance 14, 15, 16*: works by Carla Blank and Sally Gross, Lucinda Childs, William Davis, Judith Dunn, David Gordon, Sally Gross, Alex Hay and Robert Rauschenberg, Deborah Hay, Fred Herko, Tony Holder, Al Kurchin, Deborah Lee, Robert Morris, Steve Paxton, Yvonne Rainer, Albert Reid, Elaine Summers. April 27, 28, 29, 1964.

Carnegie Recital Hall, New York. *Fluxus Symphony Orchestra Concert*: works by George Brecht, Philip Corner, Dick Higgins, Yoko Ono, Nam June Paik, Robert Watts, Emmett Williams, La Monte Young, among others. June 27, 1964.

> Johnston, Jill. "Dance: Fluxus Fluxus." *The Village Voice,* July 2, 1964, p. 7.

Judson Memorial Church, New York. 2nd Annual New York Avant Garde Festival (organized by Charlotte Moorman and N. Seaman): performance of Karlheinz Stockhausen's *Originale*, directed by Allan Kaprow. August 30, 1964.

> Ashton, Dore. "New York Commentary: Recent Happenings and Unhappenings." *Studio International,* 168 (November 1964), pp. 220–23.
>
> "Avant-Garde: Stuffed Bird at 48 Sharp." *Time,* 48 (September 18, 1964), p. 81.
>
> Goodman, Susan. "Anti-art Pickets Pick on Stockhausen." *The Village Voice,* September 10, 1964, pp. 3, 8.
>
> Johnston, Jill. "Dance: Inside Originale." *The Village Voice,* October 1, 1964, pp. 6, 16.
>
> Klüver, Billy. "Letter to the Editor: More Incidents." *The Village Voice,* September 24, 1964, p. 4.
>
> "Music: Birds, Beasts, and Bach." *Newsweek,* 64 (September 21, 1964), p. 80.
>
> Schonberg, Harold. "Music: Stockhausen's 'Originale' Given at Judson." *The New York Times,* September 9, 1964, p. 46.

Washington Square Gallery, New York. Flux Fest: works by AY-O, Joe Jones, George Maciunas, among others. September 9–November 3, 1964.

Judson Memorial Church, New York. Carolee Schneemann, *Meat Joy* (kinetic theater). November 16–18, 1964.

Filmography

1958

Jordan Belson, *Flight,* color, sound, 10 minutes.

Ed Bland, *The Cry of Jazz,* black and white, sound, 35 minutes.

Stan Brakhage, *Anticipation of the Night,* color, silent, 42 minutes.

Robert Breer, *Par Avion,* color, silent, 3 minutes.

Shirley Clarke, *Brussels "Loops,"* color, silent, twelve 2½-minute loop films.

Bruce Conner, *A Movie,* black and white, sound, 12 minutes.

Morris Engel, *Weddings and Babies,* black and white, sound, 81 minutes.

Larry Jordan, *Triptych in Four Parts,* color, sound, 12 minutes.

Lionel Rogosin, *Come Back Africa,* black and white, sound, 90 minutes.

Stan VanDerBeek, *Ala Mode,* black and white, sound, 5 minutes.

1959

Jordan Belson, *Raga,* color, sound, 7 minutes.

Charles Boultenhouse, *Handwritten,* color, sound, 9 minutes.

Stan Brakhage, *Window Water Baby Moving,* color, silent, 12 minutes.

Robert Breer, *Eyewash,* color, silent, 3 minutes.

John Cassavetes, *Shadows,* black and white, sound, 81 minutes.

Shirley Clarke, *Bridges-Go-Round,* color, sound, 7 minutes.

Ed Emshwiller, *Dance Chromatic,* color, sound, 7 minutes.

Robert Frank and Alfred Leslie, *Pull My Daisy,* black and white, sound, 29 minutes.

Ken Jacobs, *Star Spangled to Death,* black and white and color, sound, variable length (2–3 hours).

Ben Maddow, Sidney Meyers, and Joseph Strick, *The Savage Eye,* black and white, sound, 67 minutes.

Marie Menken, *Dwightiana,* color, sound, 3½ minutes.

Stan VanDerBeek, *Science Friction,* color, sound, 9 minutes.

1960

Stan Brakhage, *The Dead,* color, silent, 11 minutes.

Robert Breer, *Homage to Jean Tinguely's "Homage to New York,"* black and white, sound, 9½ minutes.

Shirley Clarke, *A Scary Time*, black and white, sound, 20 minutes.

Ed Emshwiller, *Lifelines*, color, sound, 7 minutes.

Larry Jordan, *Minerva Looks Out into the Zodiac*, black and white, sound, 6 minutes.

Richard Leacock, Al Maysles, D. A. Pennebaker, Terence MaCartney-Filgate, Robert Drew, *Primary*, black and white, sound, 53 minutes.

Ron Rice, *The Flower Thief*, black and white, sound, 75 minutes.

Bert Stern, *Jazz on a Summer's Day*, color, sound, 85 minutes.

Stan VanDerBeek, *Blacks and Whites, Days and Nights*, black and white, sound, 5 minutes.

Vernon Zimmerman, *Lemon Hearts*, black and white, sound, 26 minutes.

1961

Bruce Baillie, *The Gymnasts*, black and white, sound, 8 minutes.

Jordan Belson, *Allures*, color, sound, 9 minutes.

Stan Brakhage, *Thigh Line Lyre Triangular*, color, silent, 7 minutes.

———, *Prelude: Dog Star Man*, color, silent, 25 minutes.

Shirley Clarke, *The Connection*, black and white, sound, 100 minutes.

Bruce Conner, *Cosmic Ray*, black and white, sound, 4 minutes.

Robert Frank, *The Sin of Jesus*, black and white, sound, 40 minutes.

Ken Jacobs, *The Death of P'town*, color, sound, 7 minutes.

Jonas Mekas, *Guns of the Trees*, black and white, sound, 75 minutes.

Marie Menken, *Arabesque for Kenneth Anger*, color, sound, 4 minutes.

Harry Smith, *No. 12 (Heaven and Earth Magic, The Magic Feature)*, black and white, silent, 66 minutes.

John Whitney, *Catalog*, color, sound, 7 minutes.

1962

Stan Brakhage, *Blue Moses*, black and white, sound, 11 minutes.

———, *Dog Star Man: Part I*, color, silent, 30 minutes.

Robert Breer, *Horse Over Tea Kettle*, color, sound, 8 minutes.

———, *Pat's Birthday*, black and white, sound, 13 minutes.

Ed Emshwiller, *Thanatopsis*, black and white, sound, 5 minutes.

Marie Menken, *Moonplay*, black and white, sound, 5 minutes.

Ron Rice, *Senseless*, black and white, sound, 28 minutes.

Jack Smith, *Scotch Tape*, color, sound, 3 minutes.

1963

Kenneth Anger, *Scorpio Rising*, color, sound, 29 minutes.

Bruce Baillie, *To Parsifal*, color, sound, 16 minutes.

Stan Brakhage, *Mothlight*, color, silent, 4 minutes.

———, *Dog Star Man: Part II*, color, silent, 7 minutes.

Shirley Clarke, *The Cool World*, black and white, sound, 100 minutes.

Bruce Conner, *Report*, black and white, sound, 13 minutes (first version).

Ken Jacobs, *Little Stabs at Happiness*, color, sound, 18 minutes.

———, *Blonde Cobra*, black and white and color, sound, 25 minutes.

Adolfas Mekas, *Hallelujah the Hills*, black and white, sound, 82 minutes.

Marie Menken, *Notebook*, color, silent, 10 minutes.

Ron Rice, *The Queen of Sheba Meets the Atom Man*, black and white, silent, 70½ minutes.

Jack Smith, *Flaming Creatures*, black and white, sound, 45 minutes.

Andy Warhol, *Andy Warhol Films Jack Smith Filming "Normal Love,"* color, silent, 3 minutes.

———, *Eat*, black and white, silent, 45 minutes.

———, *Haircut*, black and white, silent, 33 minutes.

———, *Kiss*, black and white, silent, 50 minutes.

———, *Sleep*, black and white, silent, 360 minutes.

1964

Stan Brakhage, *Dog Star Man: Part III*, color, silent, 8 minutes.

———, *Dog Star Man: Part IV*, color, silent, 7 minutes.

———, *Songs 1–8*, color, silent, 33 minutes.

Robert Breer, *Fist Fight*, color, sound, 11 minutes.

Robert Downey, *Babo 73*, black and white and color, sound, 57 minutes.

Peter Goldman, *Echoes of Silence*, black and white, sound, 75 minutes.

Larry Jordan, *Duo Concertantes*, black and white, sound, 9 minutes.

Stanton Kaye, *Georg*, black and white, sound, 55 minutes.

George Landow, *Fleming Faloon*, black and white and color, sound, 7 minutes.

Jonas Mekas, *The Brig*, black and white, sound, 68 minutes.

Ron Rice, *Chumlum*, color, sound, 26 minutes.

Michael Snow, *New York Eye and Ear Control (A Walking Woman Work)*, black and white, sound, 34 minutes.

Stan VanDerBeek, *Newsreel of Dreams (Part I)*, color, sound, 8 minutes.

Andy Warhol, *Batman Dracula*, black and white, silent, 120 minutes.

———, *Blow Job*, black and white, silent, 33 minutes.

———, *Couch*, black and white, silent, 40 minutes.

———, *Empire*, black and white, silent, 480 minutes.

SELECTED BIBLIOGRAPHY   Compiled by Susan J. Cooke

The first part of the Bibliography reflects the chapter sequence of the essay "BLAM! The Explosion of Pop, Minimalism, and Performance 1958–1964," followed by references for the essay "The American Independent Cinema 1958–1964." The second part contains bibliographies for the major artists discussed, in alphabetical order by artist. Catalogues and reviews for exhibitions, Happenings, and performances presented prior to 1965 are included in the Chronology section.

Introduction

"Art: Trend to the 'Anti-Art.' " *Newsweek*, 51 (March 31, 1958), pp. 94, 96.

Bailey, Anthony. "A. E. and the Hell with It!" *Esquire*, 56 (July 1961), pp. 104–6.

Calas, Nicolas. "ContiNuance: On the Possibilities of a New Kind of Symbolism in Recent American Painting and What Such Symbols Could Possibly Mean." *Art News*, 57 (February 1959), pp. 36–39.

Canaday, John. "Happy New Year!—Thoughts on Critics and Certain Painters as the Season Opens," 1959; "Perhaps Drastic—A Moratorium on Art Might Be Nice for a While, But Could Be Dangerous," 1960; "In the Gloaming: Twilight Seems to Be Setting Rapidly for Abstract Expressionism," 1960; and "Their Heart Belongs to Dada—The Cult of the Irrational Is Having a Revival—But Now It's 'Art,' Not 'Anti-art,' " 1960; in *Embattled Critic: Views on Modern Art*. New York: Farrar, Straus and Cudahy, 1962.

Constable, Rosalind. "Scouting Report on the Avant-Garde." *Esquire*, 55 (June 1961), pp. 83–88.

Dallas Museum of Fine Arts and Pollock Galleries, Southern Methodist University, Dallas. *Poets of the Cities: New York and San Francisco 1950–1965* (exhibition catalogue). Essays by Neil A. Chassman, Robert M. Murdock, Lana Davis, Robert Creeley, John Clellon Holmes. New York: E. P. Dutton, 1974.

Finch, Christopher. "The Object in Art." *Art and Artists*, 1 (May 1966), p. 18–21.

Greenberg, Clement. "The 'Crisis' of Abstract Art," in James R. Mellow, ed. *Arts Yearbook 7: New York: The Art World*. New York: The Art Digest, 1964.

Hess, Thomas B. "The Phony Crisis in American Art." *Art News*, 63 (Summer 1963), pp. 24–28, 59–60.

Janis, Harriet, and Rudi Blesh. *Collage: Personalities, Concepts, Techniques*. Philadelphia: Chilton Book Company, 1967. Revised edition.

Rose, Barbara. "The Second Generation: Academy and Breakthrough." *Artforum*, 4 (September 1965), pp. 53–63.

Rosenberg, Harold. "Action Painting: A Decade of Distortion." *Art News*, 61 (December 1962), pp. 42–44, 62–63.

Sandler, Irving. *The New York School: The Painters and Sculptors of the Fifties*. New York: Harper & Row, 1978.

Seckler, Dorothy Gees. "The Artist in America: Victim of the Culture Boom?" *Art in America*, 51 (December 1963), pp. 27–39.

Happenings

Goldberg, RoseLee. *Performance: Live Art 1909 to the Present*. New York: Harry N. Abrams, 1979.

Hansen, Al. *A Primer of Happenings & Time/Space Art*. New York: Something Else Press, 1965.

Henri, Adrian. *Total Art: Environments, Happenings, and Performance*. New York: Praeger Publishers, 1974.

Johnston, Jill. " 'Happenings' on the New York Scene." *Encore*, 9 (September-October 1962), pp. 8–13.

Kaprow, Allan. *Assemblage, Environments & Happenings*. New York: Harry N. Abrams, 1966.

———. "The Demiurge," including "Something to Take Place: A Happening" and an untitled essay. *The Anthologist* (Rutgers University), 30, no. 4 (Winter 1959), pp. 4–17. "Something to Take Place: A Happening" reprinted in Michael Kirby. *Happenings: An Illustrated Anthology*. New York: E. P. Dutton, 1966. Untitled essay reprinted in Allan Kaprow. *Untitled Essay, and Other Works*. New York: Something Else Press, 1967.

———. "The Happenings Are Dead." *Artforum*, 4 (March 1966), pp. 36–39.

———. " 'Happenings' in the New York Scene." Photographs by Robert R. McElroy. *Art News*, 60 (May 1961), pp. 36–39, 58–62.

———. "The Legacy of Jackson Pollock." *Art News*, 57 (October 1958), pp. 24–26, 55–57.

———. "One Chapter from 'The Principles of Modern Art.' " *It Is*, no. 4 (Autumn 1959), pp. 51–52.

———. "Pinpointing Happenings." *Art News*, 66 (October 1967), pp. 46–47, 70–71.

Kirby, Michael. *Happenings: An Illustrated Anthology*. New York: E. P. Dutton, 1966. Statements by Jim Dine, Claes Oldenburg, and Robert Whitman.

Kozloff, Max. "Art." *The Nation*, 205 (July 3, 1967), pp. 27–29.

Seckler, Dorothy Gees. "The Artist in America: The Audience Is His Medium!" *Art in America*, 51 (April 1963), pp. 62–67.

Wilcock, John. "What's Going on Here?" Photographs by Robert R. McElroy. *New York Herald Tribune Sunday Magazine*, May 5, 1963, pp. 4–5, 15.

Fluxus

Art and Artists, 7 (October 1972). Special issue on Fluxus; articles by Ken Friedman, Dick Higgins, Victor Musgrave, Michael Nyman, Robin Page, Tomas Schmit.

Cranbrook Academy of Art Museum, Bloomfield Hills, Michigan. *Fluxus Etc.: The Gilbert and Lila Silverman Collection* (exhibition catalogue), 1981. Edited by Jon Hendricks.

Fluxus Etc./Addenda I: The Gilbert and Lila Silverman Collection (exhibition catalogue). Catalogue by Melanie Hedlund, Jon Hendricks, Gilbert Silverman, Lori Tucci. New York: Ink &, 1983.

Friedman, Ken, and Peter Frank. *Young Fluxus* (exhibition catalogue). New York: Artists Space, 1982.

Kölnischer Kunstverein, Cologne. *Happenings and Fluxus* (exhibition catalogue), 1970. Compiled by H. Sohm.

Moore, Barbara. "George Maciunas: A Finger in Fluxus." *Artforum*, 8 (October 1982), pp. 38–45.

Museum Wiesbaden. *1962 Wiesbaden Fluxus 1982: Eine kleine Geschichte von Fluxus in drei Teilen* (exhibition catalogue). Harlekin Art, Berliner Künstlerprogramm des DAAD, 1982. Compiled by René Block.

Ruhé, Harry. *Fluxus, the Most Radical and Experimental Art Movement of the Sixties.* Amsterdam: 'A,' 1979.

Young, La Monte, ed. *An Anthology.* New York: La Monte Young and Jackson Mac Low, 1963. New York: Heiner Friedrich, 1970. Second edition.

The New American Dance

Ballet Review, 1, no. 6 (1967). Special issue on Judson Dance Theater; articles by Jill Johnston, Judith Dunn, Constance H. Poster, as well as a discussion among Judson participants and a chronology of performances.

Banes, Sally. "Democracy's Body: Judson Dance Theatre and Its Legacy." *Performing Arts Journal*, 5 (1981), pp. 98–106.

———. "Judson Dance Theatre: Democracy's Body, 1962–1964." Ph.D. dissertation, New York University, 1980.

Bennington College Judson Project. *Judson Dance Theater: 1962–1966* (exhibition catalogue), 1981. Edited by Wendy Perron and Daniel J. Cameron; essays by Jill Johnston, Sally Banes.

Forti, Simone. *Handbook in Motion.* New York: New York University Press, 1974.

Institute of Contemporary Art, Inc., Boston. *Art & Dance: Images of the Modern Dialogue, 1890–1980* (exhibition catalogue), 1982. Essays by Marianne Martin, Iris M. Fanger, Deborah Jowitt, David Vaughan, David A. Ross, Elisabeth Sussman.

Johnston, Jill. "The New American Modern Dance." *Art and Literature*, 5 (Summer 1965), pp. 118–33.

McDonagh, Don. "Notes on Recent Dance." *Artforum*, 11 (December 1972), pp. 48–52.

Rainer, Yvonne. "A Quasi Survey of Some 'Minimalist' Tendencies in the Quantitatively Minimal Dance Activity Midst the Plethora, Or an Analysis of Trio A," in Gregory Battcock, ed. *Minimal Art: A Critical Anthology.* New York: E. P. Dutton, 1968.

———. *Work: 1961–1973.* Halifax: The Press of the Nova Scotia College of Art and Design, 1974.

Tomkins, Calvin. "Profiles: An Appetite for Motion" (Merce Cunningham). *The New Yorker*, 44 (May 4, 1968), pp. 52–126.

Tulane Drama Review, 10 (Winter 1965). Special issue on dance, Fluxus, and Happenings; articles by Robert Morris and Claes Oldenburg.

Pop Art

Alloway, Lawrence. *American Pop Art* (exhibition catalogue). New York: Collier Books in association with the Whitney Museum of American Art, 1974.

———. "Pop Art: The Words" (1962), in *Topics in American Art Since 1945.* New York: W.W. Norton, 1975.

———. "Popular Culture and Pop Art." *Studio International*, 78 (July-August 1969), pp. 17–21.

Amayo, Mario. *Pop Art . . . And After.* New York: The Viking Press, 1966.

Art Gallery, University of California, Irvine. *New York: The Second Breakthrough, 1959–1964* (exhibition catalogue), 1969. Essay by Alan Solomon.

Art Gallery of Toronto, Ontario. *Dine, Oldenburg, Segal: Painting/Sculpture* (exhibition catalogue), 1967. Essays by Alan Solomon, Ellen H. Johnson, Robert Pincus-Witten. Unpublished manuscript in the Whitney Museum of American Art Library files of "The Toronto Symposium: Perishability, Pop Art, and the Happening: A New Look," organized and moderated by Brydon Smith with Jim Dine, Claes Oldenburg, and George Segal as participants, January 1967.

Art International, 7 (January 1963). Special issue on "The New Realism, Neo-Dada, Common Object Painting, etc."; articles by Barbara Rose, Pierre Restany, Sonya Rudikoff, Ellen H. Johnson, Allan Kaprow.

"Art: Something New Is Cooking." *Life*, 52 (June 15, 1962), pp. 115–20.

"Art: The Slice-of-Cake School." *Time*, 79 (May 11, 1962), p. 52.

Baldwin, Carl R. "On the Nature of Pop." *Artforum*, 12 (June 1974), pp. 34–38.

Bannard, Darby. "Present-Day Art and Ready-Made Styles in Which the Formal Contribution of Pop Art Is Found to be Negligible." *Artforum*, 5 (December 1966), pp. 30–35.

Canaday, John. "Pop Art Sells On and On—Why?" *The New York Times Magazine*, May 31, 1964, pp. 7, 48, 52–53.

Diamonstein, Barbaralee. *Inside New York's Art World.* New York: Rizzoli International Publications, 1979.

Finch, Christopher. *Pop Art: Object and Image.* London and New York: Studio Vista and E. P. Dutton, 1968.

F[rankfurter], A[lfred]. "Editorial: Pop Extremists." *Art News*, 63 (September 1964), pp. 19, 54–55.

Gablik, Suzi. "Protagonists of Pop." *Studio International*, 178 (July-August 1969), pp. 9–16.

Geldzahler, Henry, and Kenworth Moffett. "Pop Art: Two Views." *Art News*, 73 (May 1974), pp. 30–32.

Glaser, Bruce. "Oldenburg, Lichtenstein, Warhol: A Discussion." *Artforum*, 43 (February 1966), pp. 20–24. (Transcript of a radio interview originally broadcast on WBAI, New York, June 1964.) See also Bruce Glaser, "Letter to the Editor." *Artforum*, 4 (April 1966).

Gray, Cleve. "Art Centers: New York—Remburgers and Hambrandts." *Art in America*, 51 (December 1963), pp. 118–20, 123–29.

H[ess], T[homas] B. "Editorial: Pop and Public." *Art News*, 62 (November 1963), pp. 23, 59–60.

Irwin, David. "Pop Art and Surrealism." *Studio International*, 171 (May 1966), pp. 187–91.

Johnson, Ellen H. "The Image Duplicators—Lichtenstein, Rauschenberg and Warhol." *Canadian Art*, 23 (January 1966), pp. 12–19.

Karp, Ivan C. "Anti-Sensibility Painting." *Artforum*, 2, no. 3 (1963), pp. 26–27.

Kelly, Edward T. "Neo-Dada: A Critique of Pop Art." *Art Journal*, 23 (Spring 1964), pp. 192–201.

Kozloff, Max. "Art and the New York Avant-Garde." *Partisan Review*, 31 (Fall 1964), pp. 535–54.

———. "Dissimulated Pop." *The Nation*, 199 (November 30, 1964), pp. 417–19.

———. "The New American Painting: Post-Abstract-Expressionism—Mask and Reality," in Richard Kostelanetz, ed. *The New American Arts.* New York: Collier Books, 1967.

———. " 'Pop' Culture, Metaphysical Disgust, and the New Vulgarians." *Art International*, 6 (March 1962), pp. 34–36.

Kuspit, Donald B. "Pop Art: A Reactionary Realism." *Art Journal*, 36 (Fall 1976), pp. 31–38.

Lippard, Lucy R. *Pop Art.* With contributions by Lawrence Alloway, Nancy Marmer, Nicolas Calas. New York: Praeger Publishers, 1966.

Lucie-Smith, Edward. "Pop Art," in Nikos Stangos, ed. *Concepts of Modern Art*. New York: Harper & Row, 1981. Second edition.

Plagens, Peter. "Present-Day Styles and Ready-Made Criticism in Which the Formal Contribution of Pop Art Is Found to Be Minimal." *Artforum*, 5 (December 1966), pp. 36–39.

"Pop Art—Cult of the Commonplace." *Time*, 81 (May 3, 1963), pp. 69–72.

Reichardt, Jasia. "Pop Art and After." *Art International*, 7 (February 1963), pp. 42–47.

Richardson, John Adkins. "Dada, Camp, and the Mode Called Pop." *Journal of Aesthetics and Art Criticism*, 24 (Summer 1966), pp. 549–58.

Rosenblum, Robert. "Pop and Non-Pop: An Essay in Distinction." *Canadian Art*, 23 (January 1966), pp. 50–54.

Rublowsky, John. *Pop Art*. Photography by Ken Heyman. New York: Basic Books, 1965.

Russell, John, and Suzi Gablik. *Pop Art Redefined* (exhibition catalogue). London: Thames and Hudson, published in conjunction with an exhibition presented at the Hayward Gallery, 1969.

Saarinen, Aline B. "Explosion of Pop Art: A New Kind of Fine Art Imposing Poetic Order on the Mass-produced World." *Vogue*, 141 (April 15, 1963), pp. 86–87, 134, 136, 142.

Sandberg, John. "Some Traditional Aspects of Pop Art." *Art Journal*, 26 (Spring 1967), pp. 228–33, 245.

Sandler, Irving H. "New York Letter." *Quadrum*, 14(1963), pp. 117–20.

Seckler, Dorothy Gees. "The Artist in America: Folklore of the Banal." *Art in America*, 50 (Winter 1962), pp. 56–61.

Selz, Peter. "Special Supplement: A Symposium on Pop Art." *Arts Magazine*, 37 (April 1963), pp. 36–45.

"Sold Out Art: More Buyers Than Ever Sail in to a Broadening Market." *Life*, 55 (September 20, 1963), pp. 125–29.

Solomon, Alan R. "The New American Art." *Art International*, 8 (March 1964), pp. 50–55.

———. *New York: The New Art Scene*. Photographs by Ugo Mulas. New York: Holt, Rinehart and Winston, 1967.

Swenson, G[ene] R. "The New American 'Sign Painters.' " *Art News*, 61 (September 1962), pp. 44–47, 60–62.

———. "What Is Pop Art?, Part I: Jim Dine, Robert Indiana, Roy Lichtenstein, Andy Warhol." *Art News*, 62 (November 1963), pp. 24–27, 60–64.

———. "What Is Pop Art?, Part II: Stephen Durkee, Jasper Johns, James Rosenquist, Tom Wesselmann." *Art News*, 62 (February 1964), pp. 40–43, 62–67.

Tillim, Sidney. "Further Observations on the Pop Phenomenon: 'All Revolutions Have Their Ugly Aspects . . .' " *Artforum*, 4 (November 1965), pp. 17–19.

———. "Toward a Literary Revival?" *Arts Magazine*, 39 (May-June 1965), pp. 30–33.

Tuchman, Phyllis. "Pop! Interviews with George Segal, Andy Warhol, Roy Lichtenstein, James Rosenquist, and Robert Indiana." *Art News*, 73 (May 1974), pp. 24–29.

Minimalism

Battcock, Gregory, ed. *Minimal Art: A Critical Anthology*. New York: E. P. Dutton, 1968.

Blok, C. "Minimal Art at The Hague." *Art International*, 12 (May 1968), pp. 18–24.

Bochner, Mel. "Serial Art Systems: Solipsism." *Arts Magazine*, 41 (Summer 1967), pp. 39–43.

Burnham, Jack. "Systems Esthetics." *Artforum*, 7 (September 1968), pp. 30–35.

Danoff, I. Michael. *Emergence & Progression: Six Contemporary American Artists* (exhibition catalogue). The New Milwaukee Art Center, 1979.

Davis, Douglas M. "The Dimensions of the Miniarts." *Art in America*, 55 (November 1967), pp. 84–91.

Fried, Michael. "Art and Objecthood." *Artforum*, 5 (June 1967), pp. 12–23.

———. "Modernist Painting and the Formal Criticism." *The American Scholar*, 33 (Autumn 1964), pp. 642–48.

Gablik, Suzi. "Minimalism," in Nikos Stangos, ed. *Concepts of Modern Art*. New York: Harper & Row, 1981. Second edition.

Gemeentemuseum, The Hague. *Minimal Art* (exhibition catalogue), 1968. Essays by Enno Develing and Lucy R. Lippard; statements by some of the artists.

The Solomon R. Guggenheim Museum, New York. *Systemic Painting* (exhibition catalogue), 1966. Essay by Lawrence Alloway.

The Jewish Museum, New York. *Primary Structures: Younger American and British Sculptors* (exhibition catalogue), 1966. Essay by Kynaston McShine.

Judd, Donald. "Local History," in James R. Mellow, ed. *Arts Yearbook 7: New York: The Art World*. New York: The Art Digest, 1964.

———. "Specific Objects," in William Seitz, ed. *Arts Yearbook 8: Contemporary Sculpture*. New York: The Art Digest, 1965.

Kramer, Hilton. "Episodes from the Sixties." *Art in America*, 58 (January-February 1970), pp. 56–61.

Krauss, Rosalind E. *Passages in Modern Sculpture*. New York: The Viking Press, 1977.

Lippard, Lucy R. "Rejective Art." *Art International*, 10 (October 1966), pp. 33–37.

———, and John Chandler. "The Dematerialization of Art." *Art International*, 12 (February 1968), pp. 31–36.

Lucie-Smith, Edward. "Minimalism," in Tony Richardson and Nikos Stangos, eds. *Concepts of Modern Art*. New York: Harper & Row, 1974.

Morris, Robert. "Notes on Sculpture." *Artforum*, 4 (February 1966), pp. 42–44. "Notes on Sculpture, Part 2." *Artforum*, 5 (October 1966), pp. 20–23. "Notes on Sculpture, Part 3: Notes and Nonsequiturs." *Artforum*, 5 (Summer 1967), pp. 24–29. "Notes on Sculpture, Part 4: Beyond Objects." *Artforum*, 7 (April 1969), pp. 50–54.

The Museum of Modern Art, New York. *The Art of the Real: USA 1948–1968* (exhibition catalogue), 1968. Essay by E. C. Goossen. Greenwich, Connecticut: New York Graphic Society.

Perreault, John. "Union-Made: Report on a Phenomenon." *Artforum*, 5 (March 1967), pp. 26–31.

Pierce, James Smith. "Design and Expression in Minimal Art." *Art International*, 12 (May 1968), pp. 25–27.

Project Studios One, Institute for Art and Urban Resources, Inc., New York. *Abstract Painting: 1960–1969* (exhibition catalogue), 1982.

Rose, Barbara. "ABC Art." *Art in America*, 53 (October-November 1965), pp. 57–69.

———. *A New Aesthetic* (exhibition catalogue). Washington Gallery of Modern Art, 1967.

———. "Problems of Criticism, V: The Politics of Art, Part II." *Artforum*, 7 (January 1969), pp. 44–49.

———. "The Value of Didactic Art." *Artforum*, 5 (April 1967), pp. 32–36.

Sandler, Irving. "The New Cool-Art." *Art in America*, 53 (February 1965), pp. 96–101.

Solomon, Alan. "American Art Between Two Biennales." *Metro*, 11 (June 1966), pp. 24–35.

Studio International, 177 (April 1969). Special issue on Minimalism; articles and statements by Barbara Reise, Dan Flavin, Carl Andre, Donald Judd.

Tuchman, Maurice, ed. *American Sculpture of the Sixties* (exhibition catalogue). Essays by Lawrence Alloway, Wayne V. Anderson, Dore Ashton, John Coplans, Clement Greenberg, Max Kozloff, Lucy R. Lippard, James Monte, Barbara Rose, Irving Sandler; statements by some of the artists. Los Angeles County Museum of Art, 1967.

Tuchman, Phyllis. "Minimalism and Critical Response." *Artforum*, 15 (May 1977), pp. 26–31.

Wollheim, Richard. "Minimal Art." *Arts Magazine*, 39 (January 1965), pp. 26–32.

Film

The American Federation of Arts, New York. *A History of the American Avant-Garde Cinema* (exhibition catalogue), 1976.

Anger, Kenneth. *Magick Lantern Cycle: A Special Presentation in Celebration of the Equinox Spring 1966* (exhibition catalogue). New York: Film-Makers' Cinematheque, 1966.

———. *Hollywood Babylon*. San Francisco: Straight Arrow Books, by arrangement with The Stonehill Publishing Company, 1975.

Battcock, Gregory, ed. *The New American Cinema*. New York: E. P. Dutton, 1967.

Brakhage, Stan. "Metaphors on Vision." *Film Culture*, 30 (Autumn 1963).

———. *Brakhage Scrapbook: Collected Writings 1964–1980*. New Paltz, New York: Documentext, 1982. Edited by Robert A. Haller.

Carney, Raymond. *American Dreaming: The Films of John Cassavetes and the American Experience*. Berkeley: University of California Press, 1984.

Clark, Dan. *Brakhage*. Film-Makers' Cinematheque Monograph Series 2. New York: Film Culture, 1966.

Coplans, John, ed. *Andy Warhol*. Greenwich, Connecticut: New York Graphic Society, 1970.

Curtis, David. *Experimental Cinema*. New York: Universe Books, 1971.

Film Culture, 56–57 (Fall-Winter 1972–73). Articles on Breer.

Filmwise 1: Stan Brakhage. New York: Cinema 16 and Film-Makers' Cooperative, 1961. Issue devoted to Brakhage.

Filmwise 3 & 4: Markopoulos. New York: Cinema 16 and Film-Makers' Cooperative, 1963. Collection of articles on and by Markopoulos.

Gidal, Peter. *Andy Warhol: Films and Paintings*. New York: Dutton Picturebacks, 1971.

Gutman, Walter. *The Gutman Letters*. New York: Something Else Press, 1969.

Hitchens, Gordon. "Survey Among Unsuccessful Applicants for the Ford Foundation Film Grants," *Film Comment*, 2 (Summer 1964), pp. 10–32.

Hoberman, J. "The Short Happy Life of the Charles." *American Film*, 6 (March 1982), pp. 22, 34.

Jacobs, Lewis, ed. *The Documentary Tradition from "Nanook" to "Woodstock."* New York: Hopkinson and Blake, 1971.

Koch, Stephen. *Stargazer: Andy Warhol's World and His Films*. New York: Praeger Publishers, 1973.

LeGrice, Malcolm. *Abstract Film and Beyond*. Cambridge, Massachusetts: The MIT Press, 1977.

Levin, G. Roy, ed. *Documentary Exploration: 15 Interviews with Film-makers*. Garden City, New York: Doubleday, 1971.

Mamber, Stephen. *Cinema Verité in America: Studies in Uncontrolled Documentary*. Cambridge, Massachusetts: The MIT Press, 1974.

Mekas, Jonas. "Cinema of the New Generation." *Film Culture*, 21 (Summer 1960), pp. 1–20.

———. "Notes on the New American Cinema." *Film Culture*, 24 (Summer 1962), pp. 6–16.

———. *Movie Journal: The Rise of the New American Cinema, 1959–1971*. New York: Collier Books, 1972.

Renan, Sheldon. *An Introduction to the American Underground Film*. New York: E. P. Dutton, 1967.

Rice, Ron. "Diaries, Notebooks, Scripts, Letters, Documents." *Film Culture*, 39 (1965), pp. 87–125.

Riedel, Fred. "Interview with Ken Jacobs," in *Abstract Painting: 1960–1969* (exhibition catalogue). New York: Project Studios One, Institute for Art and Urban Resources, 1982, unpaginated.

Rowe, Carel. *The Baudelairean Cinema: A Trend within the American Avant-Garde*. Ann Arbor, Michigan: UMI Research Press, 1982.

Sitney, P. Adams. *Visionary Film: The American Avant-Garde*. New York: Oxford University Press, 1974.

———, ed. *Film Culture Reader*. New York: Praeger Publishers, 1970.

———, ed. *The Essential Cinema: Essays on Films in the Collection of Anthology Film Archives*. Anthology Film Archives Series 2, Volume One. New York: Anthology Film Archives and New York University Press, 1975.

———, ed. *The Avant-Garde Film: A Reader of Theory and Criticism*. New York: New York University Press, 1978.

Smith, Jack. "The Perfect Filmic Appositeness of Maria Montez." *Film Culture*, 27 (1962–63), pp. 28–32.

———. "Belated Appreciation of V.S." *Film Culture*, 31 (Winter 1963–64), pp. 4–5.

———. "The Memoirs of Maria Montez or Wait for Me at the Bottom of the Pool." *Film Culture*, 31 (Winter 1963–64), pp. 3–4.

Tomkins, Calvin. "Profile: All Pockets Open." *The New Yorker*, 48 (January 6, 1973), pp. 31–49. Profile of Jonas Mekas.

Tyler, Parker. *The Three Faces of the Film*. Cranbury, New Jersey: A. S. Barnes, 1967. Revised edition.

———. *Underground Film: A Critical History*. New York: Grove Press, 1969.

Vanderbeek, Stan. "The Cinema Delimina: Films from the Underground." *Film Quarterly*, 14 (Summer 1961), pp. 5–15.

Walker Art Center, Minneapolis. *The American New Wave, 1958–1967* (exhibition catalogue), 1982. Edited by Bruce Jenkins and Melinda Ward.

Warhol, Andy, and Pat Hackett. *Popism: The Warhol '60s*. New York: Harcourt Brace Jovanovich, 1980.

Youngblood, Gene. *Expanded Cinema*. New York: E. P. Dutton, 1970.

Selected Artists

Carl Andre

Bourdon, David. *Carl Andre: Sculpture 1959–1977* (exhibition catalogue). Foreword by Barbara Rose. New York: Jaap Rietman, 1978.

Buchloh, Benjamin H. D., ed. *Carl Andre, Hollis Frampton: 12 Dialogues, 1962–1963.* Photographs by Hollis Frampton. Halifax: The Press of the Nova Scotia College of Art and Design, and New York: New York University Press, 1981.

Develing, Enno. "Carl Andre: Art as a Social Fact." *Artscanada*, 27 (December 1970–January 1971), pp. 47–49.

The Solomon R. Guggenheim Museum, New York. *Carl Andre* (exhibition catalogue), 1970. Compiled by Diane Waldman.

Stedelijk Van Abbemuseum, Eindhoven, Netherlands. *Carl Andre: Wood*, 1978. Preface by R. H. Fuchs; statement by the artist.

Tuchman, Phyllis. "An Interview with Carl Andre." *Artforum*, 8 (June 1970), pp. 55–61.

George Brecht

Brecht, George. *Chance-Imagery*. New York: Something Else Press, 1966. Text originally written in 1957.

Martin, Henry. "An Interview with George Brecht." *Art International*, 11 (November 1967), pp. 20–24.

———, ed. *An Introduction to George Brecht's Book of the Tumbler on Fire.* With an anthology of texts by and interviews with the artist. Milan: Multhipla Edizioni, 1978.

Nyman, Michael. "George Brecht." *Studio International*, 192 (November-December 1976), pp. 256–66.

Onnasch Gallery, New York. *George Brecht: Works 1957–1973* (exhibition catalogue), 1974.

Van der Marck, Jan. "George Brecht: An Art of Multiple Implications." *Art in America*, 62 (July-August 1974), pp. 48–57.

Walter De Maria

"Art: Sculpture—High Priest of Danger." *Time*, 93 (May 2, 1969), p. 54.

Bourdon, David. "Walter De Maria: The Singular Experience." *Art International*, 12 (December 1968), pp. 39–43, 72.

Hessisches Landesmuseum, Darmstadt, West Germany. *Walter De Maria: Der grosse Erdraum: 8 Skulpturen, 44 Zeichnungen* (exhibition catalogue), 1974.

Kunstmuseum Basel. *Walter De Maria: Skulpturen* (exhibition catalogue), 1972.

Jim Dine

Calas, Nicolas. "Jim Dine: Tools & Myth." *Metro*, 7 (December 1962), pp. 76–77.

Gordon, John. *Jim Dine* (exhibition catalogue). New York: Whitney Museum of American Art and Praeger Publishers, 1970.

Gruen, John. "Jim Dine and the Life of Objects." *Art News*, 76 (September 1977), pp. 38–42.

Johnson, Ellen H. "Jim Dine and Jasper Johns: Art About Art." *Art and Literature*, 6 (Autumn 1965), pp. 128–40.

Kozloff, Max. "The Honest Elusiveness of James Dine." *Artforum*, 3 (December 1964), pp. 36–40.

Shapiro, David. *Jim Dine: Painting What One Is.* New York: Harry N. Abrams, 1981.

Smith, Brydon. "Jim Dine—Magic and Reality." *Canadian Art*, 23 (January 1966), pp. 30–34.

Solomon, Alan R. "Jim Dine and the Psychology of the New Art." *Art International*, 8 (October 1964), pp. 52–56.

Dan Flavin

Baker, Elizabeth C. "The Light Brigade." Photographs by Ferdinand Boesch. *Art News*, 66 (March 1967), pp. 52–55, 63–66.

The National Gallery of Canada, Ottawa. *Dan Flavin, fluorescent light, etc. from Dan Flavin* (exhibition catalogue), 1969. Catalogue by Brydon Smith; essays by Mel Bochner, Don Judd, and the artist.

Wallraf-Richartz-Museum and Kunsthalle Köln, Cologne. *Dan Flavin: Three installations in fluorescent light* (exhibition catalogue), 1973. Catalogue by Evelyn Weiss, Dieter Ronte, Manfred Schneckenburger; writings by the artist.

Red Grooms

Allan Frumkin Gallery, New York. *Red Grooms: The Early Sixties* (exhibition catalogue), 1983.

Glueck, Grace. "Odd Man Out: Red Grooms, the Ruckus Kid." *Art News*, 72 (December 1973), pp. 23–27.

Tully, Judd. *Red Grooms and Ruckus Manhattan.* New York: George Braziller, 1977.

Jasper Johns

Alloway, Lawrence. "The Man Who Liked Cats: The Evolution of Jasper Johns." *Arts Magazine*, 44 (September-October 1969), pp. 40–43.

Crichton, Michael. *Jasper Johns* (exhibition catalogue). New York: Harry N. Abrams, in association with the Whitney Museum of American Art, 1977.

Hopps, Walter. "An Interview with Jasper Johns." *Artforum*, 3 (March 1965), pp. 32–36.

Kozloff, Max. *Jasper Johns.* New York: Harry N. Abrams, 1969.

Rose, Barbara. "Decoys and Doubles: Jasper Johns and the Modernist Mind." *Arts Magazine*, 50 (May 1976), pp. 68–73.

Rosenblum, Robert. "Jasper Johns." *Art International*, 4 (September 1960), pp. 74–77.

Steinberg, Leo. "Jasper Johns" (1962), revised and expanded as "Jasper Johns: The First Seven Years of His Art," in *Other Criteria: Confrontations with Twentieth-Century Art.* New York: Oxford University Press, 1972.

Donald Judd

Agee, William C. *Don Judd* (exhibition catalogue). New York: Whitney Museum of American Art, 1968.

———. "Unit, Series, Site: A Judd Lexicon." *Art in America*, 63 (May-June 1975), pp. 40–50.

Coplans, John. *Don Judd* (exhibition catalogue). Pasadena Art Museum, 1971.

Glaser, Bruce. "Questions to Stella and Judd." Edited by Lucy Lippard. *Art News*, 65 (September 1966), pp. 55–61.

Judd, Donald. *Complete Writings, 1959–1975: Gallery Reviews, Book Reviews, Articles, Letters to the Editor, Reports, Statements, Complaints.* Halifax: The Press of the Nova Scotia College of Art and Design, and New York: New York University Press, 1975.

Muller, Gregoire. "Donald Judd: Ten Years." *Arts Magazine*, 48 (February 1973), pp. 35–42.

The National Gallery of Canada, Ottawa. *Don Judd* (exhibition catalogue), 1975. Compiled by Brydon Smith; essay by Roberta Smith.

Knight Gallery/Spirit Square Arts Center, Charlotte, North Carolina. *Donald Judd: Eight Works in Three Dimensions* (exhibition catalogue), 1984. Compiled by Brian Wallis.

Allan Kaprow

Alloway, Lawrence. "Allan Kaprow, Two Views," in *Topics in American Art Since 1945*. New York: W. W. Norton, 1975.

Kaprow, Allan. "Should the Artist Become a Man of the World?" *Art News*, 63 (October 1964), pp. 34–37, 58. See rebuttal by T[homas] B. H[ess]. "Editorial: The Artist as a Company Man," ibid., p. 19; and Allan Kaprow, "Editor's Letters." *Art News*, 63 (December 1964), p. 6.

Pasadena Art Museum. *Allan Kaprow* (exhibition catalogue), 1969.

Sandler, Irving. "In the Art Galleries." *New York Post*, June 16, 1963, section 2, p. 14. Interview with Allan Kaprow.

Roy Lichtenstein

Alloway, Lawrence. "On Style: An Examination of Roy Lichtenstein's Development, Despite a New Monograph on the Artist." *Artforum*, 10 (March 1972), pp. 53–59.

———. *Roy Lichtenstein*. New York: Abbeville Press, 1983.

Boatto, Albert, and Giordano Falzoni, eds. *Lichtenstein*. Collection of essays comprising *Fantazaria*, 1 (July-August 1966).

Boime, Albert. "Roy Lichtenstein and the Comic Strip." *Art Journal*, 28 (Winter 1968–69), pp. 155–59.

Coplans, John, ed. *Roy Lichtenstein*. New York: Praeger Publishers, 1972.

Lichtenstein, Roy. Talk presented at the College Art Association annual meeting, Philadelphia, 1964. Published in Ellen H. Johnson, ed. *American Artists on Art from 1940 to 1980*. New York: Harper & Row, 1982.

Loran, Erle. "Cézanne and Lichtenstein: Problems of Transformation." *Artforum*, 2 (September 1963), pp. 34–35. See reply by Max Kozloff. "Art." *The Nation*, 197 (November 2, 1963), pp. 284–87.

———. "Pop Artist or Copy Cats?" *Art News*, 62 (September 1963), pp. 48–49, 61.

Pasadena Art Museum, and the Walker Art Center, Minneapolis. *Roy Lichtenstein* (exhibition catalogue), 1967. Essay by John Coplans.

The Tate Gallery, London. *Roy Lichtenstein* (exhibition catalogue), 1968. Interviews by Gene R. Swenson and John Coplans; essay by Richard Morphet.

Waldman, Diane. *Roy Lichtenstein* (exhibition catalogue). New York: The Solomon R. Guggenheim Museum, 1969.

———. *Roy Lichtenstein*. Milan: Gabriele Mazzotta Editore, 1971.

Robert Morris

Antin, David. "Art & Information, 1: Grey Paint, Robert Morris." *Art News*, 65 (April 1966), pp. 22–24, 56–58.

Compton, Michael, and David Sylvester. *Robert Morris* (exhibition catalogue). London: The Tate Gallery, 1971.

The Corcoran Gallery of Art, Washington, D.C., and The Detroit Institute of Arts. *Robert Morris* (exhibition catalogue), 1969. Essay by Annette Michelson.

Friedman, Martin. "Robert Morris: Polemics and Cubes." *Art International*, 10 (December 1966), pp. 23–27.

Tucker, Marcia. *Robert Morris* (exhibition catalogue). New York: Whitney Museum of American Art, and Praeger Publishers, 1970.

Claes Oldenburg

"Claes Oldenburg: Extracts from the Studio Notes (1962–64)." *Artforum*, 4 (January 1966), pp. 32–33.

Johnson, Ellen H. *Claes Oldenburg*. Baltimore: Penguin Books, 1971.

———. "The Living Object." *Art International*, 7 (January 25, 1963), pp. 42–45.

Oldenburg, Claes. *Injun & Other Histories (1960)*. New York: Something Else Press, 1966.

———. *Raw Notes: Documents and Scripts of the Performances: Stars, Moveyhouse, Massage, The Typewriter*. With annotations by the author. Halifax: The Press of the Nova Scotia College of Art and Design, 1973.

Rose, Barbara. *Claes Oldenburg* (exhibition catalogue). New York: The Museum of Modern Art, and Greenwich, Connecticut: New York Graphic Society, 1970.

Store Days: Documents from The Store (1961) and Ray Gun Theater (1962). Selected by Claes Oldenburg and Emmett Williams. Photographs by Robert R. McElroy. New York: Something Else Press, 1967.

Van Bruggen, Coosje. *Claes Oldenburg: Mouse Museum/Ray Gun Wing*. Translated by Machteld Schrameijer. Cologne: Museum Ludwig, 1979.

Robert Rauschenberg

Cage, John. "On Robert Rauschenberg, Artist, and His Work." *Metro*, 2 (May 1961), pp. 36–51.

Forge, Andrew. *Rauschenberg*. New York: Harry N. Abrams (c. 1972). Autobiography by the artist. Revised edition.

Fort Worth Art Center Museum, Fort Worth. *Robert Rauschenberg: Selections* (exhibition catalogue), 1969.

Krauss, Rosalind. "Rauschenberg and the Materialized Image." *Artforum*, 13 (December 1974), pp. 36–43.

National Collection of Fine Arts, Smithsonian Institution, Washington, D.C. *Robert Rauschenberg* (exhibition catalogue), 1976. Essay by Lawrence Alloway.

Seckler, Dorothy. "The Artist Speaks: Robert Rauschenberg." *Art in America*, 54 (May-June 1966), pp. 72–84.

Tomkins, Calvin. *The Bride & The Bachelors: The Heretical Courtship in Modern Art*. New York: The Viking Press, 1965.

———. *Off the Wall: Robert Rauschenberg and the Art World of Our Time*. Garden City, New York: Doubleday, 1980.

James Rosenquist

Alloway, Lawrence. "Derealized Epic." *Artforum*, 10 (June 1972), pp. 35–41.

Geldzahler, Henry. "James Rosenquist's F-111." *The Metro-politan Museum of Art Bulletin*, 26 (March 1968), pp. 277–81.

Lippard, Lucy R. "James Rosenquist: Aspects of a Multiple Art." *Artforum*, 4 (December 1965), pp. 41–45.

Pincus-Witten, Robert. "Rosenquist and Samaras: The Obsessive Image and Post-Minimalism." *Artforum*, 11 (September 1972), pp. 63–69.

Siegel, Jeanne. "An Interview with James Rosenquist." *Artforum*, 10 (June 1972), pp. 30–34.

Swenson, Gene R. "The F-111: An Interview with James Rosenquist." *Partisan Review*, 32 (Fall 1965), pp. 589–601.

Tucker, Marcia. *James Rosenquist* (exhibition catalogue). New York: Whitney Museum of American Art, 1972.

Lucas Samaras

Alloway, Lawrence. *Samaras: Selected Works 1960–1966* (exhibition catalogue). New York: The Pace Gallery, 1966.

Levin, Kim. *Lucas Samaras*. New York: Harry N. Abrams, 1975.

Solomon, Alan. "An Interview with Lucas Samaras." *Artforum*, 5 (October 1966), pp. 39–44.

Samaras, Lucas. *Lucas Samaras* (exhibition catalogue). New York: Whitney Museum of American Art, 1973.

George Segal

Friedman, Martin, and Graham W. J. Beal. *George Segal: Sculptures* (exhibition catalogue). Minneapolis: Walker Art Center, 1978.

Geldzahler, Henry. "An Interview with George Segal." *Artforum*, 3 (November 1964), pp. 26–29.

Johnson, Ellen H. "The Sculpture of George Segal." *Art International*, 8 (March 1964), pp. 46–49.

Kaprow, Allan. "Segal's Vital Mummies." *Art News*, 62 (February 1964), pp. 30–33, 65.

Seitz, William C. *Segal*. New York: Harry N. Abrams, 1972.

Tuchman, Phyllis. *George Segal*. New York: Abbeville Press, 1983.

———. "Interview with George Segal." *Art in America*, 60 (May-June 1972), pp. 74–81.

Van der Marck, Jan. *George Segal*. New York: Harry N. Abrams, 1975.

Frank Stella

Fried, Michael. *Three American Painters: Kenneth Noland, Jules Olitski, Frank Stella* (exhibition catalogue). Cambridge, Massachusetts: Fogg Art Museum, Harvard University, 1965.

Glaser, Bruce. "Questions to Stella and Judd." Edited by Lucy Lippard. *Art News*, 65 (September 1966), pp. 55–61.

Leider, Philip. "Literalism and Abstraction: Frank Stella's Retrospective at the Modern." *Artforum*, 8 (April 1970), pp. 44–51.

Richardson, Brenda, with the assistance of Mary Martha Ward. *Frank Stella: The Black Paintings* (exhibition catalogue). Baltimore: The Baltimore Museum of Art, 1976.

Rosenblum, Robert. *Frank Stella*. Baltimore: Penguin Books, 1971.

———. "Frank Stella: Five Years of Variations of an 'Irreducible' Theme." *Artforum*, 3 (March 1965), pp. 21–25.

Rubin, William. *Frank Stella* (exhibition catalogue). New York: The Museum of Modern Art, and Greenwich, Connecticut: New York Graphic Society, 1970.

Andy Warhol

Andy Warhol. With contributions by Jonas Mekas and Calvin Tomkins. Greenwich, Connecticut: New York Graphic Society, 1970.

———. "Andy Warhol and Elvis Presley." *Studio International*, 181 (February 1971), pp. 49–56.

———. "Early Work: The Systematic Evolution of the Impersonal Style." *Artforum*, 8 (March 1970), pp. 52–59.

Crone, Rainer. *Andy Warhol*. Translated by John William Gabriel. New York: Praeger Publishers, 1970.

Geldzahler, Henry. "Andy Warhol." *Art International*, 8 (April 1964), pp. 34–35.

Gotham Book Mart Gallery, New York. *Andy Warhol: His Early Works, 1947–1959* (exhibition catalogue). Compiled by Andrea Brown.

Ratcliff, Carter. *Andy Warhol*. New York: Abbeville Press, 1983.

Tom Wesselmann

Glenn, Constance. *Tom Wesselmann: The Early Years, Collages 1959–1962* (exhibition catalogue). Long Beach, California: The Art Galleries, California State University, 1974.

Newport Harbor Art Museum, Balboa, California, and The Nelson Gallery-Atkins Museum, Kansas City. *Tom Wesselmann: Early Still Lifes, 1962–1964* (exhibition catalogue), 1970. Introduction by Thomas H. Garver.

Stealingworth, Slim [Tom Wesselmann]. *Tom Wesselmann*. New York: Abbeville Press, 1980.

Robert Whitman

The Hudson River Museum, Yonkers, New York. *Palisade: Robert Whitman* (exhibition catalogue), 1979. Compiled by Billy Klüver and Julie Marten; interview with the artist by Barbara Rose.

Segal, George. "On Whitman and Things." *Arts Magazine*, 47 (November 1972), pp. 53–55.

WORKS IN THE EXHIBITION

Paintings and sculptures are listed alphabetically by artist. Dimensions are given first in inches, then in centimeters; height precedes width precedes depth. A section on Fluxus material appears at the end without dimensions owing to the largely textual nature of the works.

Carl Andre (b. 1935)

Last Ladder, 1959
Wood, 84¼ × 6⅛ × 6⅛ (214 × 15.6 × 15.6)
The Tate Gallery, London

Pyramid (1959), reconstruction 1970
Wood, 68⅞ × 31 (174.9 × 78.7)
Dallas Museum of Fine Arts

George Brecht (b. 1926)

Repository, 1961
Mixed media assemblage, 40⅜ × 10½ × 3⅛
(102.6 × 26.7 × 7.9)
The Museum of Modern Art, New York;
 Larry Aldrich Foundation Fund

Iced Dice, realization of word event "chair"
(1961), reconstruction 1984
White wicker rocking chair, approximately
 48 × 36 (121.9 × 91.4)
Original destroyed; reconstructed for exhibition at the Whitney Museum of American
 Art

Clothes Tree (c. 1963), reconstruction 1984
Painted clothes tree with three hats, one coat,
 and two umbrellas, 72 × 27 × 29½
 (182.9 × 68.6 × 74.9)
Collection of Reinhard Onnasch; reconstructed for exhibition at the Whitney
 Museum of American Art

Walter De Maria (b. 1935)

Column with Ball, 1961
Wood: column, 96 × 12 × 12 (243.8
 × 30.5 × 30.5); ball, 2 diameter (5.1)
Collection of the artist

Rope Box, 1961
Wood box and rope: 60 × 24 × 6¼
 (152.4 × 61 × 15.9); inscribed in pencil
 near the top of the box, PULL ROPE TO
 LENGTH DESIRED
Private collection

Statue of John Cage (1962), reconstruction 1984
Plywood and wood dowels: base, 14½ × 14½
 (36.8 × 36.8); column,
 84 high (213.4)
Collection of the artist

Walls in the Desert, 1964
Graphite and colored pencil on paper,
 18¼ × 85¾ (47.6 × 217.8) framed; each of
 six drawings, 9 × 11⅝ (22.9 × 29.5)
Private collection

Jim Dine (b. 1935)

Green Suit, 1959
Oil and cloth, 62 × 24 (157.5 × 61)
Collection of the artist, courtesy The Pace
 Gallery, New York

Head (Hiding Face), 1959
Oil and pasted cloth collage on gesso board,
 26⅜ × 23 (67 × 58.4)
The Metropolitan Museum of Art, New York;
 Gift of Stanley Posthorn

Bedspring, 1960
Mixed media construction, 48 × 72 × 8
 (121.9 × 182.9 × 20.3)
Collection of Allan Kaprow and Vaughan
 Rachel

Shoe, 1961
Oil on canvas, 64 × 51½ (162.6 × 130.8)
Private collection

Black Zipper, 1962
Oil and mixed media on canvas, 96 × 72
 (243.8 × 182.9)
Collection of Ileana and Michael Sonnabend;
 on indefinite loan to The Baltimore
 Museum of Art

Double Isometric Self-Portrait (Serape), 1964
Oil with objects on canvas, 56⅞ × 84⅛
 (144.5 × 213.7)
Whitney Museum of American Art, New
 York; Gift of Helen W. Benjamin in
 memory of her husband, Robert M.
 Benjamin   76.35

Martha Edelheit (b. 1933)

Frabjous Day, 1959
Canvas, sheet aluminum, oil, and collage,
 58½ × 51½ (148.6 × 130.8)
Collection of the artist

Dan Flavin (b. 1933)

Apollinaire wounded (to Ward Jackson),
 1959–60
Crushed can, oil, pencil, on masonite, and
 plaster on pine, 12⅞ × 19⅜ × ⅞
 (32.7 × 49 × 2.3)
Collection of the artist

Gus Schultze's screwdriver (to Dick Bellamy),
 1960
Screwdriver, oil, pencil, on masonite, and
 acrylic on balsa, 15⅜ × 17½ × 1¾
 (39.1 × 44.5 × 4.5)
Collection of the artist

*icon IV (the pure land) (to David John Flavin
 [1933–1962])*, 1962
Formica and daylight fluorescent light,
 45½ × 45½ × 11⅛ (115.5 × 115.5 × 28.2)
The National Gallery of Canada, Ottawa

icon V (Coran's Broadway Flesh), 1962
Oil on masonite, porcelain receptacles, clear
 incandescent candle bulbs,
 42⅛ × 42⅛ × 9⅞ (107 × 107 × 25.2)
Collection of Heiner Friedrich

the nominal three (to William of Ockham),
 1963–64
Cool white fluorescent light, three units
 each, 96 high (244)
The National Gallery of Canada, Ottawa; reconstructed by the artist for exhibition at
 the Whitney Museum of American Art

Red Grooms (b. 1937)

Elephant, 1959
Oil on canvas, 54¼ × 48 (137.8 × 121.9)
Collection of Anita Simmons

Policewoman, 1959
Wood and metal, 45 × 29 × 10
 (114.3 × 73.7 × 24.5)
David K. Anderson Gallery, New York

Set for *The Burning Building* (Happening)
 (1959), reconstruction 1984
Mixed media; first presented at the Delancey
 Street Museum, New York
Collection of the artist

Jasper Johns (b. 1930)

Target with Plaster Casts, 1955
Encaustic and collage on canvas with objects,
 51 × 44 × 3½ (129.5 × 111.8 × 8.9)
Collection of Mr. and Mrs. Leo Castelli

White Flag, 1955–58
Encaustic and newsprint on canvas,
 52¼ × 78¾ (132.7 × 200)
Collection of Mr. and Mrs. Burton G.
 Tremaine

Gray Rectangles, 1957
Encaustic on canvas, 60⅛ × 60⅛
 (152.7 × 152.7)
Collection of Mr. and Mrs. Victor W. Ganz

Flag on Orange Field II, 1958
Encaustic on canvas, 54 × 36¼ (137.2 × 87)
Collection of Robert and Jane Rosenblum

Donald Judd (b. 1928)

Untitled, 1962
Light cadmium red oil on Liquitex, sand on
 masonite with yellow Plexiglas,
 48 × 96 × 2½ (121.9 × 243.8 × 6.4)
Private collection

Untitled, 1963
Light cadmium red oil on wood, purple
 enamel on aluminum, 48 × 83 × 48
 (122 × 210.8 × 122)
The National Gallery of Canada, Ottawa

Untitled, 1963
Light cadmium red oil on wood with
 metal lathe, 72 × 104 × 49
 (183 × 264.2 × 124.5)
The National Gallery of Canada, Ottawa

Untitled, 1963
Light cadmium red oil on wood,
 19½ × 45 × 30½ (49.5 × 114.3 × 77.5)
The National Gallery of Canada, Ottawa

Untitled, 1964
Turquoise pebbled Plexiglas and hot-rolled
 steel, 20 × 45 × 31 (50.8 × 115.2 × 78.7)
Private collection

Allan Kaprow (b. 1927)

Yard (1961), reconstruction 1984
Mixed media environment; first presented at
 the Martha Jackson Gallery, New York
Reconstructed by the artist for exhibition at
 the Whitney Museum of American Art

Words (1962), reconstruction 1984
Mixed media environment; first presented at
 the Smolin Gallery, New York
Reconstructed by the artist for exhibition at
 the Whitney Museum of American Art

Yayoi Kusama (b. 1929)

Accumulation No. 1, 1962
Paint on canvas stuffed with cotton batting,
 40 × 43 × 43 (101.6 × 109.2 × 109.2)
Collection of Mr. and Mrs. Hart Perry

No. B, 3, 1962
Eggcrates and upholstery stuffing, 78 × 70
 (198.1 × 177.8)
Collection of Mr. and Mrs. Hart Perry

Roy Lichtenstein (b. 1923)

Bugs Bunny, 1958
India ink on paper, 20 × 26 (50.8 × 66)
Collection of the artist

Mickey Mouse, 1958
India ink and pastel on paper, 19 × 25
(48.2 × 63.5)
Collection of the artist

Emeralds, 1961
Oil on canvas, 67⅝ × 67⅜ (171.8 × 171.1)
Private collection

Washing Machine, 1961
Oil on canvas, 56½ × 68½ (143.5 × 174)
Collection of Richard Brown Baker

Blam, 1962
Oil on canvas, 68 × 80 (172.7 × 203.2)
Collection of Richard Brown Baker; on loan
  to the Yale University Art Gallery, New
  Haven

Masterpiece, 1962
Oil on canvas, 54 × 54 (137.2 × 137.2)
Collection of Agnes Gund

Kiss with Cloud, 1964
Oil and magna on canvas, 60 × 60
(152.4 × 152.4)
Collection of Irving Blum

Robert Morris (b. 1931)

Column (1961), reconstruction 1984
Painted plywood, 192 × 24 × 24
(487.7 × 61 × 61)
Collection of the artist

I-Box, 1962
Mixed media construction, 19 × 12¾ × 1⅜
(48.3 × 32.4 × 3.5)
Collection of Mr. and Mrs. Leo Castelli

Metered Bulb, 1963
Mixed media construction, 17¾ × 8⅛ × 8¼
(45.1 × 20.6 × 21)
Collection of Jasper Johns

Corner Piece (1964), reconstruction 1984
Painted plywood, 78 × 108 (198.1 × 274.3)
Reconstructed for exhibition at the Whitney
  Museum of American Art

Claes Oldenburg (b. 1929)

Woman's Leg, 1959
Newspaper soaked in wheat paste over wire
  frame, painted with casein,
  38½ × 16½ × 10 (97.8 × 41.9 × 25.4)
Collection of Raymond Saroff

Light Switches—Hard Version, 1964
Painted wood, formica, metal,
  47¾ × 47¾ × 11¾ (121.3 × 121.3 × 29.8)
Private collection

Works from **The Street,** *first presented
at the Judson Gallery, Judson Memorial
Church, New York, 1960; later presented at the Reuben Gallery, New
York, 1961:*

Big Man (Big Guy), 1960
Corrugated cardboard, wood, newspaper,
  twine, painted with casein, 185 high (469.9)
Museum Ludwig, Ludwig Collection, Cologne

Car, 1960
Corrugated cardboard, painted with casein
  and spray enamel, 13½ × 30½ × 7½
  (34.3 × 77.5 × 19.1)
Museum Ludwig, Ludwig Collection, Cologne

Car (Wall Piece), 1960
Corrugated cardboard, painted with casein
  and spray enamel, 12½ × 22 (31.8 × 55.9)
Museum Ludwig, Ludwig Collection, Cologne

Fire from a Window, 1960
Paper, wood, painted with casein,
  15½ × 10½ × 4 (39.4 × 26.7 × 10.2)
Museum Ludwig, Ludwig Collection, Cologne

*MUG (Hanging Figure in the Shape of a
  Mug)*, 1960
Corrugated cardboard on wood, painted with
  casein and spray enamel, 76 × 50
  (193 × 127)
Museum Ludwig, Ludwig Collection, Cologne

Street Chick, 1960
Cardboard and wood, painted with casein,
  35 high (88.9); base, 7 × 15½ (17.8 × 39.4)
Museum Ludwig, Ludwig Collection, Cologne

Street Head (Profile with Hat), 1960
Burlap bag filled with newspaper, painted
  with casein, 76 × 46 (193 × 116.8)
Museum Ludwig, Ludwig Collection, Cologne

Street Sign, 1960
Corrugated cardboard, painted with casein,
  106 × 41 (269.2 × 104.1)
Museum Ludwig, Ludwig Collection, Cologne

Street Sign (1960), reconstruction (with altera-
  tions) 1984
Corrugated cardboard, painted with casein,
  72 × 42 (182.9 × 106.7)
Collection of the artist

Three Street Figures, 1960
Corrugated paper, wood, twine, wire, painted
  with casein, each approximately
  100 high (254)
Museum Ludwig, Ludwig Collection, Cologne

Works from **The Store,** *first included in
"Environments, Situations, Spaces" at
the Martha Jackson Gallery, 1961; later
presented at The Store, 107 East Second
Street, New York, 1961–62, and at the
Green Gallery, New York, 1962:*

Air Mail Letter, 1961
Painted plaster, 9⅞ × 5⅞ × 9⅞
  (25.1 × 14.9 × 25.1)
Collection of Marcia Marcus

Black Girdle, 1961
Painted plaster, 46½ × 40 × 4
  (118.1 × 101.6 × 10.7)
Whitney Museum of American Art, New
  York; Promised Gift of Howard and Jean
  Lipman   P.54.80

Black Ladies' Shoes, 1961
Muslin soaked in plaster over wire frame,
  painted with enamel, 5⅛ × 10⅝ × 3
  (13 × 27 × 7.6)
Collection of William J. Hokin

Blue Hat, 1961
Muslin soaked in plaster over wire frame,
  painted with enamel, 8¾ × 12 × 6
  (22.2 × 30.5 × 15.2)
Private collection

Bowties, 1961
Muslin soaked in plaster over wire frame,
  painted with enamel, 18 × 20 (45.7 × 50.8)
Collection of Mr. and Mrs. Ronald K.
  Greenberg

Bunting, 1961
Muslin soaked in plaster over wire frame,
  painted with enamel, 22 × 33⅞ × 4⅜
  (55.9 × 86 × 11.1)
Collection of the artist

Candy Counter with Candy, 1961
Enamel paint on plaster in a painted sheet
  steel and wood case, 11½ × 34¾ × 21¾
  (29.2 × 88.3 × 55.2)
Collection of William J. Hokin

Cash Register, 1961
Muslin soaked in plaster over wire frame,
  painted with enamel, 25 × 21 × 34
  (63.5 × 53.3 × 86.4)
Private collection

Cherry Pastry, 1961
Muslin soaked in plaster over wire frame,
  painted with enamel on separate red saucer,
  2½ × 2 × 5½ (6.4 × 5.1 × 14); saucer,
  8 diameter (20.3)
Collection of Robert H. Halff

Decimal Point of 9.99, 1961
Muslin soaked in plaster over wire frame,
  painted with enamel, 6¼ diameter (15.9)
Collection of the artist

Four Pies in a Glass Case, 1961
Enamel on plaster pies in painted metal and
  glass case, 5¼ × 30 × 9
  (13.3 × 76.2 × 22.9)
Collection of Robert K. Hoffman

Girl on Calendar, 1961
Painted plaster, 21 × 14 (53.3 × 35.6)
Collection of William J. Hokin

Half Cheese Cake, 1961
Muslin soaked in plaster over wire frame,
  painted with enamel, 10 × 32 × 16
  (25.4 × 81.3 × 40.6)
Collection of the artist

Ice Cream Cone and Heel, 1961
Muslin soaked in plaster over wire frame,
  painted with enamel, 22½ × 22½
  (57.2 × 57.2)
Collection of Margo Leavin

Injun Souvenir, 1961
Burlap soaked in plaster, painted with
  enamel, 8½ high (21.6)
Collection of Arthur and Carol Goldberg

Jacket and Shirt Fragment, 1961
Muslin soaked in plaster over wire frame,
  painted with enamel, 42⅛ × 30 × 6½
  (107 × 76.2 × 16.5)
Collection of the artist

Liver Sausage with Slices, 1961
Burlap soaked in plaster, painted with en-
  amel, 5 × 10 × 12 (12.7 × 25.4 × 30.4)
Collection of Mr. and Mrs. David K.
  Anderson

Lucky Strike Pack, 1961
Plaster and enamel on wood base, 5 × 3 × 1
  (12.7 × 7.6 × 2.5)
Collection of William J. Hokin

Match Cover, 1961
Muslin soaked in plaster over wire frame,
  painted with enamel, 4 × 2¾ × 1⅛
  (10.2 × 7 × 2.9)
Collection of the artist

Orange and Glass, 1961
Muslin soaked in plaster over wire frame,
  painted with enamel, 16¼ × 14 × 14
  (41.3 × 35.6 × 35.6)
Collection of Mr. and Mrs. David K.
  Anderson

Pile of Toast, 1961
Muslin soaked in plaster over wire frame,
  painted with enamel, 9 × 4 (22.8 × 10.2)
Collection of the artist

Pink Cap, 1961
Muslin soaked in plaster over wire frame,
  painted with enamel, 37 × 38½ × 11⅞
  (94 × 97.8 × 30.2)
Collection of the artist

Red Tights with Fragment 9, 1961
Muslin soaked in plaster over wire frame,
  painted with enamel, 69⅝ × 34¼ × 8¾
  (176.7 × 87 × 22.2)
The Museum of Modern Art, New York; Gift
  of G. David Thompson

Roast Beef, 1961
Muslin soaked in plaster over wire frame, painted with enamel, 14 × 17 × 16 (35.6 × 43.2 × 40.6)
Collection of Ileana and Michael Sonnabend

Sandwich, 1961
Muslin soaked in plaster over wire frame, painted with enamel, 2¼ × 6 × 5½ (5.7 × 15.2 × 14); base, ½ × 5¾ × 5 (1.3 × 14.6 × 12.7)
Collection of Margo Leavin

Sardine Can with Two Sardines on Paper Bag, 1961
Burlap soaked in plaster, painted with enamel, 3½ × 14 × 10 (6.4 × 35.6 × 25.4)
Collection of William J. Hokin

Small Beauty Parlor Face, 1961
Muslin soaked in plaster over wire frame, painted with enamel, 8 × 6 × ½ (20.3 × 15.2 × 1.3)
Collection of Raymond Saroff

Small Yellow Pie, 1961
Muslin soaked in plaster over wire frame, painted with enamel, 16½ × 17⅜ × 7 (41.9 × 44.1 × 17.8)
Collection of the artist

Stockinged Thighs Framed by Skirt, 1961
Muslin soaked in plaster over wire frame, painted with enamel, 34⅜ × 41⅜ (87.3 × 105.1)
Collection of Holly and Horace Solomon

39 Cents, 1961
Muslin soaked in plaster over wire frame, painted with enamel, 29 × 38 × 4 (73.7 × 96.5 × 10.2)
Collection of William J. Hokin

Three Ladies Stockings, 1961
Painted plaster and wood, 20⅜ × 21½ (51.8 × 54.6)
Collection of William J. Hokin

Vulgar Pie, 1961
Painted plaster on painted metal tray, 12 × 7½ × 9 (30.5 × 19.1 × 22.9); tray, 13⅞ diameter (35.2)
Collection of Mr. and Mrs. Philip Gersh

Watch in Red Box, 1961
Muslin soaked in plaster over wire frame, painted with enamel, 5¼ × 6¾ × 6½ (13.3 × 17.1 × 16.5)
Collection of Taylor A. Smith and Edward B. Smith V

The White Slip, 1961
Painted plaster, 41¾ × 29¼ × 3½ (106 × 74.3 × 8.9)
Whitney Museum of American Art, New York; Promised Gift of Howard and Jean Lipman   P.55.80

Wrist Watch on Blue, 1961
Muslin soaked in plaster over wire frame, painted with enamel, 41⅜ × 29⅛ × 5⅛ (105.1 × 74 × 13)
Collection of the artist

Pastry Case I, 1961–62
Enamel paint on nine plaster sculptures in glass showcase, 20¾ × 30⅛ × 14¾ (52.7 × 76.5 × 37.3)
The Museum of Modern Art, New York; The Sidney and Harriet Janis Collection

Floor Cone, 1962
Synthetic polymer paint on canvas filled with rubber and cardboard, 53¾ × 136 × 56 (136.5 × 345.4 × 142.2)
The Museum of Modern Art, New York; Gift of Philip Johnson

Giant Ice Cream Cone 1962
Muslin soaked in plaster over wire frame, painted with enamel, 13⅝ × 37½ × 13¼ (34 × 95.3 × 33.7)
Collection of Ileana and Michael Sonnabend; on indefinite loan to the Baltimore Museum of Art

Larry Poons (b. 1937)

Enforcer, 1963
Liquitex and fabric spray on canvas, 80 × 80 (203.2 × 203.2)
Private collection

Lee's Retreat, 1963
Liquitex and fabric spray on canvas, 80 × 80 (203.2 × 203.2)
Private collection

Robert Rauschenberg (b. 1925)

Bed, 1955
Combine-painting with bed: oil and pencil on pillow, quilt, sheet, on wood supports, 75¼ × 31½ × 6½ (191.1 × 80 × 16.5)
Collection of Mr. and Mrs. Leo Castelli

Set for Paul Taylor's The Tower, 1957
Mixed media construction, 119¼ × 16 × 48 (302.9 × 40.6 × 121.9)
Collection of Mr. and Mrs. Victor W. Ganz

Canyon, 1959
Combine-painting: oil, pencil, paper, metal, photograph, fabric, wood, on canvas, plus buttons, mirror, stuffed eagle, cardboard box, pillow, and paint tube, 81¾ × 70 × 24 (207.6 × 177.8 × 61)
Collection of Ileana and Michael Sonnabend; on indefinite loan to The Baltimore Museum of Art

Winter Pool, 1959
Combine-painting: oil, paper, fabric, metal, transparent tape, wood, on canvas, plus wood ladder, handkerchief, and button, 89½ × 58½ × 4 (227.3 × 148.6 × 10.2)
Collection of Mr. and Mrs. Victor W. Ganz

James Rosenquist (b. 1933)

The Light That Won't Fail, I, 1961
Oil on canvas, 72 × 96 (182.9 × 243.8)
Hirshhorn Museum and Sculpture Garden, Smithsonian Institution, Washington, D.C.

The Lines Were Deeply Etched on the Map of Her Face, 1961–62
Oil on canvas, 66 × 78 (167.6 × 198.1)
Collection of Mr. and Mrs. Robert Meltzer

He Swallowed the Chain, 1963
Paint, plastic, string, plus bamboo pole with canvas and wood base, 48 × 48 × 43 (121.9 × 121.9 × 109.2)
Collection of Richard Brown Baker; on loan to the Yale University Art Gallery, New Haven

Two 1959 People, 1963
Oil and assemblage on canvas, 72 × 93⅛ (182.9 × 236.5)
Rose Art Museum, Brandeis University, Waltham, Massachusetts; Gevirtz-Mnuchin Purchase Fund

Lucas Samaras (b. 1936)

Untitled, 1959
Cloth and plaster, 9¼ × 7½ × 7½ (23.5 × 19.1 × 19.1)
Collection of the artist

Large Untitled Jigsaw Puzzle, 1960
Oil on cardboard, 64 × 78 (162.6 × 198.1)
Collection of the artist

Floor Piece, 1961
Sculpmetal, 48 × 48 (121.9 × 121.9)
Collection of the artist

Great Plate, 1961
Mixed media assemblage, 18 × 15 × 3 (45.7 × 38.1 × 7.6)
Collection of the artist

Paper Bag #2 (Containing Book #2), 1962
Mixed media assemblage, 17 × 12 × 7½ (43.2 × 30.5 × 19.1)
American Friends of the Israel Museum, New York

George Segal (b. 1924)

Man Seated at a Table, 1960
Plaster, wood, glass, plastic material, 55⅛ × 37⅜ × 55⅛ (140 × 95 × 140)
Städtisches Museum Mönchengladbach, West Germany

Woman Shaving Her Leg, 1963
Plaster, metal, porcelain, and masonite, 63 × 65 × 30 (160 × 165.1 × 76.2)
Collection of Mrs. Robert B. Mayer; on long-term loan to the Museum of Contemporary Art, Chicago

Tony Smith (1912–1980)

Black Box, 1962
Painted steel, 22¼ × 24¾ × 32¾ (56.5 × 62.9 × 83.2)
Jack Tilton Gallery, New York

Frank Stella (b. 1936)

Coney Island, 1958
Oil on canvas, 85¼ × 78¾ (216.5 × 200)
Yale University Art Gallery, New Haven; Gift of Larom B. Munson, B.A. 1951

Delta, 1958
Enamel on canvas, 85⅜ × 97 (216.8 × 246.4)
Collection of the artist

Arundel Castle, 1959
Black enamel on canvas, 121⅜ × 73⅛ (308.3 × 185.7)
Hirshhorn Museum and Sculpture Garden, Smithsonian Institution, Washington, D.C.

Henry Garden, 1963
Oil on canvas, 80 × 80 (203.2 × 203.2)
Collection of Edward Cauduro

Fez, 1964
Fluorescent alkyd on canvas, 77 × 77 (195.6 × 195.6)
Albright-Knox Art Gallery, Buffalo; Gift of Seymour H. Knox, 1964

Andy Warhol (b. 1928)

Dick Tracy, 1960
Oil on canvas, 70½ × 52⅝ (179.1 × 133.7)
Private collection

$199 Television, 1960
Oil on canvas, 62¼ × 49½ (158.1 × 125.7)
Collection of Kimiko and John K. Powers

Wigs, 1960
Oil and wax crayon on canvas, 70⅛ × 40 (178.1 × 101.6)
Dia Art Foundation, New York

Twenty-Five Colored Marilyns, 1962
Acrylic on canvas, 89 × 69 (226.1 × 175.3)
Fort Worth Art Museum; The Benjamin J. Tillar Memorial Trust, acquired from the collection of Vernon Nikkel, Clovis, New Mexico

Orange Disaster, 1963
Acrylic and silkscreen enamel on canvas, 106 × 81½ (269.2 × 207)
The Solomon R. Guggenheim Museum, New York; Gift, Harry N. Abrams Family Collection

Robert Watts (b. 1923)

Whitman's Assorted Chocolates, 1963
Chrome, 8¼ × 8¼ × ⅞ (21 × 21 × 2.2)
Collection of the artist

Bread (1964), reconstruction 1984
Plaster casts in wood display case, approx-
    imately 60 × 120 (152.4 × 304.8)
Collection of the artist

Butter, 1964
Chrome, 6 × 5½ × 6 diameter
    (15.2 × 14 × 15.2)
Collection of the artist

Tom Wesselmann (b. 1931)

Portrait Collage #1, 1959
Mixed media and collage on board, 9½ × 11
    (24.1 × 27.9)
Collection of Claire Wesselmann

Still Life #24, 1962
Acrylic polymer on board with attached
    fabric curtain, 48 × 58⅞ × 7⅞
    (121.9 × 149.5 × 20)
The Nelson-Atkins Museum of Art, Kansas
    City, Missouri; Gift of the Guild of Friends

Bathtub Collage #2, 1963
Mixed media, collage, and assemblage on
    board, 48 × 72 × 6½
    (121.9 × 182.9 × 16.5)
Private collection

Interior #3, 1964
Acrylic, polished metal, and assemblage
    (including working fluorescent light and
    clock on board), 66 × 52 × 9
    (167.6 × 132.1 × 22.9)
Private collection; on loan to the Museum
    Boymans-van Beuningen, Rotterdam

Robert Whitman (b. 1935)

Set for *Mouth* (theater piece, 1961),
    reconstruction 1984
Mixed media; first presented at the Reuben
    Gallery, New York
Collection of the artist

Fluxus

Ay-O (b. 1931)

Finger Box, 1964
Brown paper tape over cardboard, with foam
    rubber contents
Collection of Gilbert and Lila Silverman

George Brecht (b. 1925)

Spanish Card Piece for Objects, 1959–60
Printed text
Collection of La Monte Young

Exit, c. 1963
Metal sign mounted on painted wood
Collection of Gilbert and Lila Silverman

Untitled, c. 1963
Matches in aluminum foil
Collection of La Monte Young

Water Yam, 1963
Cardboard box containing fifty-six orange and
    nineteen white Event cards
Private collection

George Brecht and Robert Watts (b. 1923)

Lantern Extract/An Aspect of Yam Festival,
    1962
Printed mailed envelope containing ten Watts
    Event cards and eight Brecht Event cards
Collection of La Monte Young

Dick Higgins (b. 1938)

Word compositions from Dick Higgins,
    Selected Early Works, 1955–1964, Berlin:
    Editions Ars Viva!, 1982

Alison Knowles (b. 1933)

Word compositions from 1961–65 from *by
    Alison Knowles*, New York: Something Else
    Press, 1965

George Maciunas (1931–1978)

Solo for Important Man, 1962
Printed text
Collection of La Monte Young

Spell La Monte's Name, 1962
Miscellaneous objects in a plastic box
Collection of La Monte Young

*Twelve Piano Compositions for
    Nam June Paik*, 1962
Printed text
Collection of La Monte Young

Homage to De Maria, c. 1962
Printed text
Collection of La Monte Young

Manifesto, c. 1963
Printed and handwritten text
Private collection

Jackson Mac Low (b. 1922)

Peaks and Lamas, 1965; first performed 1961
Original typed version of poem with
    accompanying chart and simultaneous
    version for performance
Collection of the artist

Performance poems from Jackson Mac Low,
    Asymmetries 1-260 (1960), New York:
    Printed Editions, 1980

Stanzas for Iris Lezak, 1960
Original typed version of poem with annotat-
    ed directions for simultaneous performance
Collection of the artist

Robert Morris (b. 1931)

Blank Form, 1960–61
Printed text originally intended for *An
    Anthology*, 1963, La Monte Young, editor;
    deleted by the author prior to publication
Private collection

Carry an Iron, 1960–61
Typed text
Collection of La Monte Young

Flag/elate, 1960–61
Handwritten text
Collection of La Monte Young

Make a Box, 1960–61
Typed text
Collection of La Monte Young

Yoko Ono (b. 1933)

Program for Carnegie Recital Hall concert,
    New York, 1961
Collection of La Monte Young

Touch Poem, c. 1961
Word compositions
Collection of La Monte Young

Grapefruit, 1964
Word compositions from 1953–64
Collection of La Monte Young

Mieko (Chieko) Shiomi (b. 1938)

Air Event, 1964
Event card with balloon with "Alison
    Knowles" written on it
Collection of Gilbert and Lila Silverman

Events and Games, 1964–65
Plastic box with label, containing twenty
    scores printed on cards
Collection of Gilbert and Lila Silverman

Robert Watts (b. 1923)

Safe Post/K.U.K. Feldpost/Jockpost, 1962
Fifteen different images printed on gummed
    and perforated paper
Collection of Gilbert and Lila Silverman

Event cards: *Bean on Plate, Car-Flashlight,
    Keycase-Moth, Mailbox Event, Page Not
    There, Position on Rain*, 1963–64
Collection of the artist

Chromed Toothbrush, c. 1964
Chromed toothbrush
Collection of Gilbert and Lila Silverman

La Monte Young (b. 1935)

Composition 1960 #7, 1960
Handwritten score
Collection of the artist

Composition 1961, 1961
Printed book score
Collection of the artist

Word compositions from *An Anthology*, 1963,
    La Monte Young, editor: *Composition 1960
    #2, Composition 1960 #3, Composition
    1960 #4, Composition 1960 #5, Piano
    Piece for Terry Riley #1, Composition 1960
    #6*
Private collection

Newspapers, Anthologies, and Documentary Materials

V TRE, 1962
George Brecht, designer and editor
One leaf printed both sides
Private collection

An Anthology, 1963
First edition, uncollated pages
La Monte Young, editor, texts by George
    Brecht, Claus Bremer, Earle Brown, Joseph
    Byrd, John Cage, Walter De Maria, Dennis,
    Henry Flynt, Simone Forti, Dick Higgins,
    Toshi Ichiyanagi, Terry Jennings, Ray
    Johnson, Jackson Mac Low, Richard
    Maxfield, Yoko Ono, Nam June Paik, Terry
    Riley, Diter Rot, Emmett Williams,
    Christian Wolff, La Monte Young
Private collection

Fluxus News-Policy Letter No. 6, 1963
George Maciunas, editor
Mimeograph printed on back of a Ben Vautier
    announcement
Collection of Gilbert and Lila Silverman

Yam Festival Newspaper, 1963
George Brecht and Robert Watts, designers
    and editors
Original collage
Collection of Gilbert and Lila Silverman

cc V TRE, Fluxus Newspaper #1, 1964
George Brecht and George Maciunas, editors
Newsprint
Collection of Gilbert and Lila Silverman

cc V TRE, Fluxus Newspaper #2, 1964
George Maciunas, editor
Newsprint
Collection of Gilbert and Lila Silverman

cc Valise e TRanglE, Fluxus Newspaper #3,
    1964
George Maciunas, editor
Newsprint
Collection of La Monte Young

Flux-Kit ('A' Copy), 1965
Vinyl attaché case with silkscreen title,
    contains objects and printed texts by Ay-O,
    George Brecht, Dick Higgins, Joe Jones,
    Alison Knowles, Takehisa Kosugi, Nam
    June Paik, Ben Patterson, Mieko (Chieko)
    Shiomi, Ben Vautier, Robert Watts, Emmett
    Williams, and La Monte Young
Collection of Gilbert and Lila Silverman

An Anthology of Concrete Poetry, Emmett
    Williams, editor, New York: Something
    Else Press, 1967